In Search of a Usable Past:

The Marshall Plan and Postwar Reconstruction Today

 by

Barry Machado

GEORGE C. MARSHALL FOUNDATION
LEXINGTON, VIRGINIA
2007

Printed in the United States of America
by The Sheridan Press

ISBN 0-935524-06-1

Barry F. Machado is emeritus Professor of History at Washington and Lee University in Lexington, Virginia, where he taught from 1971 through 2005. He received his B.A. from Dartmouth College and his M.A. and Ph.D. from Northwestern University. His teaching areas included recent U.S. history, U.S. foreign and military affairs, and the history of American business.

Writing and publication of this volume were made possible by a grant from the Smith Richardson Foundation.

For Anice
Lighter of Candles
and Molder of Many Lives
Especially My Own

Contents

The European Backdrop

Summary

In recent years the Marshall Plan has been invoked on numerous occasions as a solution for problems domestic and foreign. This study aims to establish the relevance for contemporary postwar reconstruction projects of an experimental foreign policy conceived and executed back in the late 1940s and early 1950s.

The monograph clarifies why and how the Marshall Plan was adopted, what its essential features were, and why it succeeded in western Europe, concluding that it had important and mutually reinforcing aspects—political, psychological, and economic. Fear of Communist expansion westward and the resulting containment doctrine energized its American proponents and European beneficiaries. Its principal architects were realists, motivated by enlightened self-interest. The strengths, weaknesses, and one major myth of their realism are analyzed. Features of great solidity and current relevance include the partnership of the Economic Cooperation Administration (ECA) with Congress and the American people; a multilateral, regional approach that treated western Europe as a unit; an insistence on European self-help and mutual aid; restriction of the ECA's role to a "catalytic agent" rather than a "driving force"; imposition of the highest standards for recruitment and hiring of personnel; creation of the ECA as a small, autonomous, and unbureaucratic agency; popularization of economic growth as a national priority; freedom from corruption and scandal; and an understanding of the requirements of world leadership. Further examples are provided throughout the text. Some weaknesses discovered were abuses of quantification and language, interagency feuding, and, most importantly, oversimplification of the root causes of Communist popularity in parts of western Europe.

Through the prism of four country studies—Greece, Italy, Turkey, and West Germany—the author examines how the Plan was actually implemented, demonstrating the practical limitations of conventional theories and generalizations about its impact. They were chosen for their resonance with conditions facing present-day policymakers. Such autopsies of recipient nations with different economic and political problems, and in diverse cultural regions of Europe, reveal the Marshall Plan's fundamental flexibility, its rejection of a one-size-fits-all approach, and its mixed results. While its grand intention was to promote a more cooperative and interdependent "New Europe," various relief, reconstruction, reform, and development progams encountered local resistance and failure as well as collaboration and success. Sometimes, as in Turkey, mistakes were made despite the best intentions. Or, as happened in southern Italy, the cultural challenge was too formidable for Marshall Planners. In the case of West Germany the national will to self-renewal probably determined that country's ensuing "economic miracle" more than did the amount or kind of American foreign aid. Greece was, in some respects, *sui generis* but also a practicum in workable and unworkable theories and methods of postwar reconstruction today.

Finally, for the benefit of contemporary policymakers, the monograph extracts unusable, avoidable, and usable elements from the historical record of the Marshall Plan. Arguments against its replication are also explored. Of largely antiquarian interest, the unusable characteristics involve luck, timing, and unintended consequences. The large role of seven historical contingencies is identified as contributing to the Marshall Plan's success. The avoidable features pertain to mistakes that ought not to be repeated in the future. The usable past recommends itself for incorporation by the shapers of postwar reconstruction programs today.

Acknowledgments

Many contributed to the final version of this monograph. In February 2006 in the first of two vetting sessions, American scholars provided valuable commentaries on the initial draft. Later, they read carefully its revision, from which I profited as well. For their oral and written critiques, special thanks go to participants in that two-day review in Arlington, Virginia: Ambassador James Dobbins of the Rand Corporation; John Bledsoe Bonds of the History Department at the Citadel; William H. Becker, Professor of History and International Affairs in the Elliott School of International Affairs, George Washington University; Jacqueline McGlade, Provost at Penn State University, Shenango; Jerry Rosenberg, Professor of Management, Rutgers University Business School; and Olin Wethington, former Counselor to the Treasury Secretary and Trustee of the George C. Marshall Foundation who did double duty, participating in the second session with the same insightfulness and incisiveness he brought to the first.

A second, two-day retreat took place in June 2006 in Paris, France, at an appropriate setting, Hotel de Talleyrand, one-time headquarters of the Economic Cooperation Administration (ECA) in Europe. There, European scholars passed their judgments on the revised draft, offering helpful suggestions and constructive criticisms. For enriching the document in numerous additional ways, my appreciation goes out to: Luciano Segreto, Professor of History, University of Florence; John Killick, former Lecturer in Economic History at the University of Leeds in England, who must be singled out for an extra acknowledgment for also providing me with copies of unpublished papers delivered at a fiftieth anniversary conference on the Marshall Plan held at Leeds in 1997; Athanasios Lykogiannis, historian and researcher at the Bank of Greece, Athens; and Odd Arne Westad, Professor of International History and Co-Director of the Cold War Studies Centre, London School of Economics and Political Science.

Though invited, Apostolos Vetsopoulos could not attend but kindly sent me a copy of his fine dissertation on the Marshall Plan in Greece. James Lowenstein, an old Marshall Planner, shared his recollections, and Fred Morefield, a member of the Marshall Foundation's council of advisers, sharpened my focus. Colonel George F. Oliver, Professor of Joint Operations at the Naval War College, who worked on an early alternative draft, supplied important ideas and suggested sources. I am also in their debt. Because of their gracious hospitality at the American Embassy and the Organization for Economic Cooperation and Development (OECD) while the "monograph team" was in Paris, Ambassador Craig R. Stapleton and Ambassador Constance Morella deserve the warmest gratitude.

Other big debts were accumulated at the George C. Marshall Foundation. Larry I. Bland, editor of *The Papers of George Catlett Marshall* and editorial supervisor, copy editor, indexer, and prepress producer of the monograph, contributed understanding and guidance in an optimal blend. The leadership of Brigadier General Wesley B. Taylor, President of the Foundation, has been admirable. Brian Shaw, Executive Vice President and Director of Development and Communications, extended an offer I could not resist. To preserve the memory of George C. Marshall, my retirement could wait. Together, Robert B. James, Vice President and Director of Outreach Programs, and K. Jane Dunlap, Associate Director of Development and Director of Corporate Relations, made the vetting sessions on two continents, and much more, possible. Jane excelled in checking the project's centrifugal forces, and I dubbed her affectionately "the indispensable one." Her knowledge of the relevant manuscript collections and literature made Joanne D. Hartog, Director of Research and Scholarly Programs, my valuable shepherdess while working in the George C. Marshall Library. Three Trustees—Ambassador Thomas Pickering, Dr. Thomas Henricksen, and Lieutenant General Charles W. Dyke—offered thoughtful ideas about how to improve the monograph's organization and style. Anne S. Wells thoroughly proofed the manuscript, offering numerous suggestions.

Finally, I have benefited greatly from the research conducted by my old student, previously at the Paul H. Nitze School of Advanced International Studies and currently at the University of Virginia Law School, Eric Klingelhofer. His work in the ECA's Turkish mission records at the National Archives and Records Administration, and the provisional analysis of his findings, were first-rate and of great help. James C. Warren's unflagging support for the project (I have a folder stout with his special brand of correspondence) kept my own spirits high. He attended both vetting sessions and has his fingerprints all over these pages. Not only was he a Mississippi River, in flood-stage, of information and interpretation, he knew what he was talking about. How fortunate I was to reach for the hand he extended. As another old Marshall Planner, Warren served as my constant reminder of why Emerson thought that an organization is the lengthened shadow of human beings.

Glossary

AFL	=	American Federation of Labor
AMAG	=	American Mission for Aid to Greece
CASA	=	Cassa per il Mezzogiorno (The Southern Fund, Italy)
CCMP	=	Citizens' Committee for the Marshall Plan to Aid European Recovery
CDU	=	Christian Democratic Union (West Germany)
CED	=	Committee for Economic Development
CEEC	=	Committee for European Economic Cooperation
CIA	=	Central Intelligence Agency
CIO	=	Congress of Industrial Organizations
DC	=	Christian Democrats (Italy)
DSE	=	Democratic Army of Greece
ECA	=	Economic Cooperation Administration
EPU	=	European Payments Union
ERP	=	European Recovery Program
GARIOA	=	Government and Relief in Occupied Areas (Germany)
GDP	=	Gross Domestic Product
GNA	=	Greek National Army
GNP	=	Gross National Product
HICOG	=	U.S. High Commission for Germany
JUSMAPG	=	Joint U.S. Military Advisory and Planning Group (Greece)
KKE	=	Greek Communist Party
MIT	=	Massachusetts Institute of Technology
MSA	=	Mutual Security Agency
NATO	=	North Atlantic Treaty Organization
OECD	=	Organization for Economic Cooperation and Development
OEEC	=	Organization for European Economic Cooperation
OMGUS	=	Office of Military Government, U.S. (Germany)
OSR	=	Office of the Special Representative [of the ECA], Paris
OSS	=	Office of Strategic Services
OWI	=	Office of War Information
PA	=	Procurement Authorization
PCI	=	Italian Communist Party
SPD	=	Social Democratic Party (West Germany)
UNRRA	=	United Nations Relief and Rehabilitation Administration
USTAP	=	United States Technical Assistance and Productivity Program
WFTU	=	World Federation of Trade Unions

Abbreviations used only in endnotes:

FAOHP	=	Foreign Affairs Oral History Project, Georgetown University, Washington, D.C.
GCML	=	George C. Marshall Library, Lexington, Virginia
HSTL	=	Harry S. Truman Library, Independence, Missouri
LC	=	Library of Congress, Washington, D.C.
NARA	=	National Archives and Records Administration II, College Park, Maryland
NSA, GWU	=	National Security Archive, George Washington University Washington, D.C.
RG	=	Record Group

Illustrations

Preface

Admiration for the Marshall Plan has spanned generations. Just after Congress passed legislation in the spring of 1948 creating the European Recovery Program (ERP), its official name, the usually reserved *Economist* of London called it "an act without peer in history."[1] Many years later, a central figure in the reconstruction of western Europe concurred, rating the American undertaking as "one of the great things in human history," as well as the "pivotal event" between 1914 and 1990, because it forged a "pattern of cooperation" without precedent.[2] Seven years ago, the Brookings Institution surveyed over one thousand American college professors, members of either the American Historical Association or the American Political Science Association. The Washington-based think tank asked them to select the American government's most important achievements in the last one hundred years. Nearly half the historians and political scientists responded. They put the Marshall Plan at the top of their list, grading it as Washington's greatest public policy of the past century.

One might reasonably assume that the Marshall Plan and its meaning have been and still are being taught on most American college campuses as the yardstick with which to evaluate all federal programs. With widespread academic and popular acclaim, however, have come grand expectations. Ever since the United States helped to rebuild western Europe after World War II, calls for a "new," or a "second," or a "present day" Marshall Plan have been incessant. Those invoking it, mantra-like, have done so on the assumption of its near-universal application. A mere sampling of the range of invocations includes Latin America, the Third World, global poverty, American inner cities, eastern Europe, the former Soviet Union, the Balkans, the Middle East, and, finally, Iraq.[3]

Given the lofty esteem in which the Marshall Plan is held in circles both scholarly and lay, given the many enthusiastic hopes for its reincarnations, one should be clear as to what, in its essence, the original and experimental Marshall Plan was and was not. What were its origins and genesis? How did it gain public and congressional approval? How was it actually implemented? In contrast to what was attempted, what was achieved? Notwithstanding its encomiums, to what extent did it fall short of its aims? What characteristics of the Plan best explain its successes and failures? In what ways have myths encrusted the Plan with the passage of time? Are there, upon close and careful examination, principles, values, methods, and practices around which the Marshall Plan was constructed that have relevance for postconflict reconstruction and stabilization today? These are the overriding concerns of this monograph. Each raises larger issues.

Historians have long disagreed about history's meaning. For some practitioners, recovering and verifying a factual past are all that matter. The antiquarians and chroniclers, for example, study the past primarily for its own sake. Reconstructing what took place, but in the context of what might have happened, holds greater appeal for others. Human agency is their central focus and determinism their philosophical foe. For such theorists, historical contingencies are forever beckoning counterfactual analyses. A third school, less enamored by the subjunctive, comprehends the past as an elusive yet erudite teacher, providing useful instruction and guidance to the present in its preparations for the future. Its adherents assume that the road illuminated by history can be a shortcut to enlightened contemporary policies.

Such justifications for "doing history" need not be mutually exclusive. Nor should contingency necessarily imply yesteryear's irrelevance. Uniting all three goals, this monograph is a quest for evidence of a provable, contingent, and relevant Marshall Plan. It rejects, forcefully, both a narrow utilitarianism and reductive thinking in its approach to the connection between past and present. Part One reconstructs an empirical Marshall Plan with many implicit lessons worth learning. Part Two makes the most valuable of those lessons explicit.

PART ONE: A VERIFIABLE PAST

I
Conceptualizing the Marshall Plan

War-torn western Europe experienced an unexpectedly rapid recovery right after World War II. By the end of 1945, industrial production had already bounced back to 60% of prewar output, with France, Belgium, and the Netherlands reaching 90% levels the following spring. Economic revival in Great Britain and Norway pushed production to 110–115%. In France and Italy Gross Domestic Product (GDP) rose more than 50%. Then, in early 1947, what had seemed strong proved fragile and unsustainable. A fundamentally unhealthy system relapsed. In the estimation of one historian, economic conditions on the subcontinent turned "desperate" at midyear.

Nemesis, goddess of retributive justice, made her delayed appearance two years after mass killing stopped. For many, her arrival, principally in the modern guise of malfunctioning market mechanisms, now made peace almost as bad as the war that had cursed millions of people since 1939. Six years of World War II battered and staggered Europe economically. To its survivors, the conflict bequeathed acute devastation, dislocations, imbalances, and shortages. Besides war's widespread human and material destruction, accompanied by scarcities of fuel, housing, and food, huge dollar shortages resulted from too few exports and too many imports from the United States, a "universal emporium" at the time. A massive balance of payments gap opened up, growing worse with time. A dearth of foreign exchange put grains, raw materials, and machinery from abroad, all crucial to peacetime recuperation, out of reach of the needy. The sole surplus seemed to be rubble.

Europe's structural damage was exacerbated by both the fierce winter of 1946–47 and what soon followed, crop failures and the century's worst harvest. Abruptly, its production of milk, meat, and grains fell 20% to 30%. In the frigid months of 1947, railroads could not deliver coal, then an indispensable source of heat and energy, while Germany's coal mines in the Ruhr provided but a small fraction of their potential. Symptomatic of the privation and suffering afflicting Europe's cities, Londoners tightened their belts on rationed bread and shivered without heat from 8 A.M. until 4 P.M. The French government sliced the daily bread ration of Parisians in half, to just 200 grams. Whatever their ordeal, they were still better off than Berliners living on a shoestring, homeless in bombed-out ruins. An exception to the

Vienna food protest, May 14, 1947.

general postwar upswing that stalled, Germany suffered greatly as GDP plummeted 70% between 1945 and 1947.

War's aftereffects sapped morale and bred despair as well. Underfed, unemployed, and unpaid workers meant that by late spring hope had slackened along with industrial and agricultural production. But there was still one other weakness in postwar Europe's economic system. Unlike millions of Europeans, Nemesis labored overtime. An inflationary fever spiked, depreciating incomes, currencies, and savings. In places like Germany and Austria, a sharp rise in prices, caused by an unlimited production of occupation currency by the Soviets, fostered hoarding, black markets, and labor unrest. George W. Ball, then an American lawyer working in Paris, remembered those days as "a nervous time, with the economies of the European countries declining alarmingly." One Englishman likened the crisis to "an economic Dunkirk," while a leading French economist thought that Europe in 1947 was "on the brink of the precipice."[1]

Rising prices and declining production fueled not only widespread poverty and pessimism but also its frequent companion, political extremism. The steady growth and mounting influence of indigenous Communist parties, especially in France, Italy, and Greece, mirrored popular disaffection with unregulated capitalism and visions of a better Europe. Indeed, a Communist-led insurgency, supported by neighboring Communist governments in the Balkans, had already convulsed Greece in a civil war. Another astute Englishman, the historian Arnold Toynbee, had been proven wrong. Given its hazardous economic, political, and psychological conditions, 1947 had replaced 1931 as the twentieth century's real *annus terribilis*. They were, moreover, the dire circumstances that provoked and prodded an unprecedented American action, George C. Marshall's countervision.

The (Inter)twin(ed) Goals

That the European economy might, as a consequence of enormous maladies and pressures, suffer a wholesale collapse like the 1930s seemed probable at the time to concerned Americans. Hard times, economically, and ominous trends, politically, convinced official Washington by June 1947 that an American response was imperative. With its conceptual origins and initial nurture in the State Department, the resulting Marshall Plan, it should be underscored, emerged primarily from powerful impressions and unsettling forebodings rather than hard, irrefutable evidence of an imminent western European breakdown. Upon Secretary of State Marshall's insistence, there was to be no paralysis by analysis. Perfect proof was beyond reach, and the situation was too risky to await its demonstration anyway. Who could calculate how much misery was enough?

The Marshall Plan originated, in other words, as a qualitative judgment in search of quantitative proof. Subsequently, historians and economists on both sides of the Atlantic, armed with masses of data, as well as counterfactual and econometric analyses, have taken up the question, not of contemporary perceptions, but of whether the Marshall Plan was economically necessary after all. Their quest for understanding has been an exemplary scholarly inquiry, divorced from the cynicism and denigration implied in Benjamin Disraeli's "lies, damn lies, and statistics." The historical guild sitting in judgment has yet to render its final verdict.[2]

Unlike today's historians and economists, Secretary of State George C. Marshall's principal advisers were of one mind about the absolute necessity of doing something. Various first-hand accounts, perhaps the most influential being those of William D. Clayton, Under Secretary of State for Economic Affairs, raised alarm and frightened policymakers. In response, the Marshall Plan's broad outlines were roughly sketched during the fifteen weeks between February 21 and June 5, 1947, the date of Marshall's famous Harvard Address. Under Secretary of State Dean Acheson's "Delta Council" speech, pulling together ideas from many sources, first identified food and fuel as the precarious determinants of Europe's economic well-being. In also emphasizing ample reserves of foreign exchange as critical to the resumption of a flourishing export-import trade, Acheson echoed many in his department who regarded its shortage as the "decisive limiting factor"

Recently returned from visits to Paris and Berlin and the Moscow Conference of Foreign Ministers, where he endured forty-five days of meetings, Marshall spoke to a national radio audience on April 28, 1947, regarding the conference's failures on Germany and its relation to Europe's economy. He blamed Soviet intransigence for the conference's failure to make progress on German issues. He observed: "The recovery of Europe has been far slower than had been expected. Disintegrating forces are becoming evident. The patient is sinking while the doctors deliberate. So I believe that action cannot await compromise through exhaustion."

retarding Europe's economic recovery. At the outset of the Marshall Plan, grains, coal, oil, cotton, and dollar exchange all achieved urgency as bottlenecks to be targeted and widened.

Later, in his Harvard Commencement Speech to which George F. Kennan, head of the State Department's Policy Planning Staff, and Clayton contributed substantially, Secretary Marshall highlighted the vital links between agriculture and industry, between farms and cities, in Europe's return to economic health. One of Marshall's pressing priorities, rivaled only by, or perhaps even exceeded by, his concern for Europe's psychological state ("confidence in the economic future"), was the reestablishment of balanced economies on the continent. The dual objectives of elevated morale and balanced economies guided Marshall Planners in their work, too.

At the bedrock of George Marshall's thinking about aid to Europe were two articles of faith: a devout belief in "economic health" as prerequisite to "political stability" and a conviction that western Europe could achieve neither without both initiative and cooperation. Marshall rejected as unworkable a unilateral American solution to the perceived crisis in Europe. He foresaw no lasting improvements through a strictly bilateral approach either. Only within a regional, multinational framework—and in close partnership rather than through charity—could permanent recovery emerge. Recipients had to be centrally involved in planning for their own assistance. Though written by someone else, the opening sentence of the so-called "Harriman Report" captured the crux of his creed: "Only Europeans can save Europe." A realist, Marshall knew that trying to deliver Europe from itself was folly as well as harmful to his country's true interests. America's self-assigned role was to be what Paul G. Hoffman, Marshall Plan head as Administrator of the Economic Cooperation Administration (ECA), later described in words befitting a carmaker: "a catalytic agent and never the main driving force."[3] An agriculturalist might very well regard the nearly $13,000,000,000 that the United States spent on the Marshall Plan as "seed money." Marshall, an amateur gardener, would have agreed.

Three months after "The Speech," sixteen European nations—encouraged by Ernest Bevin, British Foreign Minister, and his French counterpart, Georges Bidault—organized themselves as the Committee on European Economic Cooperation (CEEC), assembling in Paris under the leadership of Oxford don Oliver Franks. At first estimating their basic needs at $29,000,000,000 in order to return to self-sufficiency in four years, their reply to Marshall's request for a blueprint was completed, after a false start, by late September. Paring down their dollar requirements in stages by $12,000,000,000 while blending the vague with the explicit, their comprehensive report singled out for special attention bottlenecks in wheat, coal, steel, industrial equipment, and agricultural machinery, among other needed subsidies. It also provided what would be, for some, the eventual measures of a successful joint program.

In 1947, western European industrial production varied hugely among countries and industries. With wartime neutrals like Sweden and Switzerland in much better shape than former belligerents, the aggregate was just 70% of its prewar level. If by 1952 Europe surpassed 1938 levels of industrial and agricultural production by 30% and 15%, respectively, then none dare call a future Marshall Plan a failure. In addition, the Committee for European Economic Cooperation agreed to a host of reforms: expansion of foreign trade, elimination of trade barriers, reduction of inflation, and shrinkage of the dollar gap. In order to attain their targeted production figures, along with internal financial stability, Europeans promised in writing unprecedented collective action. Maximum self-help and maximum mutual aid would be the keys to a healthier continent. For the Englishman Franks, the Marshall Plan's "most remarkable feature" as it took shape was the absence of any bullying by the United States. At a time when America was "dominant" and Europe "dependent," Washington "did not assert its dominance. What it did was to urge the Europeans together." Great Power swagger was absent, along with *diktats*. Secretary Marshall and his close advisers had struck the proper note which Josef Stalin never played. From the foundation of mutual respect, the rest of the collaborative enterprise arose.[4]

On April 3, 1948, President Harry S. Truman signed into law the Foreign Assistance Act, which launched the Marshall Plan by creating the Economic Cooperation Administration. An independent government agency, the ECA would be run by an administrator, Paul Hoffman, responsible only to the President himself. It would function in an unusual triangular arrangement, with a headquarters in Washington, one in Paris under the supervision of W. Averell Harriman, and country missions in sixteen (ultimately, seventeen) European capitals. Duties were apportioned, with Hoffman attending to Congress and the American public while Harriman dealt with recipient nations. For the first fifteen months of its operation Congress provided $5,300,000,000. All subsequent appropriations would be determined annually after a yearly review, and in gradually scaled-back amounts. A section of the Act merely rephrased the goals spelled out earlier in the CEEC's report, with Congress largely mandating what the Europeans had recommended. With his signature, President Truman broke fundamentally and irreversibly with America's isolationist past. A sense of national emergency had redefined traditional foreign policy.

While altruism comprised one motive, the commitment of the Marshall Planners to reconstruct western Europe using a European template was also impelled by minor and major anxieties. The minor worry was over the long-range domestic impact of the possible loss of America's traditional trading partners and their big market. After all, in 1947 the United States exported to Europe twice as much as it imported, providing an $8,000,000,000 surplus and stimulus. Winning the peace was crucial, but sliding back into the economic stagnation of the 1930s was intolerable. "Our export market," the

Above left: *William D. Clayton, Under Secretary of State for Economic Affairs, 1946–47.* Above right: *George F. Kennan, Soviet expert and head of the State Department's Policy Planning Staff, 1947–49.*

Below: *Secretary of State George C. Marshall walks to the Harvard University postgraduation Alumni Ceremony to receive an honorary degree and to deliver a short speech, June 5, 1947.*

State Department's Ernest Gross reminded his colleagues, is in "an exposed and unsatisfactory position."[5]

The major unappetizing prospect that justified preemptive action was that serious market dislocations in western Europe might facilitate Soviet ambitions and Communist electoral victories. With his Marxist blinders in place, Josef Stalin was anticipating capitalism's imminent collapse. To nudge history along, and to promote the illusion of independent western European Communist parties, he decreed for a time that the faithful involve themselves in "popular fronts," as well as policies of moderation and reformism. The dread and specter of an ideological foe energized lifeless exchange rates, dry export figures, and bloodless trade deficits. American fears, probably justified, overrode the possibility that Communist governments in France and Italy might—in practice—be travesties of Leninism and Stalinism, given their respective cultures and customs. Apprehension had been growing ever since the end of the war. In October 1945 in France's elections for the National Assembly, the French Communist Party (PCF) received 26% of the vote and the highest percentage of seats. The following November Communists increased their electoral strength, getting 29% of the vote and electing numerous mayors and other local officials throughout the country. In 1946 and 1947 they were France's largest political party. In May 1947, the French government had five Communist ministers in its ruling coalition cabinet. The head of the Communist Party served as Deputy Premier, and the Minister of Defense was also a Communist. On the eve of Marshall's Harvard Speech, the 618-member Parliament included 182 Communists.

In Italy, Communists obtained a troubling 19% of the vote in the June 1946 general election for the Constituent Assembly. In the fall's municipal elections a disturbing swelling in Red popularity occurred, with more Communist gains in regional elections in Sicily the following spring. By 1947, the Italian Communist Party (PCI) was widely regarded as larger and more powerful than its French counterpart. Besides being the most formidable in all of western Europe, it seemed to be the boldest. In May 1947, Palmiro Togliatti, popular leader of Italy's Communist movement who had spent the war in Moscow, announced openly that "direct action" by his followers was a possibility. What also distressed the State Department were Communist-dominated unions that fomented chaos in both countries in 1947. They flexed their power in food riots and a series of strikes and work stoppages—by railroad workers, dock workers, and garbagemen.[6] At the end of the *annus terribilis,* George Kennan of the Policy Planning Staff interpreted a Marshall Plan yet to be passed by Congress as an "effective tool in the strategy of containment."[7]

American historian Melvyn P. Leffler believes that one of the two primary motives behind the Marshall Plan was fear that the "Communist left would triumph, perhaps even through free elections" and that the "appeal of Communist parties" had to be "undermined" in western Europe. Prior to his

President Truman signs the Foreign Assistance Act, authorizing the Marshall Plan, April 3, 1948. The audience includes (left to right), Under Secretary of State Robert A. Lovett, Senator Arthur Vandenberg, Treasury Secretary John Snyder, Representative Charles Eaton, Senator Tom Connally, Secretary of the Interior Julius A. Krug, Representative Joseph Martin, Secretary of Agriculture Clinton Anderson, Representative Sol Bloom, Attorney General Tom Clark, and Postmaster General Jesse M. Donaldson. Marshall was in Bogotá, Colombia, attending the Ninth International Conference of American States.

trip to Cambridge, Secretary Marshall warned Italy's Prime Minister, rather fittingly on May Day, that additional American aid hinged on the exclusion of the radical left from the ruling coalition. Shortly thereafter, Marshall's Ambassador in Paris told the French Premier: "no Communists in gov. or else." Before the month of May was over, Marshall did authorize more emergency assistance to Italy because Communists were in fact barred from the cabinet. At the end of that extraordinary year, Robert A. Lovett, Marshall's right-hand man, confided to his diary that Marshall Plan assistance would be contingent on Communist-free governments.[8]

As Averell Harriman prepared to assume his duties at the ECA's Office of the Special Representative (OSR) in Paris, he too conceived of the Marshall Plan as a strategic weapon in the emerging Cold War. "Stalin was convinced he could move into Western Europe," recalled America's wartime ambassador to the Soviet Union. He elaborated on this point in the same interview:

Stalin was "undoubtedly told by leaders in the Communist parties in Italy and France that their organizations were very strong" and that "with some help they would be able to take over Italy and France." Though certainly arguable, in Harriman's judgment "they would have done so if it hadn't been for the Marshall Plan." Writing in 1978, the journalist Theodore H. White, who lived in Paris from 1948 until 1952, painted the European scene with a broader brush than even Harriman had. "The Marshall Plan was," he declared, "the most successful anti-Communist concept in the past fifty years."[9]

Like DNA's double-helical molecular structure, the strands of economics and politics are apparently discrete yet tightly linked. They were frequently treated by Marshall Planners as separate yet generally understood by them as inseparable. Perhaps no more profoundly than by the realist George Kennan before he left the State Department and by Lincoln Gordon, Director of the Program Division at OSR during 1949 and 1950, most grasped that he who pursues economics without reference to politics pursues essentially a construct of the mind. The Marshall Plan's second-in-command in Paris, Milton Katz, understood the "heart" of American policy from 1947 until 1952 to be "the integration of economic, political and psychological factors." The difficult "German Problem" constantly reminded Kennan, Gordon, and Katz that postwar European politics demanded regional economic integration for a lasting solution. In the end, they would fail to achieve some of their intertwined goals, but not because the concept of political economy escaped them.[10]

Elaboration

Keeping with the original CEEC diagnosis of Europe's condition and the follow-up prescription by its successor organization, the Organization for European Economic Cooperation or OEEC, the first fifteen months of the Marshall Plan involved mostly emergency commodity relief. The Four F's—foodstuffs, feed, fuel, and fertilizers—comprised 60% of all aid. Such assistance also helped to close the dollar gap. Since few dollars, in effect, crossed the ocean, exchange and convertibility barriers were effectively bypassed. Afterwards, America's reformist zeal took over and the emphasis switched to subsidies and expenditures that promoted economic development, enhanced productivity, battled inflation, expanded intra-European trade, built self-sustainable and balanced national economies, provided technical expertise, fought protectionism, and pushed regional economic integration through new mechanisms. All of these manifold objectives were pursued by means of an ultimate mix of 90% grant and 10% loan, and by regulating the uses to which counterpart funds in local currencies were put (see Chapter III).[11]

While the Marshall Plan was much more than an economic enterprise, in the late 1940s there existed, at least in theory, a variety of ways to get a conceptual handle on Europe's predicament. Since national income accounting was, as David Reynolds has pointed out, "still in its infancy," a fairly crude method—heavily dependent on shaky projections—was adopted. To attain the overriding goals of expanding industrial and agricultural production beyond the levels of 1938, which the CEEC recommended, the OEEC later ratified, and Congress ultimately required, Marshall Planners settled on Europe's war-induced balance of payments gap that had opened wide in 1946 and 1947 as the appropriate problem to solve. They selected each recipient nation's trade deficit as the principal determinant for apportioning Marshall Plan aid: the greater the estimated shortage of dollars, the larger the ECA's allotments. To the chagrin of some nations, measures of national income played no part in their calculations. Western Europe's investment needs were simply disregarded or downplayed.[12]

As recovery progressed towards the 1938 figures—in effect back to the future—concerns about permanence, about sustaining and improving upon those gains, came to the fore. Lincoln Gordon thought that "the ECA job in the first two years was deceptively easy, since it was essentially a restoration of pre-war economic conditions." Fellow Marshall Planner Van Cleveland regarded the first phase of the Marshall Plan as briefer, lasting just nine months rather than until the end of 1949.[13] Whichever the case, a reorientation did occur in the ECA's point of view, towards what some have called an investment banking perspective. In order to establish preconditions for continuous growth, ideas changed about how to program assistance. In pursuit of ends more complicated than 1938 production levels—creating sound and convertible currencies, liberalizing European trade and stimulating intra-European trade, controlling inflation, and improving standards of living, for example—the balance of payments method and the goal of a continental balance of payments equilibrium were absorbed into a national accounts–national income approach. Keynesianism eventually reigned supreme in the ECA's decision-making process.

Head of economic planning in Washington was a transplanted professor of economics at the Massachusetts Institute of Technology, Richard Bissell. After graduation from Yale, Bissell studied for a year at the London School of Economics. During the 1930s, to the dismay of his staunch Republican father, a wealthy Hartford insurance executive, he sympathized with Franklin D. Roosevelt's New Deal, as did many future Marshall Planners. As a new convert to an old progressive faith in the beneficence of government intervention in the economy, Bissell actually taught the very first course on Keynesian economics at Yale, once the pulpit for William Graham Sumner's *laissez faire* doctrines. In the United States, World War II validated Keynesian doctrines to the extent that by 1948 most government economists considered themselves disciples. Not surprisingly, Bissell employed Keynesian analysis in co-authoring the influential Harriman Report.

With his "strong background in Keynesian doctrine and a consequent belief in the value of governmental activism," Bissell made the Marshall Plan into a proving ground for the monetary and fiscal ideas of John Maynard Keynes. Employing the master's tools, he and his cohorts sought to balance Europe's need to achieve high levels of investment required to modernize its economy with its requirement to keep inflation, trade deficits, unemployment, and especially dollar shortages under control. With their expertise in taming business cycles and managing demand, they confidently prescribed economic measures for national and regional growth in western Europe. Often, the skills of a nimble juggler were essential.[14]

By fall of 1949, with Hoffman and Bissell in the forefront, Marshall Planners were already pushing strenuously for greater European production, productivity, and economic interdependence as antidotes to the poisons of class consciousness and class hatreds that circulated widely throughout European society. Indeed, they sought to foster new values among Europeans towards market forces, particularly towards the expansion of Gross National Product (GNP). According to Paul Hoffman, the ECA's "end goal" became truly ambitious, "nothing less than the creation of a 'new' Europe."[15] For the European historian David Ellwood, the Marshall Plan now "aim[ed] to change attitudes and outlooks, aspirations and mentalities . . . [and] wants [and] needs" of European businessmen and workers, rendering the former more enlightened and the latter less revolutionary. The Americans had rolled the dice in a high-stakes game. After all, a transformed western Europe would not only be less distinctive, politically and culturally, but also much better able to challenge the United States for global economic supremacy. In the context of the Cold War, the gamble seemed worth it.[16]

But before Phase Two had a fair chance to play itself out, war on the Korean peninsula gradually redefined the Marshall Plan after the midpoint of its projected four-year life. Thereafter, concerns for international security and the defense of western Europe inexorably transformed the ECA into a quasi-armaments program that undercut its purely economic and political objectives in the prewar era. In October 1951, Congress passed the Mutual Security Act, abolishing ECA as an independent agency and making it a part of the Mutual Security Agency, or MSA. In a practical sense, the Marshall Plan as an economic recovery program with accompanying political aims ended prematurely. After forty-five months, the Plan officially shut down on December 31, 1951. By that time, the impact of the "catalyst" had been profound, justifying the difficulties of its installation. To get congressional and public approval, and then to make it function properly, had called for a great mobilization of effort in both the United States and western Europe.[17]

II

Selling the Marshall Plan

At Home

Warren Buffett's father, Howard, represented Nebraska's Second Congressional District in 1948. Like many Midwesterners whose civic bible was the *Chicago Tribune*'s editorial page, the Republican congressman embraced and preached a hard-shell gospel of isolationism. His was the sensibility of an older America. In Howard Buffett's faith neither America's prosperity nor its security depended on what transpired in Europe. A strident foe of the Marshall Plan, he belittled it as "Operation Rathole," condemning as well the "barrage of propaganda . . . drench[ing] this country" and assailing the "tricks of political terrorism" supposedly being employed to gain its passage.[1]

About one of his criticisms Congressman Buffett was correct. The Republican 80th Congress and the public were in fact targets of a prodigious outpouring of propaganda, the purpose of which was to guarantee that the uninformed, along with the isolationists and pro-Communists, did not defeat Marshall Plan legislation. Another angry opponent of the Marshall Plan, Representative Fred Busby of Illinois, agreed with Buffett. "Never," he complained, "has Congress been so bombarded with propaganda." Since the conservative Class of 1946 had campaigned successfully on shrinking big government, slashing federal spending, cutting taxes, and rolling back the New Deal, a Democratic administration faced a daunting task in winning approval for its unexampled foreign aid program.

Marked by a proliferation of committees and lobbies, both public and private, the ensuing campaigns of education and manipulation constituted the second of America's two containment policies in the late 1940s. The first, dating from George Kennan's pseudoanonymous article signed "X" in the July 1947 issue of *Foreign Affairs* and embodied in the Truman Doctrine, was directed at containment of communism abroad. The second, less known, was aimed at political isolationists, like Buffett and his brethren, at home. Before the Marshall Plan could mold a "New Europe," a "New America" had to be promoted. Voices of an "Old America," loudest in the heartland, had to be marginalized. At the kickoff of the campaign the power of the isolationist opposition was considerable and the public's apathy not inconsequential.[2]

After World War II, with the exception of the eastern seaboard, America's sense of world responsibility still suffered from stunted development.

Witness the popular philosophy of Robert R. McCormick, then owner and publisher of the *Chicago Tribune*, herald of the country's most isolationist region. McCormick comingled national aloofness with illusions of invulnerability and omnipotence. "We can work out our own [national] salvation," he declared, "independently of what happens elsewhere in the world." The Truman administration and friends of the Marshall Plan could not have disagreed more. But to implement and sustain their grand foreign policy, Truman and Marshall first had to master common domestic politics. In one of America's most unusual feats of leadership, they made the latter servant to the former. Harmonizing means and ends proved as crucial as it was rare. By summer of 1947, they were organizing coast-to-coast efforts to convince the people and their elected representatives about the feasibility and rightness of their cause, and to accept, instead of a promised federal tax cut, the likelihood of higher taxes. Mobilizing favorable public opinion and bipartisan support thus began and ended in Washington.[3]

The Government Campaign

Overseen by Under Secretary Robert Lovett, a Republican, the State Department went to work independently, and in concert with various interdepartmental working committees in the Executive Branch, collecting economic and financial information. A European recovery program acceptable to a Congress full of isolationists and fiscal conservatives presupposed an immense amount of knowledge, as well as a sound basis on which to make cost projections. A Herculean effort of research, documentation, and analysis, led by Charles Kindleberger, Paul Nitze, and others, produced the legendary "Brown Books." Deciding to err on the side of too many rather than too few statistics, government officials simply overwhelmed skeptical Congressmen with detailed country studies on commodities, balance of payments, and trade that measured three inches in thickness. The scale and thoroughness of the State Department's homework and preparations helped to overcome some of its unpopularity on Capitol Hill, "amazing," in particular, Republican Senator Arthur Vandenberg of Michigan, a former isolationist whose support was indispensable.

After Secretary Marshall's Harvard speech, President Truman also appointed three bipartisan governmental advisory groups to examine the feasibility of massive foreign aid to Europe. He asked Julius Krug, Secretary of the Interior, to chair a committee to assess its impact on America's natural and national resources. He nominated Edwin Nourse, head of the President's Council of Economic Advisers, to investigate its consequences for the health of the domestic economy. The third set of advisers he called into existence was put together from a list of prominent Americans compiled by Dean Acheson and chaired by the Secretary of Commerce, Averell

Harriman. Their charge was to review the CEEC proposal and determine the limits and appropriate shape of Marshall's ideas. How much, for example, could the United States spend without bankrupting itself?

In terms of laying the groundwork and influencing Congress and the press, contemporaries regarded the Krug and Nourse committees as minor players. The third committee, however, the "President's Committee on Foreign Aid," better known as the "Harriman Committee," complemented Foggy Bottom's marketing and was by far "of very great importance." Working from late August 1947 until publication of its results in early November, it cooperated behind the scenes with State Department working groups and utilized their expertise. Its essential findings that European self-help was mandatory, the expense was not prohibitive, and a "new" Europe "with a common economic market and strong political ties" had to replace "the old, compartmentalized pre-war Europe" were greeted by widespread applause and accolades in the press. More than any other government document, the final report of the Harriman Committee converted the press to the cause of the true believers.[4]

The Harriman Committee consisted of around twenty members. Representing business, labor, and academia, its personnel "inspired confidence" in a Congress that largely lacked confidence in the State Department.[5] According to the MIT economist who, as the committee's executive secretary, directed its research and deliberations, and collaborated in drafting its final report, the group was "rather conservative" and, in at least one crucial way, well prepared for its task. The attitudes of many members had already been molded by "experience in governmental policy" in World War II. Their service in wartime agencies with limited purposes and life spans left two fortunate legacies: inoculation against simplistic, clichéd thinking and sloganeering about the federal government often heard in the private sector and a good understanding about how a government adhocracy functioned.[6]

Not only did the committee's bipartisan makeup and recommendations impress journalists and legislators alike, but two of its leading participants, Averell Harriman and Paul Hoffman, went on their own personal crusades to win acceptance of the Marshall Plan in the business community. Although he was a poor public speaker, appearing to some as inarticulate, no one was more zealous in promoting the objectives of the Marshall Plan, or more committed to its congressional passage, than Harriman. After his committee's report was finished, he flew all over the Midwest and West drumming up support in the months leading up to the vote in Congress. Flying great distances in an unpressurized DC-3, he adhered to what one of his companions considered a superhuman speaking schedule. Every day for several weeks he made three stops—in unglamorous cities like Fargo, Boise, and Walla Walla, bastions of isolationism.[7]

Also delivering scores of speeches to audiences in need of conversion was Paul Hoffman, head of the Studebaker automobile company and one of

Barry Machado

the founders in 1942 of the Committee for Economic Development (CED), an organization of liberal businessmen. Six years later, his connections with the CED turned highly beneficial. According to an associate, a determined and tactful Hoffman "kept the business community behind the Plan . . . in the beginning," using "liberal businessmen as the cutting edge to get united support."[8] Public relations was Hoffman's great gift. Some who knew him well deemed him "little short of a genius" in its employment. To Dean Acheson, he was an "evangelist" spreading the gospel.[9]

In the Truman administration's self-appointed mission to awaken the American public from its isolationist slumber, World War II's organizer of victory, General Marshall, led by example. In October 1947 he broke with precedent and, in search of organized labor's backing, he addressed the annual Congress of Industrial Organizations (CIO) convention. From January until May 1948 he campaigned as virtually a one-man talkathon. An impeccable reputation as a nonpartisan aided his arguments immensely. Marshall's whirlwind swing around the country took him to a chamber of commerce here and a church group there, as well as to business councils, university faculties and student bodies, farmers' associations, and women's clubs. Besides testifying regularly on the Hill, he carried the State Department's message coast-to-coast: from New York, Pittsburgh, and Atlanta, to Chicago and Des Moines, and on to San Francisco, Los Angeles, and Portland.[10]

There were businessmen and congressmen, like Everett Dirksen of Illinois, who were persuaded neither by the torrent of speeches nor by George Marshall's prestige. Rather, they underwent self-conversion, switching from an isolationist to an internationalist faith by the baptism of first-hand experiences. In the late summer and fall of 1947 not a few Representatives and Senators, particularly members of the fact-finding House Herter Committee, traveled to Europe to take the measure of the continent's misery. What Dirksen and others observed of life among the ruins moved them profoundly. Unmediated observations abroad exceeded in power any abstractions that Harriman or Hoffman or even Marshall might discuss at home.

The Quasi-Private Offensive

The spearhead to reeducate the nation on the grand scale was the ad hoc "Citizens' Committee for the Marshall Plan to Aid European Recovery" (CCMP). Established in late October 1947 by prominent liberal Eastern internationalists and members of the Council on Foreign Relations, the CCMP had its headquarters in New York City, a busy office in Washington, and regional and local chapters in places like Baltimore and Philadelphia. From there it ran a massive, well-organized assault on unfavorable domestic sentiments towards the Marshall Plan. Top-heavy with corporate and labor leaders in provisional alliance with one-time government officials—Robert

Secretary Marshall and Under Secretary Lovett testify in favor of the emergency aid bill—$597,000,000 for France, Italy, and Austria—November 10, 1947.

Patterson and Dean Acheson, for instance—CCMP epitomized bipartisanship. While more than half of its general membership were businessmen, in contrast to only 6% labor union officials, its National Council was divided evenly between Democrats and Republicans.

Though ostensibly a nongovernmental organization, and though bankrolled by big donors like John D. Rockefeller as well as by small private contributions, in many ways the distinguished private citizens who led the organization actually fronted for a State Department legally barred from engaging in propaganda. To sway public opinion, the CCMP ran ads, press releases, and editorials in both big city and country newspapers, paid for radio broadcasts, and hired its own news and speakers bureaus. Publicity entailed sending spokesmen to women's clubs, church councils, and public affairs groups. Dean Acheson followed in the footsteps of Harriman and Hoffman, undertaking his own speaking tour of the Midwest and West. He addressed audiences in Palo Alto, Portland, Spokane, Minneapolis, and Duluth. Will Clayton stumped parts of the country as well. In January and February 1948 a CCMP field staff visited additional areas of the Midwest to mobilize local support. Winning the hearts and minds of fellow Americans also meant circulating more than a million pieces of pro–Marshall Plan publications—booklets, leaflets, reprints, and fact sheets. The primary focus was frequently on elite opinion, but the grassroots were cultivated, too.

The preliminary bout on the legislative fight card was an Interim Aid bill. After the warm-up, congressional debate and committee hearings on the Marshall Plan began in earnest in January 1948. The main attraction lasted for six months, until June. Thanks to the fair-minded leadership of Vandenberg in the Senate and the elderly Representative Charles Eaton in the House, neither steamroller nor filibuster occurred. Early on, however, reluctant members of Congress made it clear that their vote for passage depended on the ultimate shape of the program. Finding the Harriman Committee report particularly handy, the CCMP assembled and briefed a cross-section of private organizations as witnesses. In all, twenty-six members of the CCMP testified before congressional committees, representing organized labor, farmers' associations, industry, and religious groups.[11]

Clearly, President Truman, Secretary Marshall, and their advisers wisely decided to commit the citizenry to an ambitious, unprecedented public policy before committing the nation to sacrifice money and manpower on its behalf. Selling the Marshall Plan at home required compelling arguments as clinchers. Those used by the administration's front, the CCMP, appealed, sometimes indiscriminately, to America's idealism, self-interest, and ideology. Humanitarian and economic reasons predominated, while an ideological consideration surfaced much less often, at least until troubling events took place in Czechoslovakia in late February. Before then, the notion that the Marshall Plan might serve as a "bulwark against Communism" was mentioned but not dramatized.[12]

Interestingly, in its press releases and talking points the CCMP did not play heavily on an anti-Communist theme; indeed, it forsook the shrill, hard sell. Allen Dulles, among the organization's founders and most active members and a future head of the Central Intelligence Agency (CIA), suggested in coaching his congressional witnesses that the Marshall Plan could in fact speed up the decline of communism already underway in western Europe, adding to some recent setbacks. To Dulles, the mere prospect of the Marshall Plan had inflicted "a body blow" on the Communist parties in France and Italy "from which it is staggering." As cause for optimism, he pointed to the failed Communist-led strikes in France and Italy in December 1947, especially the fact that French Communists called off their strikes, opening fractures in the French labor movement. Dulles eschewed scare tactics, recommending instead ample forethought and proper planning. "We should not embark on a Marshall Plan program," he cautioned, "until we have counted the effort, the cost, and the sacrifice that we are disposed to put into it."[13]

After February 25, when a coup in Czechoslovakia put Communists in power, fear supplanted prudence—and emotion suppressed reason—in public discussions of the Marshall Plan. A war scare swept the country for a while. Prague was perceived as another Munich. With resounding thuds, Josef Stalin had a knack throughout the early Cold War years for regularly slamming down the wrong card on the table. Once proponents of the Marshall Plan picked up the first "Uncle Joe" card, they held a winning hand. In the Soviet dictator the CCMP, along with the State Department, had found perhaps its most effective salesman. Over the duration of the Plan Stalin repeatedly misplayed his hand in Yugoslavia, Germany, and Korea, on each occasion with maximum beneficial effect on Washington's goals abroad.

The shrinking percentage of Americans who had not heard of the Marshall Plan clearly reflected the impact of the CCMP's first-rate public relations and publicity blitz. Between July and December 1947, as measured by Gallup Polls, the number of Americans unaware of the Plan fell from 51 to 36% nationwide. Suggestive of the combined effect of CCMP activities along with the release of the Harriman Committee report in November, the percentage of Americans who favored it jumped from 47 to 56% between November 1947 and February 1948. Then, before Stalin lent his helping hand, only 29% of Americans still had not heard of the Marshall Plan. By the time of the first congressional vote in late March, one major pollster determined that three-fourths of the public with an opinion preferred the Plan, which was only slightly higher than among business executives. Farm organizations backed it strongly while the press, both editors and reporters, provided powerful support as well. Dissenters in the fourth estate made for strange bedfellows, with the *Daily Worker* joining the McCormick, Hearst, and Knight newspaper chains as the most notable opponents.[14]

An intensive five-month campaign of discussion, debate, and persuasion won for the Marshall Plan broad public endorsements. The exertions of good salesmen with good selling points sold their product. Of course, the Truman administration's willingness to concede a great deal to the concerns and biases of Congress in jointly crafting the final, compromise version of the ERP bill secured additional votes. Congress was always actively engaged in the process of revision, and the enabling legislation bore numerous congressional fingerprints: the program would not be run out of the State Department, its director would be a respected businessman from the private sector, appropriations would be for one year only with annual reviews of how money was spent, guidelines and safeguards for disbursing funds would be imposed, aid would be denied to governments which went Communist, counterpart funds would be required, and American shipping would be employed. When the House and Senate approved the Foreign Assistance Act, 329–74 and 69–17 respectively, Marshall Plan supporters stretched across occupational and political spectrums. Powerful interest groups closed ranks around it. An unusual feat had been achieved: the American Bar Association in common cause with the United Auto Workers, farmers organizations united with Americans for Democratic Action, and the hands of the

American Legion joined with those of the National Planning Association. Even an unenthusiastic National Association of Manufacturers went along with the shift in opinion. "The CCMP's work," Michael Wala has written, was "crucial in passing the Marshall Plan."[15]

When time finally arrived to implement the Plan, the ideal in America's foreign affairs had been realized: a genuine consensus with the people, the press, the Congress, and the administration unified and committed to the same policy. Because of lengthy, open debate and tough congressional questioning, the nation undertook the Marshall Plan with eyes wide open. In the history of the republic, it was a rare moment. As some illustrious public servants have maintained, the propaganda campaign that took the issues straight to the rank-and-file as well as to elites perhaps best explains "the broad and deep interest" that Americans invested in foreign affairs during the early Cold War era, in sharp contrast to both earlier and later periods in the nation's history.[16]

As the final congressional votes approached, with passage a certainty, Congressman from Vermont Charles Plumley offered his own assessment of why isolationism was a spent force and the curtain was falling on an older, inward-looking, provincial America. Echoing his Republican colleagues, Howard Buffett and Fred Busby, Plumley felt he was living in unexampled times. "There was never," he groused to fellow members of the House, "such propaganda in the whole history of the nation as there has been for the Marshall Plan." Unbeknownst to Representative Plumley, a novel sales campaign all across the United States was just a rehearsal, a warm-up, for an even bigger sales campaign that attended the implementation of the Marshall Plan in western Europe. In the idiom of vaudeville, the distinguished gentlemen from Vermont, Nebraska, and Illinois hadn't seen nothin' yet.[17]

Abroad

A most knowledgeable European historian has called the Marshall Plan "the largest international propaganda operation ever seen in peacetime."[18] While credible, a question his claim does raise is whether its author has ever had access to Cominform records in Moscow. The Marshall Plan may not deserve its first-place standing. After all, to the Plan's American architects and implementers, the Information Divisions that attached themselves to every country mission were simultaneously involved in a sales campaign and a counteroffensive. The latter originated in the October 1947 announcement by Stalin's favorite henchman, Andrei Zhdanov, that the Comintern had been resurrected. Renamed the Cominform—Communist Information Bureau— the heir to the agency for exporting Communist revolution soon functioned as a conduit for Soviet funds and the latest party line to Moscow-directed Communist parties in western Europe. No longer could Georges Bidault insist, as he did in a conversation four months earlier with the chief foreign correspondent of the *New York Times*, that "neither [Maurice] Thorez nor

"Sixteen in a Circle"—Pravda *satirizes restrictions on the amount of Marshall Plan aid the U.S. was willing to extend to CEEC nations in mid-1947.*

the French Communist Party worked on direct orders from Moscow." ECA headquarters in Washington considered Zhdanov's public pledge to destroy the Marshall Plan with propaganda the first shot fired in the propaganda wars. The need to counteract Soviet distortion of American actions justified the magnitude and cost of the counterattack.[19]

With its own wire service linked to a network of hundreds of Communist daily newspapers and magazines, the Cominform was directing an empire of misinformation and disinformation long before the Office of the Special Representative (OSR) opened for business in Paris. Integral to the Cominform's enormous effort to defeat American objectives were attacks on American motives, tactics that proved effective, particularly among receptive French workers and peasants, Parisian intellectuals, and students at the Sorbonne. With political and cultural animosities combining, the ERP, in Tony Judt's view, "faced the greatest popular criticism" in France. Shortly after the Cominform launched its anti-American offensive, the National Security Council in Washington adopted the view that a revived Comintern had selected Italy rather than France as its highest priority in a strategy of spreading communism westward.[20]

The head of the ECA's Information Division in Rome appraised the Cominform's investment in Italy as a "stupendous effort" with its goal to "undermine the Marshall Plan by distorting our objectives and procedures."[21] ECA Washington actually believed that, in the propaganda contest in western Europe, the Cominform's budget exceeded its own. What lends plausibility to the notion that the Soviets outspent the Americans on the propaganda front are recent revelations by a former Central Intelligence Agency official that in the months prior to the April 1948 elections in Italy, the Soviet compound in Rome transferred $8–10,000,000 per month to Palmiro Togliatti's Communist Party, the PCI. The Cominform's "black bags" are alleged to have been even bulkier than the ones the CIA delivered to four anti-Communist parties.[22]

Whether Marshall Planners merit first or second place in the annals of peacetime propaganda is at least arguable. What should not be is that their own undeniably stupendous effort was part of the dynamic that drove much of the Cold War, an escalating cycle of rhetoric and response, and of action and reaction. Subversives begat countersubversives, while disinformation necessitated information. Largely on the defensive at first, they eventually constructed a vast counterpropaganda machine, perhaps the envy of the Cominform. The information branch grew steadily until it ranked as one of the two largest staffs at OSR, Paris. By 1951, out of 600 Americans employed by OSR 180, or 30%, were in propaganda. To advance Washington's purposes, and to thwart Moscow's, they enlarged the battlefield in countries which were picked for psychological struggle, particularly Italy. They assembled a bigger arsenal, with more and better weapons.[23]

And they brought greater ingenuity to bear. One combatant in the war of words and images recalled the American campaign as "rather free-wheeling" and his cohorts as "in the main, [with] very little bureaucratic experience." Supposedly "greenhorns" in the field of foreign propaganda, with little to unlearn, they developed "fresh, invigorating, and oftentimes wonderfully effective techniques." In fact, Thomas Flanagan and Lawrence Hall, who ran the Information Division in Ankara, regarded the "ECA propaganda machine" as "far superior to anything previously developed by the US government." The non-civil service personnel involved, especially the large number of professionals from the working press, explained why.[24]

The leaders of America's information campaign were, in most respects, anything but novices in the dissemination of news and ideas. With its value recently demonstrated on the homefront, the importance of winning hearts and minds in Europe was recognized almost immediately. Only accomplished professionals were hired for leadership positions. The men put in charge in Washington and Paris, as well as those selected as heads of the Information Divisions in the country missions, possessed outstanding qualifications. Paul Hoffman later boasted that "we recruited talent from the top American newspapers, magazines, radio networks and movie concerns." Credentials in courting public opinion overseas were difficult to come by, so trained and experienced print and broadcast journalists, along with successful advertising executives, filled the ranks.[25]

At age thirty-six, in mid-1948, Alfred Friendly was appointed initial Director of Information at OSR, Paris, with Wally Nielsen as his Deputy. After a year, Friendly was replaced by Roscoe Drummond, a respected columnist for the *Christian Science Monitor,* who retained Nielsen as his own Deputy. During the ECA's final year an experienced Nielsen ran the Office of Information. A brief look at the first of the three commanding officers should capture the assets and advantages the American side brought to the battlefield.

Beginning his thirty-five-year newspaper career as a cub reporter with the *Washington Daily News* in 1936, Friendly switched to the *Washington Post*

President Truman, Secretary of State Marshall, ECA Administrator Paul Hoffman, and W. Averell Harriman, ECA's Special Representative in Europe, confer on the Marshall Plan in the White House Oval Office, November 29, 1948.

three years later. In the late 1930s his reputation grew as he covered extensively America's preparedness and mobilization for World War II, an event that drew him into probably the most secret and select of all wartime operations, ULTRA. Formally attached to the Army Air Forces, the Amherst graduate spent most of the war at Bletchley Park in England, "involved in the breaking of sophisticated German military codes" encrypted by the Enigma machine. After V-E Day, with his brilliance certified, he returned to the *Post,* where his erudition, investigative skills, and lucid writing caught the publisher's attention. Alfred Friendly is best remembered, however, for his association with the *Post* after his one year of active service in the Marshall Plan. In 1952 he became Assistant Managing Editor. Three years later, he rose to Managing Editor, a position he held until 1965. A Pulitzer Prize for international reporting awaited him in 1967. Since his death in 1983, ten fellowships per year for print journalists in the developing world have been named in his honor.

So when Friendly arrived in Paris, his career was on its rapid, upward trajectory—yet he was still without any managerial or administrative training. What he brought to the workplace amounted to the newsroom atmosphere of the *Post* wedded to the informality and semichaos of a Bletchley Park hut. The loose structure turned out to be an ideal incubator of ideas. About the content of his craft the Director knew a great deal. The arts of spreading, leaking, and concealing information he had already mastered. He could grasp and convey the big picture. Keeping secrets was another of his specialties. And he spoke German well and French passably. Until he resigned in mid-1949, Friendly did double duty. One responsibility was to win the battle in Europe by keeping Europe's public sufficiently informed and in receipt of enough favorable publicity to assure their cooperation and conversion. The second was to keep the homefront apprised in order to sustain congressional and political support—with ample funding—for the continuation of American generosity abroad.[26]

During the Plan's crucial first year, Friendly's British connections from wartime served him well. His Anglophilia may not have. In his later recollection, and in disregard of the terms of the bilateral treaties that all recipients signed, "Britain alone was willing to do a reasonable information program about the Marshall Plan." Having lived in Paris throughout the Marshall Plan years, Theodore White corroborated Friendly's version of events. "What the Plan was, and what it was doing," White lamented, "was scarcely ever reported factually in the Paris press." Not until 1950 did the French government "embark on any extensive publicity campaign" on the Marshall Plan's behalf. The rest of the ECA countries basically reneged on their legal requirement, leaving the Americans to carry the brunt of the propaganda load for the first two years. It all struck Friendly as a "damn shame." There was, however, another way of looking at the situation that bothered Friendly. Since all ECA expenses involved in the information campaign were defrayed out of the 5% set aside by law from counterpart funds for administrative expenses—5% of $8,600,000,000, or approximately $430,000,000—the other fifteen countries might have simply regarded their obligations as satisfied in full and their promises invalidated.[27]

High-caliber recruits also filled up the staffs of the Public Information Division. Press, radio, and documentary film sections were generally thought to have done superb jobs. Quality individuals provided a quality product. The press section effectively cultivated relations with and planted news stories in the local press. It targeted American readers, too. While serving as second head of OSR's Information Division, Roscoe Drummond wrote a weekly column, entitled "State of Europe," that appeared every Saturday in the *Christian Science Monitor*. The radio section put on popular weekly radio programs and occasionally special programs broadcast in the vernacular by local stations in sixteen countries. They attracted a regular European listening audience in the millions. Its challenge also entailed satisfying the demands of ECA Washington, which never lost sight of the need to retain public support for the Marshall Plan at home.

The radio section consequently produced programming in English— updates on ECA progress on the continent—for consumption via transmissions from Paris to NBC and CBS hook-ups for rebroadcasts back in the States. The Mutual Broadcasting System ran another weekly radio program

Marshall Plan publicity—a parade in the Netherlands.

which was recorded in France and aired there first. Robert Mullen, ECA's Information Director in Washington from 1949 to 1952, quickly adjusted to the new technology of television by arranging with ABC to televise for two years a series on the Marshall Plan. Supplying information to junketing Congressmen could also be a fulltime job for mission chiefs. In 1949, between June and December, 166 Senators and Representatives visited London with questions about ECA operations. All received personal briefings from John Kenney, head of mission. Such continuous, vigilant attention to domestic opinion had its desired results. Between 1949 and 1951 popular approval of the Marshall Plan ranged from 61% to 79% in the United States.[28]

The propaganda war's true hero was the documentary film section which was run, in succession, by Lothar Wolff, Stuart Schulberg, Nils Nilson, and Albert Hemsing. Its productivity, personnel, policies, and practices placed it on the front line of the conflict and made the visual medium the most effective. The foremost authority on Marshall Plan films has put their output at over three hundred. A few fiction and technical information films were commissioned, while two monthly newsreel series, "ERP in Action" and "Marshall Plan at Work," were produced in 1950 and a third, "Changing Face of Europe," the following year. But the great majority of the celluloid weapons used in battle with the Cominform were documentaries on specific ECA projects. In keeping with the injunction that only Europeans could save

Europe, most were made under contract by Europeans, with guidelines and supervision provided by American superintendents and their staffs. Certainly, the defining feature of Marshall Plan films was that they were made by and for Europeans. This decision ranks among the shrewdest in the life of the Marshall Plan, for the local directors, cameramen, and producers who were hired tended to be either Europe's finest documentarians or else gifted stars on the rise. Victor Vicas, the expatriate Hungarian John Halas, Holland's John Ferno, Vittorio Gallo and the Vitrotti brothers of Italy, Peter Baylis (head of Associated British Pathé) and Cliff Hornby of England are but a small sample of the deep well of cinematic talent that was drawn upon.

Some creations were country specific. Others were "trans-European." Most were reminders that the Marshall Plan was making a difference. About half of the films played in countries other than the subject country. Not only was distribution widespread, reaching tens of millions, but exceptional technical artistry added to the allure of Europe's most popular postwar art form. It can still be appreciated in *The Shoemaker and the Hatter,* a prize-winning animated cartoon that pitched free trade and mass production and was distributed in 1950 in eleven languages to movie houses throughout western Europe; or in *The Story of Koula,* about a Greek boy and his American mule, another favorite that circulated in nine languages. *The Island of Faith,* about reconstructing the dike system in the Netherlands, played to audiences in nine nations and was dubbed in eight languages. A moving French production, *The House We Love,* was viewed in eight countries. Typically eleven to fifteen minutes in length, almost all played as shorts alongside features, usually American-made, in local cinemas, a format that maximized their viewers as well as their intended impact. The generally favorable impression of daily life in the United States conveyed by Hollywood directors reinforced the ECA's message.

One source of the films' popularity, their artistic qualities, derived from two inspirations: the creativity of the European filmmakers and the sophistication of their American supervisors. If one's political aim in the pretelevision age of the late 1940s were to mold the consciousness of millions and to sway mass opinion, then imaginative techniques like special effects, animation, original musical scores, and Technicolor made for receptive moviegoers. So, too, did the subtlety of the essential messages. The genius of the Americans in charge was their eye for talent in very different nations and cultures, while their true good sense was in their realization that subtlety can be best achieved from within those diverse cultures. Americans established the agenda—the themes of self-help, solidarity, and cooperation; of a consumer ethos of "more, bigger, better" and greater prosperity; of optimistic and can-do attitudes; of improving conditions and rising expectations. Homegrown directors had to figure out how, through European symbols, images, and accents, as well as the pace of the film itself, to enter regional psyches and thereby overcome varieties of resistance in Rotterdam, Florence, and Cherbourg to the producers' messages. Sometimes, as in Italian director Jacopo Erbi's neorealist *Aquila,* a new film aesthetic solved the problem.[29]

Surely to the chagrin of numerous Congressmen who expected their constituents' generosity to have the highest profile, Americans in Paris instructed their European partners in the keys to maximum effectiveness: understate and underplay the ECA's role, render the ECA a subtle presence, put a premium on good taste, and do not push their underlying purposes too often or too hard. "An unwritten ECA law," Stuart Schulberg later acknowledged, "stipulate[d] that the Marshall Plan . . . will not be mentioned more than twice in a one-reeler and three times in a two-reeler." America's penchant for hype was in fact curbed. How, prior to sallying forth in their culture war, did those American supervisors acquire such valuable insights?[30]

An answer can be located in their distinctive backgrounds. None of them were plucked out of Zanesville, Ohio, and dropped into Paris. Neither Babbitts nor philistines who arrived across the Atlantic wide-eyed and innocent from small-town America, they had instead a European outlook and sensibility, much like the Marshall Plan's inspirators—Harriman, Acheson, Lovett, and Kennan. In the manner of Evan Thomas and Walter Isaacson's *Wise Men,* Wolff, Schulberg, Nilson, and Hemsing were Euro-Americans, or Europhiles, or cosmopolitans, a word unfortunately debased by both Hitlerism and Stalinism. They all spoke several Continental languages, had lived in Europe for years, and understood the tones, textures, and taboos of its cultures. The patriarch of the motion picture branch, Lothar Wolff, was born in Germany and immigrated to the United States in 1936 after working as an editor and publicist in Germany and France. A Jewish émigré in flight from nazism, Wolff was soon hired as chief film editor of the monthly "March of Time" newsreel series. The genre he came to know most personally in the late 1930s, the fifteen-minute short, later became the Marshall Plan's signature film. And it demonstrated that Wolff "understood how to address European audiences."

Wolff's successors and protégés were all in their late twenties or early thirties with promising futures when employed by the ECA. His deputy and replacement, Stuart Schulberg, though a native Californian, was schooled in Switzerland where he acquired fluency in French and German. After World War II, he worked in Berlin for the Office of Military Government, U.S. (OMGUS), running for several years their film unit and producing two first-rate documentaries, *Nuremberg* on the war crimes trials and *Me and Mr. Marshall.* From Berlin he went to Paris to assist Wolff. Schulberg's own deputy, Nils Nilson, also worked for OMGUS after the war in its Information Office. He too personified America's rich diversity and multiculturalism and the ways they can be exploited in foreign crises. The melting pot had its extra hidden benefits. With a Swedish father and German mother, three points of view coexisted in Nilson's makeup. When Nilson succeeded Schulberg, he elevated Albert Hemsing to his second-in-command. Like Wolff, Hemsing was born in Germany. Like Nilson, his parents and their heritages—a French mother and a German father—broadened his perspective after the family immigrated to the United States when he was a child. During wartime Hemsing had worked in the Motion Picture Branch of the Office of War Information (OWI). Afterwards, he was an independent filmmaker and professor at City College of New York's Film Institute. Under the collective aegis of the four directors of ECA's Documentary Film Section in Paris, America's propaganda offensive made its greatest advances.[31]

Only around the ECA's pioneer program of Labor Information did controversy swirl. Setting itself clearly apart from the State Department, which lacked a "labor information" officer abroad, Marshall Planners had actually "invented the title."[32] Some labor historians, Anthony Carew among them, regard its activities as having had a profound long-term impact on the self-image of Europe's organized labor movement.[33] Critics, however, have been strident. Indeed, nobody has expressed greater disappointment, and administered lower marks, in response to its allegedly poor performance than did Alfred Friendly. According to its overseer, the Labor Information branch did not carry its weight in the campaign for European acceptance of facets of The American Way. Friendly's unfriendly verdict was: "a shameful boondoggle and waste of time and money," for while "they may have had entrée to . . . I doubt that they had any influence on European labor thought."[34]

Whatever Labor Information's proper grade might be, an ECA-sponsored opinion poll in mid-1950 revealed that 75% of those polled "approved" of the Marshall Plan. In all, two thousand Europeans residing in six countries—France, Norway, Denmark, Holland, Austria, and Italy—were interviewed. The results suggested that ECA propagandists had bested their competitors in the Cominform. The striking exception was France, where interviewees registered widespread disapproval and 40% of Parisians opposed the Marshall Plan. A reasonable inference to draw from such figures, notwithstanding their skimpiness, is that the sequel to the prodigious American campaign to sell the Marshall Plan at home also succeeded abroad.

Closer inspection of the results, however, raises reservations, for among workers and peasants, the primary targets of Cominform propaganda, the Marshall Plan garnered its least support. The consensus fashioned in large part by the domestic offensive did not fully materialize in its foreign redux. In one sense, the 1950 poll validated an earlier impression shared with his colleagues in the General Counsel's office at OSR headquarters by Henry Reuss, Harvard Law School graduate and future fourteen-term congressman from Wisconsin. "The European worker listens listlessly," Reuss observed, "while we tell him we are saving Europe, unconvinced that it is his Europe we are saving."[35] Did Marshall Plan propaganda fail to erode the support of workers for communism? Might the polling data have been otherwise? What more could have been done in publicity and public relations campaigns? At the very least, the Marshall Plan's impressive but qualified success in a very costly struggle with the Cominform for western Europe's hearts and minds invites analyses of the Plan's overall strengths and weaknesses.

III

Analyzing the Marshall Plan

In an atmosphere of great urgency the Economic Cooperation Administration was designed and organized in 1948 to achieve explicit economic objectives, as well as implicit psychological and political aims. In order to evaluate the extent to which the ECA succeeded or failed in accomplishing its goals, the ambitiousness of its architects and engineers must first be appreciated. Otherwise, too narrow a basis for passing historical judgment results. An appropriately comprehensive basis for determining the Marshall Plan's impact needs to be established next. What criteria, for instance, define success and failure? Is the Plan's meaning in the short term or long run? Or in an economic, psychological, or political sense? If principally political, what stakes matter most? Are they the conflict between communism and anticommunism? Or perhaps a resolution of the postwar "German Problem" that required Germany's reconciliation with its neighbors and France's abandonment of its punitive German policy? Should the Plan also be judged in terms of whether it created European goodwill for America? Such issues have to be clarified prior to parsing evidence.

This monograph is not intended to plunge into the deep end of the historical disagreements that have been erected on such analytical foundations. Suffice it to say that an era of generally sweeping superlatives, when an American writer once gushed about "the boldest, most successful, and certainly most expensive foreign policy initiative ever attempted in peacetime," is essentially over. Among contemporary commentators, the German Professor of Public Finance who wrote in 2004 of the Marshall Plan as "amazingly successful" is probably in the minority.[1]

The last twenty years of scholarship on the Marshall Plan have expanded and refined the questions being asked of source material. Recent research has even led one economist to conclude that "we cannot conclude that Marshall aid was a substantial direct stimulus to growth."[2] Neither personal witness nor self-evidence can any longer go unchallenged. The word of the Dutch Foreign Minister from 1948 until 1952 that the Marshall Plan was "the only way in which we could have overcome our difficulties" is now open to question. In the published version of a speech commemorating the thirtieth anniversary of Marshall's Harvard Address, Sir Oliver Franks captured the verities of his generation. Explaining to his audience why he judged the

Marshall Plan a success, he declared: "The facts speak for themselves." What were those "facts," his indisputable proof? With great selectivity, Franks then provided two statistics, both short-term economic measures, to clinch his case. He cited industrial production 25% higher than prewar figures two years into the Marshall Plan and a dollar deficit that had dropped to $1,000,000,000 from $8,500,000,000 by the end of 1950.[3]

Furthermore, Franks indicated no difficulty whatsoever in grasping how such a seemingly small amount of Marshall Plan aid—$12,500,000,000 was the equivalent of little more than 2% of western Europe's national income from 1948 to 1951—might be crucial in Europe's reconstruction and growth. The former Oxford don did not need any quantitative economic models, agreeing completely with Dean Acheson that "nations exist in narrow economic margins," such that what appears marginal may nonetheless operate decisively. Two percent went a long way, when used wisely and productively.

In narrow economic terms, the Marshall Plan can, as Franks suggested many years ago, be viewed as practically an unqualified success in both the short term and long run. Statistics tell favorable stories. Between 1947 and 1950, industrial production in western Europe leapt 45%. By March 1951 it was 39% above its prewar level; four months later 43% above that benchmark. At the end of the year it had risen 55% since 1947 and stood 41% greater than 1938 levels. In 1950, exports from Marshall Plan recipients, the key to dollar reserves, were over 90% greater than in 1947, while intra-European trade in 1951 surpassed the 1938 baseline by 36%. Franks could have added that agricultural output grew more slowly, but by the end of 1951 was nearly 10% above 1938 totals, missing by 5% the target figure. Like agriculture, coal production fell slightly below projections. Perhaps more significantly, western Europe's aggregate GNP rose 32% while the Plan was in existence. Long-term statistics measure remarkable revitalization as well. Spurred by soaring productivity, unprecedented economic expansion took place in western Europe. For two decades beginning in 1953, the GDP's rate of growth "accelerated to an astonishing 4.8% per year."[4]

Despite insistence by Imanuel Wexler and other scholars that the Marshall Plan must be understood as essentially an "economic enterprise,"[5] broader perspectives have their serious proponents. On the basis of personal observation while Averell Harriman's assistant in Paris for two years, Vernon Walters has maintained that "the most important achievement of the Marshall Plan was not so much the material aid it gave as the rekindling of hope, the rekindling of energy." Drawing on historical research rather than firsthand experience, historian Tony Judt recently echoed Walters. "Any attempt to reduce it," Judt has argued persuasively, "misses its most important characteristic," which was psychology. In his estimation, the Plan was "perhaps above all psychological" by boosting public confidence, optimism, and morale in a vital way at a critical time. As inspiration the Marshall Plan had a huge and incalculable impact, so that by this criterion, too, the

Marshall Plan made a big difference. Still others have maintained, employing yet a third criterion, that success inhered in the stabilization of a European politics veering towards a totalitarianism that was the mirror image of wartime fascism. In Italy and West Germany, for example, the Plan empowered and entrenched centrist, pro-American political parties.[6]

Given the inconclusiveness to date of the scholarly debate about the Marshall Plan's provable impact on the economies of recipient nations, counsel from the economist Charles Kindleberger, an early formulator of the Plan, merits heeding at this juncture. His informed view that "it may never be possible to form a judicious estimate" about the success of the Marshall Plan—particularly in light of the shift to remilitarization after the Korean War broke out—makes eminently good sense. Because the Marshall Plan was not "an isolated plan of assistance," but rather a wholly new beginning in a sequence of postwar aid that included United Nations Relief and Rehabilitation Administration (UNRRA), Interim Aid, Government and Relief in Occupied Areas (GARIOA), the Export-Import Bank, and the World Bank, a final judgment may never be rendered. There are simply too many variables to account for. "The Marshall Plan was necessary," Kindleberger has concluded, "though not sufficient to achieve the economic recovery of Europe." Besides "amen," a sensible response might be to stretch the meaning of Europe's recovery to include psychological and political factors.[7]

Strengths

For what reasons did the Marshall Plan achieve necessity, though not sufficiency, in the revival of western Europe's economy, the return of hope and optimism among its people, and the containment of Communist advances in several of its nations? Its successful outcome was, in crucial ways, fixed at the beginning. The first, and perhaps most obvious source of strength, was that the Marshall Plan was in fact a "plan." Within American guidelines, the OEEC required every Marshall Plan country to formulate a four-year program that was reviewed, revised, and approved before being amended by the ECA. OEEC established broad outlines, which the ECA later invoked in pressuring compliance in specific ways. Well known, of course, is Harlan Cleveland's pronouncement that, in a conventional sense, it was not a plan, because of "frequent course corrections" during its lifetime. A sticky, semantic wrangle is easy to dodge because Richard Bissell's one-time Executive Assistant went on to reclassify the Marshall Plan as "real planning," an example of a "brilliant series of improvisations" that followed a "general sense of direction." Putting greater emphasis on its "direction" and its explicit four-year deadline, others have detected adjustments, but little of the ad hoc, or stopgap, or seat-of-the-pants in its extended operation.

The Marshall Plan was comprised of structured and disciplined programs. The ECA and OEEC negotiated and coordinated all projects, with

ECA Washington evaluating their regional impact. The sunset provision made European self-help a believable requirement. Since American aid was conditional, there was also a premium on accountability. Bilateral agreements spelled out the obligations of all sixteen recipient nations. Both donor and recipient, in other words, collaborated on specific goals. The ECA could, at any time, discontinue or abridge an aid package for default on terms of mutual consent. The leverage that conditionality bestowed on the donor extended to the threat of impounding counterpart funds. Setting the Marshall Plan apart as well was the general coherence of methods and goals. Had the ratio of financial assistance been tilted more heavily toward long-term loans, recipient nations would have assumed a debt burden jeopardizing future economic growth. In the case of Secretary Marshall's vision, a formal plan and "real planning" ultimately reinforced each other.[8]

In their recollections, very few Marshall Plan alumni fail to commend its unbureaucratic quality. While a plan preceded it, and "real planning" attended it, the deadweight of bureaucracy did not handicap its execution. This was largely attributable to happenstance. The ECA's separate existence owed more to the "low esteem in which the State Department was [then] held by Congress" than to any appreciation of the superior qualities of an independent agency. Whatever the motive, separating the ECA from the State Department was a sound decision. Running the Marshall Plan out of a brand-new government agency meant that it conducted business without typical bureaucratic inertia and was spared the hardening of the arteries that debilitated other long-established, old-line departments. Built to act immediately, it was able, generally speaking, to respond to problems quickly throughout its life. Bureaucracies, according to William Pfaff, have a dual nature. The first is "to live off received ideas from the past, to which organizations and individual careers are attached." The second is "to defend those ideas when they are challenged, since new ideas are dangerous and usually make trouble." Marshall Planners were neither chained to old notions nor threatened by novel ones.[9]

The bureaucratic structure that did exist made sense. Milton Katz, Harriman's right hand man at OSR, looked upon the ECA's decision to copy how American armed forces organized themselves abroad as inspired. Maximum feasible autonomy in the field meant that the perspective in western Europe generally took precedence over the point of view at an ECA desk in Washington. The so-called "theater command concept" also functioned effectively for overseas civil administration. Eliminated was constant reference to Washington for decisions that could be better made on the spot. Because "the nearer the project, the closer the appreciation of realities," decentralized theater command enhanced operational understanding, efficiency, accountability, and speed. After the ECA, the concept fell out of favor in foreign aid circles, and a format discarded which had once been a significant governmental asset.[10]

A former information officer at both OSR and the French country mission summarized the Marshall Plan as "unlike your standard government bureaucracy" because "new ideas were encouraged and welcomed, red tape was virtually non-existent," and, best of all for creative individuals, "you were left alone to get the job done."[11] According to the former head of a country mission, who served in that capacity for almost four years, another big advantage of an independent agency was its ability to focus near-total attention on the delimited task at hand. The State and Commerce departments, by contrast, had to deal with too many competing problems to achieve the same efficiencies as the ECA. Moreover, with a deadline on its activities, and self-liquidation a matter of law, the ECA sidestepped the perils and pitfalls of careerism. Marshall Plan officials abroad could afford "to stick out their necks to get results" in ways that middle-grade Foreign Service Officers in the State Department often could not.[12]

For most of its life, the ECA's relatively small size preserved its unbureaucratic character, and was a decided advantage. Initially, Paul Hoffman impersonated Jimminy Cricket, assuring Congress that he could administer the Marshall Plan with around five hundred people. It turned out to be wishful thinking and an overly sanguine prediction. In early 1949 the ECA's total payroll, home and abroad, had still not surpassed fifteen hundred. But near the end of its second year, roughly a thousand people worked in the Washington office and another twelve hundred throughout Europe. At its peak, during its heyday of power and influence, the combined American staff at headquarters in Washington, OSR Paris, and the seventeen country missions never exceeded twenty-four hundred. Never as lean as Hoffman envisioned, it still retained a human scale until absorption by the Mutual Security Agency. Much like the Marine Corps, a small, elite organization bred the virtues of high morale, a gung-ho attitude, and genuine camaraderie. Such qualities took time to emerge in Paris. At the outset, OSR suffered greater turnover in the "middle command" than Washington did. Three of its divisions, in fact, had three chiefs before the first year ended. Still, the initial instability in Paris never affected its top-level or junior-level recruits.[13]

A linkage between leanness and speed was also forged at the outset, setting a pattern and tone for the future. At Washington's Miatico Building, ECA applicants for foreign assignments experienced a most unbureaucratic treatment. There, in a one-stop service and in no more than two days, they were hired, processed, and medically examined; received almost immediately their security clearances; obtained their passports and travel vouchers; and were propelled on their way to their European posts. Indicative that a second Red Scare was not yet at high tide, appointments were made subject to a full Federal Bureau of Investigation background check at a later time. The potential for acute gridlock and a gigantic snarl was thereby sidestepped.[14]

The ECA's premium on speed had become a habit in official Washington by the summer of 1948. Compared to the American response to the 1970s energy crisis, a policy that took four years to develop after the October 1973 oil embargo, only ten months elapsed between Marshall's Harvard speech and the creation of the ECA. For reasons of the ECA's size and sensibility, "large ideas [could be] translated into action so much more quickly then than [the United States] can now." Not only do large established organizations generate massive amounts of information, but they also serve up "too rich a diet of facts and theories" to decision makers. In heavily bureaucratic structures too much knowledge can be as bad as too little, clogging the process of decision making.[15]

In truth, after two to three years the size of the ECA bureaucracy did become a noticeable problem, but not in Washington. OSR in Paris, where Averell Harriman was in charge, became organizationally flabby towards the end of its existence. By then, its unwieldy staff was comprised of 630 Americans and 800 Europeans, numbers that convinced Richard Bissell back in the States that "OSR had gotten out of hand as to size." One Marshall Plan insider has conjectured that had the Department of Commerce—ironically, Harriman's former department—been given the assignment to oversee the Marshall Plan, ECA's officialdom "would have numbered in the tens of thousands." It was heading in that direction. Primary responsibility for the ultimate bloat in Paris lay with the man authorized by Congress to hire personnel in Europe, the former Secretary of Commerce himself.[16]

Forever reminding his assistants that he wanted "a very small staff," Harriman's intentions were never the issue. He allowed the situation to balloon because he was, at bottom, "positively subversive of good administration."[17] Conditions in Paris might have been even worse, except that Vernon Walters joined Harriman's inner circle as his personal interpreter. Reassigned from Army intelligence, Walters did the work of at least six translators. Credentialless, with degrees from neither high school nor college, Walters was a phenomenal linguist, able to converse in sixteen languages with native fluency in six western European tongues. His immense value as a public servant during the Marshall Plan continued for the remainder of his life.

Nothing increased the likelihood of the Marshall Plan's success more than two factors: overwhelming domestic backing and the high quality of the recruits which public popularity helped to generate. The ECA had, as Melbourne Spector rightly underscored, "complete and unswerving support from the White House," as well as from the Congress and the public. The high command—Truman, Marshall, and later Acheson—cared deeply and were inspirations. Located in the Miatico Building, at the corner of 17th and H Streets, ECA's offices were less than a five-minute walk to the White House. Their proximity went well beyond symbolism. "If I wanted to see [President Truman] on anything," ECA's Chief of Mission in London recalled approvingly, "I never had as much as 24 hours wait to get in to see him." The Chief of Mission in The Hague regarded the Marshall Plan's "greatest single asset" to be the "enthusiastic sense of mission" that its top people instilled. If executive leadership had not been so concerned, and had the public been indifferent, then the rank-and-file might have not volunteered, or lacked conviction, or else in short order lost heart. Truman, Marshall, and Acheson imbued their undertaking with a special spirit and vitality.[18]

ECA's employment policies helped greatly, too. Until his resignation in January 1949, Secretary of State Marshall never meddled in the administration of the plan bearing his name. He never proposed to Paul Hoffman, the man in charge, a single appointment, and not once did he tell him how to run his agency. With a free hand in hiring, Hoffman established ground rules for all recruiters. According to his biographer, Hoffman wanted "our ablest citizens" to staff ECA. To a degree, the right connections did matter, but only when talent and experience were more imposing parts of the mix. Former colleagues and prior professional associates headed his list. A division of labor prevailed, with Hoffman wooing leading businessmen and bankers (and one college president) for whom he could vouch. They filled an estimated 60% of the leadership and management positions. Bissell hired most of the policy-making staff. A former Harvard law professor, Milton Katz recruited for OSR some of his finest law students, like Kingman Brewster and John McNaughton. For program officers assigned to country missions, Lincoln Gordon hand picked economists he knew personally, preferably just like himself, an academic economist with practical experience in a wartime agency. Gordon's staff was "about half and half from universities and government agencies."[19]

Hoffman's Rules approximated the democratic ideal, a situation rare in the annals of government recruitment. They governed the web of mutual respect and friendship, the personal "old school–old boy–word-of-mouth network," and the more formal application process operating side-by-side. Hoffman's principles of broad representation, diverse backgrounds, and exceptional merit, along with his bans on political patronage, party hacks, nepotism, and cronyism, guided the selection process. "In screening [personnel]," Hoffman explained, "our idea was that the choices must reflect America—including government, business, labor, agriculture, education, etc." Given Hoffman's commitment to a national cross-section, his "etc." requires elaboration.

ECA extended rights of admission to New York and Boston law firms, all regions of the country, all religions, and both political parties. Alan Valentine, first chief of mission in The Hague, actually received his offer to join ECA while at the Republican Party convention in Philadelphia nominating Thomas Dewey. "There were," Lincoln Gordon recalled, "no political tests whatsoever," and party loyalists received no preferential treatment. Selectivity was stringent. Of the 70,000 applications received during the first six months of the Marshall Plan, only 350, or 1 out of 200 who applied, were hired. Personnel applications were still running at around 25,000 in early 1949. Not too great an exaggeration was the recollection of one Marshall Planner that "everybody wanted to work" for ECA in its early years. Richard Bissell remembered that recruitment was "very easy" because the popular ECA was "a glamour agency for a time."[20]

By and large, the major regulations imposed by Hoffman assured positions of authority and power to the meritorious from various professions, occupations, and colleges. Rather than merely a Yale reunion, like the CIA at the time, a meritocracy of ability and high achievers eagerly took up responsibility. Graduates from the Ivy League, and other elite educational institutions, were prominent but never monopolized the important positions in the Marshall Plan. The poster boy for the diversity of its personnel was Paul R. Porter. A graduate of the University of Kansas, where he had been a "militant socialist," Porter later published trade union newspapers in Kenosha, Wisconsin, before working as an official in both American Federation of Labor and Congress of Industrial Organizations unions. Porter's unusual background never prevented him from holding three major positions: Mission Chief in Athens, Assistant Administrator in Washington, and Acting Head of OSR in Paris. In fact, Harriman selected him to head the Athens mission because he had "a labor, socialist background" and therefore "might be a little bit tougher on the Greeks" than his predecessor, an investment banker, had been.[21]

For many new recruits to the ECA, government service on the homefront in World War II had been the rehearsal and test that they passed with distinction. Their wartime auditions assured them their later peacetime positions. Very few amateurs ever gained employment. Though Richard Bissell and Samuel van Hyning worked for the War Shipping Administration, the most favored of all wartime agencies was the War Production Board (WPB), where more than fifteen Marshall Planners, including Milton Katz and Lincoln Gordon, served their apprenticeships. Calling ECA the WPB Alumni Association was not far-fetched. Prior experience in the federal government proved invaluable. (See Appendix A.)

Another hard-and-fast condition for employment was that there were to be no outside pressures, particularly no political meddling or influence-peddling in staffing positions.[22] This was a great taboo. One incident illustrates its rigid and ironic enforcement. In May 1948, a member of the Senate's inner circle, old friend of President Truman, and senior Democrat from New Mexico, Carl Hatch, pressed the ECA's Director of Personnel and Administration to hire his son-in-law for the unfilled position of Chief of Mission in Athens, a decision ultimately in Averell Harriman's hands. Hatch was best known in Washington as the legislator who had authored in 1939 the Hatch Act, banning federal government employees from political campaigning. Reforming dubious political practices was not on his mind nine years later.

In possession of exceptional qualifications, Senator Hatch's son-in-law happened to be a fine candidate on paper. He had an M.A. in Public Administration from the Maxwell School at Syracuse, and he had already spent three years in Athens, two in relief work with UNRRA and one as a United Nations adviser to Greece. Nonetheless, Hatch's meddling constituted a potentially dangerous precedent, his family relation was passed over, and a Chicago investment banker with experience in the War Production Board was hired instead. The applicant thus paid for his father-in-law's transgression. Not even ranking Senators received free passes from Averell Harriman. The closest Hoffman ever approached favoritism was co-opting Maurice (Tex) Moore as his Special Assistant. Senior partner in Cravath, Swaine and Moore and consummate Wall Street lawyer, Moore helped the administrator spot good managerial talent. He also happened to be Studebaker's high-priced counsel. More importantly, he was Henry R. Luce's brother-in-law and chairman of the board of Luce's Time, Inc. Moore's business association, friendship, and family ties linked his boss/client to a powerful media voice. In the Special Representative's office, Harriman ignored the rules at least once when he selected as a special assistant Michael Forrestal, the twenty-one-year-old, inexperienced son of his friend, the Secretary of Defense.[23]

Because the Republican 80th Congress, appropriator of funds in 1948, distrusted the State Department, a tacit understanding shaped staffing. There was to be no wholesale relocation of personnel. Although they provided advice and counsel, or like Harold B. Cleveland, assisted on "temporary detail," few ranking officials either transferred outright into ECA from State, or else were permitted to wear two hats. C. Tyler Wood, Philip Bonsal, and later Henry Labouisse were three notables who made the move. Out of sheer necessity, State did loan a handful of mid-level specialists to ECA to set up a foreign service personnel system for its country missions. They modeled the new structure on State's traditional arrangements. Except for a raid on the Division of Investment and Economic Development that netted Program Review Officers for missions in Copenhagen and The Hague and added Hubert Havlik to OSR's staff, those early helpful advisers were just about the only other civil servants hired out of Foggy Bottom. ECA's mission chiefs were almost all from private life, ranging from college presidents (Alan Valentine), to corporate executives (James David Zellerbach), to union officials (John E. Gross).[24]

Also beneficial was the prohibition on hiring openly partisan applicants. Hoffman, a Midwestern Republican moderate, and Harriman, an Eastern Democrat, symbolized the bipartisan spirit that shaped employment procedures. While certainly not a partnership of opposites, ECA's leadership exhibited how the duty of citizenship and a common identity superseded political, regional, and educational differences. Hoffman was a University of Chicago dropout, a salesman and manufacturer, and no admirer of the New Deal in the 1930s. In fact, he had backed Wendell Willkie in 1940 and Thomas Dewey in the most recent presidential election. Harriman was Groton–Yale–Skull and Bones, an investment banker, an early supporter of the New Deal, and an admirer of Franklin D. Roosevelt. Like the other "Wise Men," Harriman was always more attracted to *realpolitik* than ideology. Even though Republicans definitely outnumbered Democrats as ECA managers, political friction in a Democratic administration was minimal. The absence of partisanship, or its transcendence, at least as witnessed by Henry Reuss while working for ECA in Paris, contributed to a distinctive sense of teamwork. A future fourteen-term congressman, Reuss came to know something about the corrosive quality of partisanship in government.[25]

The Hoffman Rules helped to put decision making in the hands of a remarkable group of Americans. The egocentric did not volunteer, and very few dim lights went to work for the ECA. Europeans who dealt with them on a daily basis over a long period later paid them high compliments. The Federal Republic of Germany's representative to ECA Washington from 1949 until 1952, Gunther Harkort, has provided a revealing, nuanced performance review. Harkort began by conceding that "giving aid to foreign countries is not easy." He then emphasized that "whoever wishes to help quickly and efficiently and who at the same time calls on the receivers for self-help, needs great persuasive power, ample subject knowledge and a good deal of psychological skill." Did the Hoffman team possess such attributes? "On the whole," the German official concluded, "the American personnel . . . did justice to their task." The head of the section in the Dutch Ministry of Foreign Affairs responsible for the Marshall Plan was even more complimentary of the country missions. Ernst van der Beugel "never [saw] an example of a difficult job so well performed as in most ECA missions." Admiration stemmed from his realization that "if they would have been less tactful, there could have been very, very great difficulties." Instead, "the job they did, the people they sent, were absolutely outstanding."[26]

David Halberstam once applied the term "best and brightest" to John F. Kennedy's foreign policy team, but it is a much better fit for the Marshall Planners. (See Appendix B.) Three typical examples are Lincoln Gordon—Rhodes Scholar, Harvard professor, and future President of Johns Hopkins University; Thomas Schelling—Yale and Harvard professor and in 2005 Nobel laureate in Economics; and Richard Bissell—MIT professor, manager of the U-2 Project after joining the CIA in 1954, and utterly indispensable to ECA's success, yet someone who "shunned self-promotion and avoided publicity." Reassured by public approbation, Marshall Planners mixed pragmatism with idealism, and a missionary spirit with first-rate brains. They were not self-serving, believed in the value of government activism and enlightened public policies, and picked the nation's welfare over narrow personal or group interests.[27]

The motives of the recruited obviously varied, but some like Lincoln Gordon were impelled by history's powerful sway. Gordon sensed quite personally the long shadow cast by Versailles. As a Rhodes Scholar in the 1930s, he had traveled throughout Europe as a student tourist, a first-hand encounter with the folly of the past. He came to believe in a national imperative not to repeat the supposed blunders and mistakes that his country had committed after 1918. "I was very conscious," Gordon has revealed, "that what had been done after World War I was absolutely awful." Postwar American policies had, in his judgment, "created the mess that led to the depression . . . and . . . World War II." So, in the summer of 1947, at age thirty-four, off he went to Washington from Harvard's cloistered campus, driven by his sense of history's lessons to get it right and win the peace this time around.[28]

George C. Marshall supplied the vision for a historically minded Gordon. At ECA, brilliant and motivated thinkers made his abstractions concrete, revolutionizing the business of foreign aid. American crusaders produced novel concepts and significant advances in the mechanisms of helping Europeans. Their refinements and innovations brought the curtain down on stodgy, old-fashioned relief efforts, especially the simple bank-transfer method previously utilized by UNRRA. The most inspired changes introduced by Richard Bissell's policy staff included commitment letters, procurement authorizations, counterpart funds (mandated by Congress), conditional aid, and drawing rights. There was also the European Payments Union (EPU), the Marshall Plan's showpiece, as well as technical assistance.[29]

Innovations

Of course, the process of allocating American aid originated with Europeans themselves. Once OEEC's proposal for collective European recovery received final ECA approval, recipient nations organized their orders through state-run purchasing missions in the United States, dealing with ECA Washington on strictly government-to-government terms. ECA then followed a series of original steps. First, a general agreement or "commitment letter," essentially a promise to pay, was issued to the purchasing mission covering specific allotments in the annual grant and approving negotiations with American suppliers. If a sale resulted, then a "procurement authorization," or PA, was granted to the same governmental mission or private European purchaser, specifying the price that ECA would pay for a particular commodity or machine. Cashable at a designated American or European branch bank, the PA converted into dollar payments for American sellers. Authorized banks also compensated non-American suppliers in dollars, since during the Marshall Plan's first year only 66% of all orders for commodities were placed in the United States. The rest were contracted offshore, in Canada, Latin America, and wherever non-American oil might be obtained globally.[30]

In the last step of the purchasing process, participating banks redeemed their PAs at the U.S. Treasury, reimbursed from ECA dollars on account, a fund to which every American over the life of the Marshall Plan contributed roughly eighty dollars. The method developed by ECA greatly delighted a still frugal and waste-conscious Congress whose leadership included some notorious penny-pinchers. New York's John Taber, the prickly Chairman of the House Appropriations Committee and supervisor of all foreign aid, stood out. The new techniques appealed to Congressman Taber because relatively few dollars ever left the United States or even passed through foreign hands—by program's end an estimated 83% of all dollar purchases were spent in the United States. What also pleased Congress were well-designed and rigorous accounting controls that were adopted upon arrival of ECA commodities abroad. The entire system virtually eliminated the perennials of foreign aid—corruption, black marketeering, and scandal.[31]

In fact, the Marshall Plan was a model of incorruptibility. What ECA administrators spent in four years, translated into contemporary dollar equivalence, totaled nearly $100,000,000,000, a powerful temptation to wrong-doing and peculation. Yet, in Lincoln Gordon's summation, "by and large this was an incredibly clean operation," marred by a solitary financial scandal involving Austrian cabinet ministers and their diversion of counter-part funds. Leading members of the OEEC, with a different perspective, agreed with Gordon. A United Kingdom Treasury official, R. W. B. Clarke, offered the Marshall Plan one of many fitting epitaphs: "a remarkable success in avoiding scandals." Perhaps with Lyndon Johnson's Great Society as his unspoken yardstick, an American journalist extended the ultimate praise. "Most liberal high purpose collapses in fraudulent accounting," Theodore White wrote in retrospect, but "the Marshall Plan did not."[32]

To remedy the balance of payments problem, the Marshall Plan provided gifts to nations of goods pegged ultimately to private or public purchases. Inasmuch as the owners of commodities upon their delivery in cargo ships at European ports were technically the various recipient governments, the next ECA innovation involved resale of American "gifts" to local importers for equivalent value in local currencies. The transaction generated government income called "counterpart." One of the Marshall Plan's lesser appreciated features was the bedrock assumption on which it was predicated, and upon which it relied, namely, "sufficient purchasing power of the [European] population" allowing Washington's overall strategy to play out properly. Proceeds from local purchases, acting much like a tax transfer, were deposited in local banks as a counterpart fund. Whether designated for debt reduction or domestic investment by recipient nations, its use was sub-ject to ECA veto, one more deterrent to corruption.[33]

Another of its myriad strengths was the considerable flexibility that ECA permitted in the purposes to which these special accounts were put locally. Some nations used them to battle inflation by reducing budget deficits and slowing down their printing presses. Others financed reconstruction proj-ects and improvements in infrastructure. The French, for example, used 7% of their counterpart funds to rebuild their railroad system and 27% to devel-op an electric power network, each in service to their own Monnet Plan. The Monnet Plan's Deputy Commissioner during the Marshall Plan years later confirmed that "Marshall funds were allocated according to the Monnet Plan with the understanding of the ECA people." Nearly half of all public invest-ment authorized by the Monnet Plan from 1948 through 1951 can be traced to ERP aid. Italy invested 26% of its liras in modernizing transportation and 20% on improving agriculture, while England spent 97% of its pound sterling account on shrinking its huge public debt, obviating astronomical taxes.

France: Above—U.S. Ambassador Jefferson Caffery welcomes the first shipload of Marshall Plan grain. Right: Aunay-sur-Odon, completely demolished during the war, being rebuilt. Below: Paris rail yard after reconstruction.

Norway used all its counterpart for debt retirement. In such manner, Marshall Plan grants did double duty with extra value as economic stimuli. Since loans required no counterpart, and because over $1,000,000,000 in counterpart was either not released or else not spent, $11,700,000,000 in grants morphed into more than $20,000,000,000.[34]

Ever since the end of World War II, currency convertibility posed a severe stumbling block to Europe's rehabilitation. As a temporary and limited solution, and as a prod to Europeans to help each other, Marshall Planners introduced the applied concept of drawing rights. Their purpose was to reduce dollar deficits by expanding credits in Continental currencies. The device called into existence a distinction between direct or unconditional aid, and indirect or conditional aid. Besides their normal direct assistance, Europe's developed, industrial nations received indirect aid if they accepted responsibility for its redirection to the ECA's developing, debtor countries. Such aid usually took the form of industrial products and expertise that might otherwise be blocked from Europe's export-import channels. In practice, it meant a "mini-Marshall Plan" with the U.K., France, and Belgium creating credit margins, from dollar balances favoring the United States. They then granted to, say, Greece and Turkey drawing rights in their respective currencies in order to manage the convertibility problem, freeing up greater intra-European trade. Resting on bilateral balance of payments and hard bargaining, drawing rights allowed some Marshall Plan nations to purchase industrial products in Europe rather than the United States or the dollar region. Because this effectively took business and sales away from American companies to expand intra-European commerce and facilitate greater European interdependence, Marshall Planners elevated national ideals above narrow, short-term self-interest in implementing this innovative idea.[35]

In September 1950, Marshall Planners upped the ante of America's unselfishness, scrapping drawing rights and replacing the device with a vast improvement for intra-European trade that functioned efficiently for over eight years. ECA earmarked a $600,000,000 grant, about 15% of all Marshall Plan appropriations for 1950, to fund a revolutionary mechanism, the European Payments Union. Of that amount, the EPU received $400,000,000 over the next two years. (See Appendix D.) Richard Bissell later boasted in his memoirs that the EPU rated as nothing less than "the greatest achievement of the Marshall Plan." Boast it certainly was, for the EPU was the brainchild of Bissell's own creative staff at ECA's Washington headquarters. With Ted Geiger playing a valuable role in its conception, it was American by initiative as well as by design. More significantly, it allowed OEEC to acquire its greatest credibility. The former Director of its Economic Division, Alexander Cairncross, has pointed to the EPU's response to West Germany's 1950 balance of payments crisis as proof of a maturing European sensibility, "the first occasion of successful self-help among the European countries." "The USA stood back from participation in this," the Englishman recalled

Austrian electrical engineers study a new generator at the General Electric plant at Schenectady, New York, under the Technical Assistance and Productivity Program.

with satisfaction, leaving European countries "to rescue the Germans."[36]

A major breakthrough, the EPU knocked down traditional barriers to multilateral trade by making all European currencies readily convertible, a solid foundation on which subsequent European economic growth depended. It had as well an important German angle, freeing West Germany from its prewar and wartime "debt overhang." Thus unbound, German industrialists became the nitroglycerine for an extraordinary explosion in intra-European trade. But the resulting Continental prosperity was also at America's expense, with the ECA waiving some American rights and further weakening its trade figures. As a supreme act of American self-confidence and altruism, it rivaled or perhaps even surpassed Lend-Lease during World War II.[37]

Robert Marjolin, the OEEC's indispensable secretary general, has pointed out in his own memoirs that the EPU aided a future "formidable competitor" while inflicting short-term economic injury on the United States. Like drawing rights, EPU disadvantaged American business, this time by excluding convertibility of European currencies into dollars. In addition to sanctioning temporary discrimination against the American currency, it restricted American imports in order to stimulate greater European exports. Congressional admiration for the EPU proved to be far less than it was for PAs and counterpart funds. Over time, however, limitations on American imports were phased out and eliminated. Eventually, in 1958, western Europeans adopted a general convertibility that included the dollar.[38]

With its delayed fuse, the United States Technical Assistance and Productivity Program, or USTAP, qualifies as the Marshall Plan innovation with the biggest bang for the buck. Under its auspices more than six thousand European managers, workers, educators, and engineers visited the United States to learn production and construction methods by the end of 1951. They toured factories, conversed with businessmen and labor leaders, and attended management-labor seminars. The program traveled a two-way street, as hundreds of American specialists also went to Europe to teach and demonstrate the American System and know-how to Marshall Plan recipients. European engineers took crash courses, for example, on highway improvements, courtesy of ECA. When they completed classroom curricula, they put theory to practice, undertaking field work in the United States. To increase the flow of dollars into the European economy, ECA also established technical assistance training in the field of tourism, with Austria a primary beneficiary. Besides building new roads and launching new industries, the purpose of all the instruction and retraining was to boost European productivity through adoption of American practices.[39]

Although begun in the fall of 1948, technical assistance was promising yet inconsequential at first. By the end of 1949 only $5,000,000 was budgeted for USTAP. By the time the Marshall Plan ended on December 31, 1951, its expenditures totaled just $30,000,000, or less than 1%, out of the billions spent. It was an amount regarded by Imanuel Wexler as too paltry to modify long-established European attitudes towards business. The response, actually, was mixed. British and French management put up an especially stiff resistance to copying Yankee business practices and managerial styles while West German management was avidly receptive. Much more inclined to follow the American example, they had better results than their British and French counterparts.[40]

Its value underappreciated by Marshall Planners, USTAP expanded dramatically after MSA absorbed ECA. The brand new concept it embodied then caught on, and its potentialities were fully realized. In 1953, with creation of a European Productivity Agency, the number of technical missions visiting the United States soared. To a large degree, western Europe's subsequent adaptations of American methods and ideas stemmed from the greatly enlarged technical assistance program originating during Marshall Plan days. In keeping with George Marshall's core conception, in the interaction of cultures in the 1950s neither American imposition nor full-fledged European adoption occurred. Technical assistance was a tale of voluntary, selective, and partial adaptations of Yankee models. Europeans embraced what conformed to their needs and values. Admittedly, from 1953 until 1958, when USTAP shut down after an additional $154,000,000 had been invested in its numerous projects, it "generated" in Jacqueline McGlade's findings "only modest [American] business participation and support." Concerns about compromising their trade secrets, losing their competitive advantages, and industrial espionage led some executives to withdraw their cooperation. This meant that after 1950 ECA's search for business consultants led increasingly to business schools rather than corporate boardrooms. Many prominent American businessmen, however, were willing to help potential European rivals by disclosing their latest equipment and manufacturing techniques.[41]

Weaknesses

The temporary national sacrifices built into technical assistance programs, drawing rights, and the EPU drew angry denunciations in Congress and the press, particularly among unreconstructed isolationists and xenophobes. However, such altruism in service to larger national purposes ought not to be considered a Marshall Plan weakness. Plenty of legitimate criticisms can be made of Washington's most acclaimed public policy of the last century. Praiseworthy is not synonymous with perfect. The Plan did and does have its faults and critics. With Congress and seventeen national economies to take into account, deficiencies naturally existed in its conception, and shortcomings weakened its execution.

The Marshall Plan exhibited the uses and abuses of quantification, along with the illusion of mastery that figures can foster. Of no small consequence were the imprecise statistics on which initial congressional authorization rested. In his memoirs, Charles Kindleberger confessed that he "felt like hell" fudging the numbers submitted to Congress to justify ECA appropriations for the first year. By his own admission, his final estimate of Europe's balance of payments needs was "phony," despite many all-night sessions on Pentagon computers crunching the data.

The initial CEEC and OEEC proposals, together with aspects of subsequent national planning, also witnessed the exaggerated value of quantification. In the absence of reliable documentation from numerous member countries, creative accounting and euphemisms mocked Marshall Plan methodology. In some instances, figures either grossly overstated or understated the economic situation. According to a Dutch delegate to the CEEC and OEEC, not only did "everybody cheat like hell in Paris, everybody," but he had "never seen so much cheating." To process an economic survey from the American State Department, the French government selected a foreign service officer. The diplomat subsequently confessed to Paul Nitze that "none of his figures had any basis in hard data. Rather, as Nitze has disclosed, the Frenchman "concocted out of his head what appeared to him to be reasonable estimates." Rendering his own country's numbers "pure guesswork," a Greek delegate to the CEEC filled out an important questionnaire himself rather than send it on to his government in Athens. "True," he admitted, "I have to invent a good bit . . . but do you think that in Athens they know more than I do?" Since Rome's statistical services needed upgrading, the Italian government's official statistics were likewise "of doubtful reliability." Italian historian Vera Zamagni has observed that the "chaotic state of the statistical publications" put out in 1948 and 1949 by ISTAT, Italy's National Institute of Statistics, led to their "political" use by those invoking them. Marshall Planners, as a consequence, insisted on compiling their own economic data. In the additional case of Turkey, economic measurements under review by the Americans were actually "made up." As not infrequently happened in the Marshall Plan's early years, vital information, like the 1947 per capita income for Turkey, Greece, and West Germany, was derived from highly elastic "estimates."[42]

The companion of soft statistics was the squishy metaphor. For public consumption, though not necessarily in private conversation, the basic problem confronting Marshall Planners was how to restore western Europe to prewar economic conditions, a dubious guide for the Europe of 1952. Quickly becoming a cliché, the preferred figure of speech for selling the Plan to Congress and the average citizen entailed, in the words of Secretary Marshall, "getting Europe back on its feet." In fact, the reality on the continent was much more complicated, and the poor metaphor chosen invoked the wrong anatomical part and implied that a crutch might be sufficient. Before World War II, Europe was on its economic and financial buttocks rather than its feet. Its severe structural problems in the 1920s and 1930s did not magically disappear in 1938, the standard selected as baseline for measuring success or failure. In consequence of a politically convenient but flawed diagnosis, maldistribution of income, low standards of living, high unemployment, medieval farming practices, and even inflation never received early on the highest priority they deserved, especially when their pursuit undercut anti-Communist politicians and parties. "Perhaps a deficiency of ECA," a former head of the Program Review Division in the Athens Mission, Helene Granby, has noted, "was in not having clearer social goals." Predictably, after four years of the Marshall Plan, Italy and West Germany still had destabilizing levels of unemployment, while France and Greece continued to experience severe inflation. Rising prices threatened to roll back the gains of greater productivity. Indeed, Professor Randall Woods has concluded that "curbing inflation was not one of the ERP's major successes."[43]

Ambiguities and contradictions matched such questionable reasoning and language. Professions of Marshall Planners did not always square with their practices. There is considerable merit to Michael Hogan's idea that the Marshall Plan was, in many ways, the New Deal switched to an international setting, a European extension of the Public Works Administration, Rural

Electrification Administration, and National Labor Relations Board. Certainly, Averell Harriman thought in such terms, and some country mission chiefs, like John Nuveen in Athens, for example, had been ardent supporters of Franklin Roosevelt and the New Deal. Both the Marshall Plan and New Deal originated in attempts to reconcile free markets with government planning and ended up a Keynesian shuffle. Throughout its existence the Marshall Plan's balancing act rivaled the New Deal's juggling of a mixed economy. Its twin aims of recapturing the fictional European free markets of the 1920s and 1930s (with eastern Europe deleted from the script) *and* engaging in elaborate collective planning struck some economists, like Germany's proponent of supply-side policies, Ludwig Erhard, as contradictory. This is also a judgment that applies to professing globalism ever since Bretton Woods yet practicing regionalism in western Europe.[44]

There was furthermore a latent problem with ECA personnel that manifested itself after two years of operation. A limited pool of expertise in the United States left the Marshall Plan vulnerable to outside events. It always took a special person to accept the calling to fulfill George Marshall's vision, and the reservoir of qualified, motivated missionaries, never huge, approached depletion by late 1950. Just before the Korean War broke out, Averell Harriman confided to C. L. Sulzberger that "most of the people who [now] offer themselves for government jobs are not much good in private life." Three reasons existed for the waning of the vision's appeal and the thinning of quality in the ranks: the North Atlantic Treaty Organization (NATO), the Korean War, and the Mutual Security Agency. Establishment of NATO headquarters in London took some of the original luster off ECA and diluted its applicant pool. In the recruitment of personnel NATO operated as a competitor with OSR, Paris, rather than a complement. It did not help either that Averell Harriman, in open disagreement with Paul Hoffman, tilted towards NATO as having a more important responsibility than ECA in the Cold War. The Korean War slowly transformed the Marshall Plan into a more military-oriented, less economic-minded enterprise. For some, ECA's enlarging role in European rearmament took the bloom off their crusade. The final deterrent to the continued recruitment of an elite, independent force was MSA's absorption of ECA, removing it from the public spotlight. By 1951, an unglamorous State Department had reasserted its power over the business of foreign assistance.[45]

Additional flaws surfaced in ECA's dealings with other government departments. Interagency rivalry, as much a bane of the republic as partisanship, impaired the workings of the Marshall Plan. Mutual support and cooperation occasionally broke down after ECA became operational, with the incessant squabbling in West Germany between OMGUS and ECA a national disgrace and an object of European befuddlement. A few jurisdictional battles, at times a lack of coordination, and some friction as well as bitter feuding between country missions and local embassies blemished its record. For example, Ambasssador Henry Grady and Chief of Mission John Nuveen clashed in Athens, each withholding cooperation. Grady insisted on Nuveen's ouster, but Paul Hoffman rejected his demand for six months. Finally, in the summer of 1949 Nuveen was transferred to another ECA mission. In Rome in April 1951, Ambassador James Dunn, a career foreign service officer, severed all embassy ties with ECA's Information Division in retaliation for allegedly disparaging stories about him in the press. Convinced that the division chief, Frank Gervasi, fed their contents to muckraker Drew Pearson, Dunn wanted him fired, too. A one-time foreign correspondent with an international reputation, the much-admired Gervasi retained the support of his bosses in Rome, Paris, and Washington. When Ambassador Dunn left his post in 1952, Gervasi was still running ECA's best information operation.[46]

"There was," Milton Katz has recalled, "no one United States approach" to European problems. Well known is the State Department's objection to, and lack of sympathy with, ECA's promotion of Europe's regional integration, beginning with Paul Hoffman's famous October 31, 1949, speech in Paris. About this objective, State and ECA seldom occupied the same page. But ECA's most serious failing was its deviation from orthodox foreign policy, which led to tense and troubled relations with the State and Treasury departments. Since Bretton Woods the United States had sworn allegiance to economic internationalism, a goal upheld by State and Treasury after World War II, but flaunted by ECA. A hotbed of regionalists with its own distinctive approach to problem solving, the ECA refused to coordinate its development of the European Payments Union with any other government agency, believing that its pragmatic, short-term thinking took precedence over long-run, global thinking at State and Treasury. In other words, EPU at least temporarily had to eclipse the General Agreement on Tariffs and Trade (GATT) in importance. In a brazen power play, Richard Bissell and cohorts ran roughshod over both agencies, generating considerable enmity. EPU was Bissell's finest hour during his years at ECA, but his tactless clash in 1950, particularly with an incensed and more legalistic Treasury Department, was not.[47]

The Myth of Belly Communism

One of the Marshall Plan's goals, according to Melvyn Leffler, was "to undermine appeal of Communist parties" in western Europe. Six months into the ECA's existence, Averell Harriman, with the Greek Civil War clearly on his mind, stretched that ambitious aim to encompass "arresting and defeating Communist internal aggression."[48] Did the Marshall Plan actually achieve those political and military objectives?

The affirmative side has long cited the dramatic defeat by the Christian Democrats of the Communists in the April 1948 Italian elections and the victory in September 1949 by the Greek National Army over Communist insurgents as compelling evidence of success. One Marshall Plan official summarized in the 1950s what many Americans still believe—"without the Marshall Plan, Italy would have gone over to Communism." R. W. B. Clarke, British Treasury Department official, saw the Marshall Plan's triumph in even grander terms: "a stupendous and unqualified success in . . . stop[ping] Communism in Europe." More recently, Curt Tarnoff has found proof of that achievement in an allegedly 33% decline in Communist popularity in West Europe between the 1946 and 1951 general elections, when the "combined pro-Western vote was 84% of the electorate."[49]

To be sure, the postwar Center-Left-Communist political alliance throughout much of West Europe came apart under Marshall Plan and other pressures, relegating Communist parties after 1948 to a permanent minority role in government. There are, however, problems with generalizations about the appeal of a Soviet-style system. Credible is the notion that wherever Socialists were strong, Communists were usually weak, as the Belgian Socialist Paul-Henri Spaak liked to point out. Moreover, in some parts of Europe, the United Kingdom for instance, Communists never commanded much of a following after World War II. By contrast, Communist parties in Benelux and Scandinavian countries wielded for a time surprising strength: they obtained 13% of the vote in Belgium in 1946, 8% in Denmark the following year (along with influence in the trade unions), and 10% of the electorate (and 10% of the legislative seats) in Norway prior to the Marshall Plan. These were all high-water marks for Communist political power.[50]

On closer inspection, the Marshall Plan's impact on the growth of indigenous Communist movements in Italy, France, and Greece, where their threat was greatest, seems far less impressive. Like a barnacle, a myth—the myth of "belly communism"—has even attached itself to the Plan and been carried along for years. Besides introducing counterpart funds, technical assistance programs, and the EPU, Marshall Planners fashioned an enduring misconception that their diagnosis of the sources of Communist power was sound: poverty, hunger, unemployment, and misery functioned as the incubators of Red fascism. Achievement in their clash with communism was always more modest than the public claims on its behalf. They did cap or slow Communist growth, undeniably, but in their containment of the threat they also benefited greatly from outside events, frequently unrelated, which they never fully appreciated or acknowledged. The myth finally needs dislodging.

Consider, for instance, Communist political fortunes in Italy, France, and Greece during and after the Marshall Plan. Prior to the April 1948 elections, and with the Marshall Plan just a few weeks old, Secretary Marshall reminded all Italians that a Communist victory at the polls meant self-disqualification from the new American aid program. Later in the year, America's Ambassador in France repeated the tactic, warning the French government that continuation of dollar grants depended on retention of a ban on Communists in the Cabinet. Undoubtedly, the Marshall Plan effectively blocked Communists from participation in the ruling coalitions in Rome and

Paris. And western Europe did move Right during its existence. But did American ultimatums, along with the arrival of massive amounts of free American commodities in Italian, French, and Greek ports over the next four years, "undermine" Communist strength in those three countries?[51]

The answer revealed in voting data is a surprising "no." As George Quester has remarked, during Marshall Plan days Communists had an "irreducible appeal" at election time. In the much-misunderstood 1948 Italian elections, Communists actually increased their percentage of the vote over 1946. Responsibility for swinging the election to the Papal favorite, the Christian Democrats, rested with the Vatican's unprecedented intervention in the campaigning. In C. L. Sulzberger's meeting with Pope Pius XII two months before the election, the Pontiff related that the Catholic Church was "doing everything possible to prevent" Communists from coming to power. With a 92% turnout on election day, the outcome hinged on "getting out the abstainers and faint-hearted, not on reducing the left, which basically held its vote." By mobilizing the middle class and the previously uncommitted, the anticommunists prevailed.[52] Additionally, after 1946 Socialists gravitated to the Centrist parties, further enlarging their ranks. Though not greatly, Communist Party tallies climbed again in the 1953 elections, when over six million Italians voted the Communist ticket, and then remained at around 24% of the electorate in the 1958 parliamentary contest. Rather than weaken, Communist Party support showed great durability throughout the late 1940s and 1950s. During those years the Mayor of Florence was a Communist, and a Communist rally in his city attracted five hundred thousand supporters in September 1949.[53]

A similar situation prevailed in France. Maurice Thorez, a former miner and the Stalinist leader of the French Communist Party, sat in the Chamber of Deputies from 1946 until 1958. From his political perch, the man who had spent World War II in the Soviet Union parroted the latest Moscow line, continually assailing the Marshall Plan as "an American project to colonize Europe," a sentiment echoed in the Communist daily, *l'Humanité*. His graffitists scrawled ironic "Ami, Go Home" slogans on the walls of Paris. In February 1949 he escalated his agitprop, publicly proclaiming that French workers were prepared to welcome the Red Army into Paris as liberators. Thorez's radical rhetoric only solidified the party faithful. With the exception of a 13% drop at the polls in 1951, from 1945 until 1958 France's Communist Party endured as impressively as its Italian counterpart, commanding the allegiance of between 25 and 30% of French voters. In 1956, it was still the country's most popular party. Smash-up did not finally occur until November 1958, when the Gaullists crushed the Communists.[54]

The strangest political situation took place in Greece. Notwithstanding its defeat on the battlefield, its leadership in exile, and American largesse approaching $1,000,000,000 for the anticommunist government, support for the Greek Communist Party, the KKE until reconstituted as the EDA after its official ban, ranged between 9.5 and 10.6% in the elections of 1946, 1950, 1951, and 1952. In May 1958, the EDA won a stunning 20% of all parliamentary seats. William McNeill, who did extensive research and field work in the summer of 1956 in Greece for the Twentieth Century Fund, marveled at "the apparently solid character of the Communist hard core" despite its setbacks. As of 1956, McNeill concluded, "the Communist problem [had] not been really solved."[55]

David Ellwood's research on the effects of the Marshall Plan on the Emilia-Romagna region of northern Italy, where Communists probably wielded their greatest political power in the country, reaffirmed the meaning of parliamentary election statistics. In "Red Emilia" Communist Party membership did not fall, despite the Marshall Plan, until 1951–52, a period which happened to be, economically, the worst years for the region in the entire postwar era. As production increased and other indices of economic health improved between 1948 and 1951, communism retained its appeal to the people. They elected a Communist Mayor of Bologna and gave control of the town council in Modena to Communists as well. With the onset of depression, class consciousness finally lost some of its old luster.[56]

At least in Italy, Ellwood's study refutes, in effect, the concept of "belly communism," which Marshall Planners embraced simplistically and believed uncritically. Hard times did not necessarily "feed communism." Ellwood has shown that the ECA's best intentions and methods were still not enough to roll back the advance of the Communist Party in Italy.[57] Many years ago, Averell Harriman anticipated that historical verdict, telling his staff in Paris in mid-1950 that he was sorry that the Marshall Plan had not combated communism more vigorously by elevating living standards of Italian and French workers and peasants. Later, in his first of many oral histories, Harriman repeated his regret that "we didn't reduce Communist influence . . . as much as we had hoped," adding another personal disappointment over the fact that "the core of the trade union movement in France is still considerably in the hands of the Commies."[58]

The Marshall Plan's success in "curbing" the growth of communism is well established. Its failure to "undermine" popular support for Communist parties in Italy, France, and Greece is not and can be traced to several sources. Curiously, Marshall Planners understood the motives and mindset of their principal enemy only partially, at best. ECA's propaganda campaign did win over the previously uncommitted, including those who felt that their vote had not mattered in the past. They could not change the minds of the already committed, however. Defections and desertions from the Communist movement were minimal. ECA could never figure out how, economically, to attract workers and peasants away from their Communist allegiance. Why French workers who flocked to the Communist Party regarded the Russians as "liberators," not in 1945 but in 1949, confounded them. Their blindspot, it seems, was of their own making, for their challenge to the roots of Communist strength never went beyond the substitution of economic growth for the Marxist redistribution of wealth. Marshall Planners believed that enlarging the economic pie assured automatically a better society.

Paul Hoffman, for example, always professed that "the way to combat Communism is with prosperity," while his disciples put their faith into improving European living standards. When Richard Bissell admitted in passing in October 1952 that "Communists still get nearly a third of the popular vote in France and Italy," he never asked why communism continued to thrive in those two countries despite his best efforts, or why Frenchmen and Italians, no longer hungry, still voted "Red" and continued taking instructions from Moscow and Kremlin collaborators.[59]

Easy assumptions about "belly communism" simply went unchallenged by Marshall Planners. Had they listened carefully to their isolationist foes during their year-long public debate, they might have been less self-assured. Embedded in some crackpot notions, valid isolationist criticisms of "belly communism" were leveled. Congressman Fred Busby of Illinois, for example, warned that "we cannot stop an ideology with money," only with a "better ideology." Europeans, of course, had to be the judge of what was "better." Busby's colleague from Minnesota, Harold Knutson, elaborated wryly on his point. "If Communism could be halted with money," he lectured the House of Representatives, "there would not be any communism in Hollywood, where many of the communists are down to their last yacht." Such arguments were no match for the will to believe in the omnipotence of economic change.[60]

Historical, cultural, and religious reasons for both western European acceptance and rejection of a Marxist-Leninist creed commanded scant interest. During the life of the Marshall Plan not a single, serious in-house investigation into why 25 to 30% of Frenchmen voted the Stalinist line was ever undertaken. For American crusaders, ideological blinders coexisted with their vaunted pragmatism. Richard Bissell's close assistant at ECA headquarters in Washington, Samuel van Hyning, his "quantitative man," later concluded that ECA's response to communism stemmed from a "greatly oversimplified" notion that "greater availability of the better things of life would result in a lessening of Communist influence." With hindsight, van Hyning recognized such mainstream thinking as flawed—as well as a brand of neo-Marxism in its own economic determinism. While Harriman felt that they never received adequate emphasis, van Hyning judged rising living standards in Europe as overrated at ECA. For him, materialism was only a part of the solution to the Communist protest.[61]

The complex sources of the challenge emerge in the remembrances of a pro-Communist Parisian living in France during the Marshall Plan years. From middle rather than working class, she was attracted to Marxist revolution for a cluster of nationalistic, idealistic, utopian, and cultural reasons. Patriotic admiration for Communists as wartime Resistance fighters came first. In fact, for many Frenchmen, as for many Greeks, World War II put halos on their hammers and sickles. Patriotism and communism were compatible causes. The second was disdain for French businessmen for supposedly "betray[ing] their republican ideals" in World War II. The third was a sense of social injustice—the mistreatment of workers—that seemed to offend only Communists and their "progressive" allies. She had been won over by their sermons and their promised land. Her fourth motive was romanticism, a dream of a classless society that contrasted with the ECA's vision of a prosperous consumer culture. Placing her in the company of Jean-Paul Sartre and other Parisian intellectuals and artists, her final impulse was anti-Americanism, a desire to defend her culture against supposed debasement by crass American values. She said not a word about a full dinner pail or an empty belly.[62]

As one pro-Communist's self-image suggests, the Marshall Plan's interaction with European culture and history was understood in oversimplified terms. When the American historian Arthur Schlesinger, Jr., who worked for OSR Paris in the summer of 1948, wrote fifty years later that "Marshall aid reduced Communism's appeal to the working class," he purveyed a half-truth and perpetuated a myth.[63] The complexities of institution building, nation building, and region building after World War II, and the questionable nature of certain assumptions, achieve much greater clarity when efforts on their behalf in four specific Marshall Plan countries—Greece, Italy, Turkey, and West Germany—are examined closely.

ECONOMIC COOPERATION ADMINISTRATION
HEADQUARTERS
WASHINGTON, D.C.

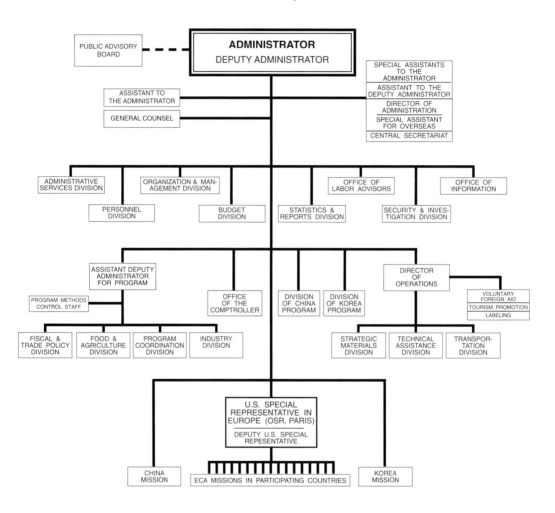

ECA organization as of March 15, 1949

IV
Implementing the Marshall Plan

Compelling reasons exist for performing careful historical autopsies on nations that once benefited from Marshall Plan aid. After all, distances between intention and effect, as well as between conception and execution, need to be understood. But what countries to select for study? Singled out were ones with the greatest resonance for the challenges of postwar reconstruction and stabilization today. In the first place, three of the four nations chosen had been ravaged by World War II, with two being vanquished enemies in need of political reinvention and economic stability. The third struggled, simultaneously, to rebuild itself, pursue economic development, and fight a bloody civil war against Communist insurgents. The relevance of the fourth was its non-Christian, non-Western culture co-existing with a commitment to modernization. The case studies also possessed the virtues of variety—a western European, two southern or Mediterranean European, and an essentially Middle Eastern society—which promised to reveal the Marshall Plan's practical limits along with the ways weakness could be strength. Finally, all shared at least one characteristic: they experienced "economic miracles" in the 1950s.

The four Marshall Plan countries selected for close examination— Greece, Italy, Turkey, and West Germany—once posed distinctive challenges and special problems to the American specialists whose assignments were to expand their economic production and stabilize their politics. In multiple aspects, each is a reminder of two truths: first, in searching for historical generalizations nothing is quite so universal as the particular; and second, particularism's tendency to run riot must be checked for the sake of the "big picture." The countries will be analyzed on a continuum from the Plan's mixed results in Greece to its outstanding success in West Germany.

Greece then straddled the cultural divide between West and Middle East, as it does today. To a country of eight million people with a feeble political center, Marshall Plan aid was fundamental to national survival. It had to be rescued from both economic collapse and internal aggression. Paul R. Porter, one-time head of ECA's Athens mission, thought that "without American economic and military aid, Greece would have spent the next forty years on the wrong side of the Iron Curtain." The former chief of the mission's Import Program Office agreed: "Greece would have gone down the tube."[1]

In Italy, a nation securely in the West and with a strong political center, any possibility of a violent overthrow of the government ended in the elections of April 1948. By then, the Italian economy was, despite high unemployment, on a generally sound footing. How to rapidly develop a society of forty-five million inhabitants split between a modern north and a traditional south, and against the will and fears of a pro-American government, was the ECA's central dilemma. The difficulty faced in Turkey, a secular Islamic country aspiring to be Western, but one that also remained on the sidelines as a neutral during World War II and experienced no destruction, was how to modulate the economic ambitions of Turkish authorities. As a vital military ally in the Cold War, facing intimidation by the Soviet Union, twenty million Turks needed a stronger, more modern economy. For Marshall Planners, pursuing a national security goal with economic means had its bumper crop of unintended consequences.

Unlike Greece, Italy, and Turkey, which quite often turned out to be contests of ingenuity and will, pitting the ECA mission and the local government against each other over methods or money, West German and American officials generally saw eye-to-eye about reintegrating the Federal Republic back into the European mainstream. As in Athens, from September 1949 until 1952 the ECA dealt with a semisovereign government in Bonn. For the prior fifteen months its relations with the American military governor of Bizonia probably qualified as the most trying in Marshall Plan annals. The reason was simple. The stakes there were the greatest, for the fate of ECA's vision of a "new Western Europe," economically self-sufficient and politically stable, hinged on the outcome of its policies towards World War II's villain. In the design of the Marshall Plan's elaborate structure, West Germany fit as the ironic but critical keystone.

Greece

In a chronology of postwar assistance to Greece, the Marshall Plan stood third in line, a Johnny-come-lately. Before the ECA Mission to Athens arrived in the summer of 1948, UNRRA and the American Mission for Aid to Greece, or AMAG, had been extending a helping hand. UNRRA administered, in effect, first aid, while in 1947 AMAG, a combined military and civilian mission formed under the Truman Doctrine, connected Greece to a life-support system that barely sustained arguably the most devastated country to emerge from World War II. Under the direction of Dwight Griswold, former Governor of Nebraska, AMAG was a full-blown aid program with a $300,000,000 congressional appropriation. Upon finally shutting down, its projects and most of its personnel transferred to ECA Athens. The Marshall Plan's first Chief of Mission in Greece, John Nuveen, described the transition succinctly: "I inherited [Griswold's] staff." By August, when Griswold departed, Nuveen was assembling his own. During the rest of the mission's first year a large turnover in division directors took place, with AMAG holdovers later distinguishing themselves in service to the Marshall Plan.[2]

Despite UNRRA's and AMAG's best efforts, Greece was still bankrupt and convulsed by civil war when they turned their economic and technical assistance programs over to Marshall Planners. Driven by its supreme can-do attitude, ECA strove to transform a basket case living hand-to-mouth into a showcase. The year before ECA replaced AMAG, Greece had attained just 40% of its prewar national income.[3] Seventy percent of all Greeks were then one-crop farmers. The country had virtually no industry, foreign exchange, or exports of manufactured goods. Just eight million arable acres, a token infrastructure, rampant inflation, almost no bank deposits, capital flight, and a currency distrusted by everyone meant that American money was wagered on a long shot. A pervasive national fear worsened the odds. Greece's dread of the future had a golden color and the shape of a British sovereign, preferred by its people over the drachma. Undaunted, Marshall Planners provided Greece with $700,000,000 in grants over the next four years. (See Appendix D.) That was half West Germany's allocation, amounting to 5.5% of all ECA assistance and making Greece the sixth largest recipient.

In spite of some glaring failures, the country mission beat the unfavorable odds, accomplishing more structural reform than ever seemed possible. Moreover, a stabilization program, bent on controlling inflation and halting the sale of gold sovereigns, started in earnest in late October 1951, as the Marshall Plan wound down. The following year, after ECA lost its independence, American-sponsored currency reform finally stabilized Greek finances, ushering in fifteen years of a respected drachma and the so-called "Economic Miracle" of the 1950s and 1960s. Remarkably, Greece's rate of real national per capita income growth rivaled West Germany's over that span. There was a catch, however. American achievements raised Greek expectations unrealistically, laying a groundwork for bitter disappointment ahead. Delayed in its billing, the Marshall Plan's hidden cost was a heavy toll in Greek goodwill.

Like Greece's resistant political culture, inheritances of World War II made ECA's successes problematical from the start. That catastrophe left America's wartime ally in shambles. A former State Department official regarded Greece as the "most thoroughly destroyed, disorganized, and demoralized country in Europe" at war's end. After a half century, a like-minded European historian revised only slightly the sad appraisal: Greece "probably suffered more war damage than any other European economy except Russia." Occupied simultaneously by three Axis powers for four years, the Greek people were truly star-crossed, on a par perhaps with the hapless citizens of Warsaw and Manila. Not only did 8 to 10% of its citizens perish in World War II, but when the Germans, Italians, and Bulgarians finally retreated, they imitated Vandals and Huns, destroying or looting everything they could. Bridges, canals, railroads, tunnels, and harbor facilities lay in ruins. Infrastructure, like the port of Piraeus serving Athens and the three-mile-long Corinth Canal, a shipping artery, was left unusable. Bulgarians added a final indignity. To get their Greek booty home, they built a railroad. When they finished pillaging, they dismantled the railroad and took it across the border.[4]

By the time of Secretary George Marshall's Harvard speech, the situation in Greece was uniquely tragic. A fierce civil war raged, compounding the suffering already inflicted by massive wartime destruction. Since April 1946, when Communist-led insurgents launched an uprising backed actively by Yugoslavia's Marshal Tito, the very survival of a fragile Athens government was in doubt. Calling themselves the Democratic Army of Greece (DSE), rebels had a fighting force of around fifteen thousand and supporters numbering seven hundred thousand, compounded of peasants, workers, intellectuals, and retail merchants. At the end of 1947 one of their Moscow-trained military leaders announced creation of a "free" government that contested the constitutional monarchy's legitimacy.[5]

Why the formidable strength of the Communist insurgency? First of all, World War II had conferred its usual postwar halo on Communists for leading the Resistance movement against the Germans and Italians. But, foremost, with only a tiny middle class, combustible disparities of wealth separated the few and the many in Greece, an injustice exacerbated by widespread tax evasion by the well-to-do. Substantial contributors to the insurgency, principally as aids in recruitment, were also defects in the constitutional monarchy. "Incompetent, reactionary and obstructive," an American-supported, royalist regime alienated a sizeable minority of the population at a time when Embassy personnel regarded Greek politics as national sport, even a wonderland. Actually, it was deadly serious, with the well-being of extended families hanging in the balance. The parliamentary system in place, with its proportional representation and 354 members in a single chamber, rendered effective governance and needed reforms nearly impossible. Amidst an excess of democracy and empty political speeches, thirty to thirty-five splinter parties commonly held parliamentary seats. Queen Frederica confided to George Marshall that her nation's political leadership was simply "hopeless." Like the Corinth Canal, legislative channels in Athens were impossibly clogged after the war, not by debris but by internal dissensions which left holders of power out of touch with most people outside the capital.[6]

The upshot was acute political instability and incapacity to solve fundamental economic problems, particularly the drachma's demise. Between 1944 and the end of 1951, twenty-six different governments held power in Greece, with some ruling coalitions surviving just days or weeks. The dizzying merry-go-round and dance of the cabinet ministers always taxed the

Clearing the Corinth Canal, April 9, 1948.

patience and fortitude of ECA's chiefs of mission and their staffs. Paul R. Porter, who served after Nuveen as Chief for fifteen months, recalled the extra burden he carried in trying to meet Marshall Plan objectives. During his tenure he had to deal with no fewer than seven different governments. The political situation in Athens encouraged disrespect in Washington and Paris.[7]

Remaking Greece depended on a secure environment. Pacification came first. Not until October 1949, with Communists defeated and civil war over, did Marshall Planners shift their highest priority from assisting the war effort and providing for the security craved by people in the countryside to reconstruction, reform, and development. In the meantime, even though ECA tempered its ambitious economic agenda, the country team operated on two tracks and tackled numerous problems. ECA strove to improve economic conditions as the fighting worsened. The mission regulated imports, boosted exports, improved public health, and ameliorated labor relations.

Surrounded by hit-and-run guerrilla attacks, and with the Greek National Army (GNA) commanding a huge chunk of the national budget, the Food and Agriculture branch and road-building corps performed wonders. Mission officials visited villages all over the country coaxing increased production through improved farming methods. For the crop year ending August 31, 1949, farmers produced more food, feed, and fibers than they had averaged during the prewar period, 1935–38. American agricultural specialists also started to mechanize the plains areas of Greece, lowering costs and expanding output. Between 1947 and 1951 over 5,000 tractors were imported under ECA auspices. At the end of World War II only 420 operated in the entire country. Marshall Planners were unsung heroes in keeping a 200,000-man National Army well fed and highly mobile in the field.[8]

The Athens mission was likewise instrumental in solving an enormous refugee problem spawned by civil war, a crisis born of two fathers. An unannounced goal of the Communists in fighting was to eliminate private ownership of farms preparatory to eventual collectivization of agriculture. In this objective their destruction of pro-government villages received unsolicited help from the National Army. Its own deliberate policy of clearing the countryside of potential sources of food, animals, intelligence, and recruits for the DSE led to forced evacuation of thousands of villages. Tactics on both sides left 25% of the population homeless, set in motion a huge internal migration, and bred anarchy in rural areas. In all, between 670,000 and 700,000 villagers were uprooted and relocated out of the war zone and into refugee camps at Lamia and other centers. In the winter of 1948–49 an estimated 2,500,000 Greeks depended on government support of some kind. Two months before fighting ceased, 178,000 farmers, along with their families, still lived in various relocation facilities. By June 1950, just 5,000 had yet to be resettled or repatriated.

Caring for refugees with food rations that included millions of cans of evaporated milk, providing resettlement allowances, and then speedily returning rural folk at great expense to their old villages commanded ECA's biggest commitment during the insurgency. Its valuable work certainly enhanced, indirectly, the war effort and did not end until the camps emptied of all displaced people. It meant too that ECA's efforts were, in a large way, engaged in 1948, 1949, and early 1950 with issues of food, clothing, and housing—and other necessities for refugee survival. About 50% of all counterpart funds during the life of the Marshall Plan went for "care and housing of refugees," social welfare programs on their behalf, and work relief when they returned home. An all-out attack on Greece's seemingly insoluble macroeconomic problems awaited the last provision of humanitarian relief.

Greek workmen grade the street in front of new housing
constructed with the help of Marshall Plan funds

Delay had its unfortunate consequences because it put a premium on haste in the Marshall Plan's remaining years.[9]

If the country mission's role in the civil war's outcome has been under-appreciated, the military performance of the National Army and the advisory role of the American Army under General James Van Fleet have been generally overplayed. An official American version at the time, that "the Greek people . . . drove Communism from their land," was both misleading and oversimplified. Among decisive factors in the Communist defeat were two internal decisions, along with an equal number made well beyond the battlefield. Changes in tactics and command by insurgents helped to doom their cause. Pressured against his better judgment by Nikos Zahariadis, leader of the Greek Communist Party (KKE), the insurgency's experienced military head since the fall of 1946, Markos Vafiadis, switched from effective guerrilla tactics to conventional warfare that played disastrously into the GNA's strength in firepower. A second mistake was replacing Vafiadis with Zahariadis, a slavish Stalinist whom historian John Iatrides has described as "much more a Soviet agent than a Greek." Both errors left the rebels highly vulnerable to outside events: Stalin's break with Tito, who was expelled from the Cominform, and a revised Cominform line that Macedonia would be a separate nation at the close of hostilities. Unintended consequences of these distant decisions also abbreviated hostilities.[10]

The influence of Tito's heresy on the Greek civil war was probably not as pivotal as the Cominform's new position on the Balkans. When Zahariadis and the KKE eventually sided with Stalin, who first denounced Tito in late June 1948, they in effect committed suicide in Greece's northern mountains. Tito's revenge and retaliation proved as destructive as the new GNA strategy under Field Marshal Alexander Papagos. By shutting the Yugoslav-Greek border in June 1949, denying the rebels sanctuary, and stopping all aid to the insurgents, Tito accelerated their defeat. Neither Albania nor Bulgaria could replace what was lost in matériel. Besides the unexpected actions of the "Luther of the Communist World," the equally surprising announcement in January 1949 by Zahariadis that the KKE favored the Moscow line on an independent Macedonia, one incorporating Greek lands, sealed the fate of his Communist forces. It was, for good measure, a final ruinous blunder, precipitating desertions, weakening morale, and fracturing the revolutionary movement. Opposed to the Macedonian autonomy scheme, a pro-Tito Vafiadis was expelled from the KKE. Its public disclosure transformed a civil war still going badly for the Athens government into a holy, national crusade to save the patrimony, galvanizing Greek patriotism and nationalism. Nine months later, what remained of the revolt fled into Albania and Bulgaria.[11]

Without a switch in enemy tactics and command, and *sans* back-to-back *deus ex machinas* in the first half of 1949, protracted warfare now seemed likely. When Prime Minister Themistocles Sophoulis announced enthusiastically in late August 1948 "the end of the battle of Greece," he was thirteen months premature. As late as December, insurgents still held the upper hand. ECA personnel could not travel more than twenty miles outside Athens without military escort. "By the end of 1948 and the beginning of 1949," according to Field Marshal Papagos, commander of national forces in the conflict's final stage, "the whole situation was deteriorating." Neither Papagos nor General Van Fleet, who headed the American military advisory group, Joint U.S. Military Advisory and Training Group (JUSMAPG), after February 1948, ever gave credit where credit was due. Both always denied the importance of external decisions, simply disregarding the Macedonian factor. Van Fleet viewed closure of the Yugoslav border as a Communist admission of defeat, not a cause of their failure. The claim that Tito's "defection" assured GNA victory struck him as "ridiculous." While JUSMAPG upgraded the training of Greek soldiers, modernized their weaponry, and elevated their morale, such improvements had limited effect. Despite Papagos's and Van Fleet's denials, the Marshall Plan in Greece may never have progressed very far beyond pacification had it not been for fortuitous events in the Communist world. They led, after all, to denial of safe haven to the insurgents in their military operations and the KKE leadership's implosion at rebel headquarters. Once again, the United

Workmen repair a bombed bridge in Macedonia.

States drew a wild card from the Cold War deck, one with "Uncle Joe's" picture on both sides.[12]

With the civil war finally won, internal security achieved, and a little over two years left in the life of the Marshall Plan, ECA turned its full, undivided attention at last to nation building, whose foundations were equated with a modern transportation and communications infrastructure, scientific agriculture, public health and power, a balanced economy, collective bargaining, a sound currency, equitable taxes, and American-style democracy. The mission was in an understandable rush to uplift Greece by, in effect, grafting the New Deal onto an old political economy. Some programs now given priority, like rebuilding Greece's transportation system, had been started by AMAG in collaboration with the U.S. Army Corps of Engineers, with most construction contracted out to American companies on cost-plus bases. Rebuilding and expanding roads, railways, bridges, canals, airports, and port facilities "grew directly and largely out of military needs" but merged with or folded into ECA activities. Picked up and completed by the Athens mission, transportation projects were "mammoth": 13,000 kilometers of roads, with 3,500 rebuilt and paved. New unpaved roads ended forever the isolation of Greek villages. 250 highway bridges were also reconstructed. When completed, Greece's highways formed an integrated national system for the first time. Its damaged railroads were also restored. In all, 2,000 kilometers of trackage were repaired or replaced but with one odd feature: in the drive to completion and in deference to local preferences, three different track gauges were adopted. Another first in Greek history, a genuine national market for farmers and businessmen depended on these major improvements in land transportation.[13]

The Marshall Plan's greatest contribution to Greece's modernization was not, however, upgrades in transportation. Development of a national, state-owned electric power grid earned that honor. A few Marshall Planners considered it a "carrot," or at worst, "nearly a boondoggle," an expensive means to get the Athens government to cooperate on other, more essential matters. But electrification promised to greatly spur economic growth and to diversify the Greek economy, especially by encouraging needed light industry. Inspiration for development of water power resources and production of cheap energy was, of course, the New Deal's Tennessee Valley Authority. Guiding forces behind the $100,000,000 project were AMAG alumnus Ken Iverson and Walker Cisler, President of Detroit Edison, whose advisory role also laid the groundwork for Greece's Public Power Corporation, created in 1951.

The original ECA plans in 1949 called for five major hydroelectric generating stations to end Greece's dependence on expensive oil and coal imports. In July 1950, a scaled-back proposal for a 150,000-volt transmission system for distributing power from four new generating plants—three hydroelectric (cut from five) and one coal-fired—was approved with the main contract given to an American firm, EBASCO. The Greek government was required to defray one-third the cost of the project. Construction got underway the same year. In December 1952 the first power plant came on line. Four months later, a second joined the system. Both did so ahead of schedule. When the whole net was finally completed by 1956, a basic precondition for future Greek industrialization was in place. Electrification ranked as a priceless Marshall Plan legacy and an extraordinary engineering feat as well.[14]

In keeping with its aim of balancing industry and agriculture in an overwhelmingly rural country, the country mission brought Greek farming out of the middle ages and into the second half of the twentieth century. Looking back on his time as a field adviser and head of the Food and Agriculture branch, Brice Mace felt proudest about successfully introducing an American-style agricultural extension service throughout the country. Using the U.S. Department of Agriculture's long-established program as a model, ECA did not offer it as a quick fix but rather phased it in over a two-and-a-half-year period. Its gradual acceptance and adoption guaranteed its permanence in Greek life. The whole undertaking demonstrated yet again that patience in a traditional society is a cardinal virtue. Ultimately, the Greek parliament in 1950 created another government agency to house agricultural extension agents who embodied a novel, imported concept. Its creation fixed a highwater mark in promoting self-help, a virtue more forgotten than remembered in the Athens mission. Mace's accomplishment was exceptional because he overcame the customary self-image of Greek bureaucrats that government officials were "public masters" rather than "public servants." The crucial breakthrough for Mace and his colleagues was persuading a reluctant Greek Minister of Agriculture to do the unthinkable: take to the fields to personally demonstrate proper planting techniques, uses of fertilizer, artificial insemination, and other applications of scientific knowledge. As hoped, the greater agricultural productivity that resulted did benefit all Greeks.[15]

While ECA's well-drilling program qualified as a big success in the countryside, providing villages with potable water, cooperative marketing proved a major failure, largely because long-established buyers controlled markets and resisted reform. Americans did achieve lasting fame and a permanent memorial, though, by bringing to Greek farming practically a brand-new crop. Walter Packard, the mission's irrigation and production specialist and veteran of the California Irrigation Service, is credited with the so-called "Rice Miracle." Under his supervision, ECA undertook a major land reclamation program, converting 82,000 acres of previously worthless, salty soils in river basins and deltas into rice culture. The Marshall Plan turned salt flats into paddies and farmers, whose rice output had been negligible, into producers of a surplus for export. National production expanded from 4,000 metric tons in 1935–38 to 75,000 in 1952. Until Packard's exploits, Greece had imported most of its rice. In the village square of Anthili in central Greece a bust was subsequently erected to honor Packard for his exceptional service to the nation's agriculture. Brice Mace has long deserved one, too.[16]

Seemingly with maximum economic leverage at their disposal, ambitious Marshall Planners prodded Greek politicians to rewrite their income tax laws and reform their governance. Exposing a conception of the social contract very different from their own, their attack on an unfair and unenforceable tax system, and the maldistribution of wealth it shielded, ended in failure. They also targeted national and local political structures, as well as the electoral system. Their push for better government—which meant more decentralized, democratic, and efficient—is a curious story of temporary success, Greek backsliding, and American disappointment, although a few transformations of note did occur. Long-postponed municipal elections, for example, were finally held in April 1951. And parliamentary representation eventually switched from a proportional to a district system with majority rule, a new arrangement that reduced somewhat the chronic instability at the top. The status of some municipal government officials—village presidents and city mayors—also changed from appointive to elective.

Paul Hoffman (center), the Greek government ECA liaison (left), and
C. Tyler Wood (right) view a Marshall Plan publicity display, October 1950.

After John O. Walker joined ECA's Civil Government branch in Athens in late 1948, the only division of its kind in the entire Marshall Plan set-up, he and Russell Drake spearheaded an effort to modernize and revitalize local government by decentralizing authority. Emboldened by ECA's other successes, reformers pressed forward at the grassroots, launching an assault on the nomarch system next. Their campaign turned into a battle of wits with defenders of the status quo, interminable delays, and a bewildering encounter with Athenian "psychology" and its allergy to plain speaking.

Pre-Walker Greece had been broken up into forty-seven political divisions, each called a "nomos," roughly comparable to an American county. All were administered by governors, or "nomarchs," who were usually hacks appointed by the Ministry of Interior in a giant spoils auction befitting New York's storied Tammany Hall. With cooperation from sympathetic politicians who passed, after much procrastination, a civil service law in 1952, Walker and Drake managed to depoliticize nomarchs temporarily. Younger, well-trained career men were then appointed on the basis of merit, but fatal flaws in ECA-sponsored legislation soon became apparent. First, cabinet ministers controlling counterpart funds denied the new breed of nomarchs control over public expenditures, weakening thereby the value of decentralization. Second, and more Machiavellian, politicians created a new class of political appointees called governors-general. By placing them directly over nomarchs, Athens checkmated the Americans. Old political habits were indeed resilient, as the toppled patronage system slowly reconstituted itself. In December 1952, government appointees replaced once again elected mayors. Two years later, the Ministry of Interior rescinded the "career nomarch" legislation, dismissing careerists and reviving the spoils system. In the end, reform backfired, leaving behind two stifling layers of centralization instead of one. The civil service remained woefully bloated and inefficient. And American-style democracy was still an elusive goal. Perhaps Greece's central statistical bureau, which facilitated reliable agricultural and national censuses and made possible the first national budget on record, qualified as ECA's most lasting achievement in governmental and administrative reform. One imposing monument to America's four-year presence was scientific budgeting. Like the agricultural extension service and the big rice crop, it had never been a feature of Greek life prior to the Marshall Plan.[17]

Also transforming traditional ways of transacting business in Greece were non-Communist trade unions, masterminded largely by a former official of the United Auto Workers, Douglas A. Strachan. Head of the Labor and Manpower Division and AMAG holdover, Strachan stood apart as the mission's senior member. Since his hiring in July 1948, he worked tirelessly for four years, with partial success, to build "a real labor movement." To Strachan, an old Socialist, "real" meant anti-Communist and independent. A hatred in Greece for Communist labor organizers insured him substantial local cooperation. Once again, Communists behaved as their own worst enemy. Prior to the outbreak of civil war, and in preparation for an eventual takeover of government, they had assassinated well over one hundred trade union leaders. "Real" also meant that Strachan strove to organize his fledgling Greek unions in the image of America's AFL and CIO—and on the basis of their antiideological, bread-and-butter philosophy. Despite his persistence, Greece's labor movement rid itself of Communist influence but not of its government control.[18]

One other extraordinary American achievement and legacy involved the Public Health Division's four-year campaign against malaria, which ended in the 100% eradication of the mosquitoes carrying the parasites that caused it. Later a villain of the environmental movement in the United States, the real hero then was DDT. The antimalaria campaign began under UNRRA and was inherited by ECA. Before the disease was targeted by UNRRA and the mission team headed by Dr. Oswald Hedley, another AMAG alumnus, roughly half the Greek population suffered from its periodic attacks of chills and fever. Although they failed to reform health care administration, public health officials battled tuberculosis, launched a nursing profession, and modernized hospitals and clinics.[19]

When time ran out on the Marshall Plan, Greece still had a worthless currency and an unemployment rate around 17%—and was nowhere near the goal of a self-sustaining economy. But the changes in Greek society were immense nonetheless. The Plan helped to derail a Communist revolution, promoted market farming,

Greek Army minesweeper.

improved agriculture and public health, rebuilt infrastructure, brought electrical power to the country, improved to some degree political structures and administration, founded a non-Communist trade movement, and provided more aid per capita than in any other Marshall Plan country. Moreover, chances for homegrown development turned especially favorable in 1952 when currency stabilization succeeded in dulling at long last the British gold sovereign's luster. Between 1953 and 1968 Greece experienced "almost the highest rate of real per capita economic growth of any country in the OECD, save Germany and Japan."[20] Why, then, were so many Greeks, both leaders and plain folk, either ambivalent about Americans or else downright anti-American, by the mid-1950s?[21]

An American aid official in Greece from 1947 until 1949, John O. Coppock, has shed light on the paradox. In his judgment Marshall Planners lost their way and abandoned their credo in Greece. A violation of George Marshall's First Commandment—Europe Shall Save Itself—was committed inasmuch as the Plan functioned as the "main driving force" it was never supposed to be. For one thing, the Yankee presence was simply too big, too visible, too intrusive, and too deeply involved in governmental affairs to constitute a genuine partnership. Statistics reveal the magnitude of American domination: its aid was 25% of Greece's GNP, financing 67% of all Greek imports.

The sheer bulk of the Athens mission on Churchill Street reflected its oversized influence. To a gathering of ECA mission chiefs in February 1949, John Nuveen avowed that "by a strange anomaly I represent the smallest country but the largest mission." His country team fluctuated in size between 183 Americans (and 523 Greeks) inherited as civilian personnel from AMAG and 131 a year later. But at the time Paul R. Porter replaced him in September 1949, with the civil war's end in sight, the American staff had ballooned to 240 people, three times the size of the Italian mission and nearly

Greek Army engineers repair a road.

five times its Turkish counter-part. The passage of fifty years apparently fogged Porter's memo-ry, for in 1998 he wrote that "at the peak" ECA Athens employed 181 Americans and 48 Greeks. He was mistaken. Even in ECA's last year of operation, 1951, its staff continued to number 215 Americans and 410 locals, pre-senting an overwhelming physi-cal reminder of a sovereignty more forfeited than abridged. Such mass and visibility were never Washington's intention.

The report which called forth AMAG had recommended a mission of "modest size," with no more than 50 people plus a single chief. Its author, Paul A. Porter, proved prescient. "The Greek public, whatever its initial reaction, would probably not take kindly," he predicted, "to an overly large group of Americans." Except for the single chief, nobody heeded his advice.[22]

To Coppock, the Athens mission evolved as "a thing apart," described by some as either a shadow government or how one of many ambivalent Greek officials during the Marshall Plan years, the Minister for Coordination and Economic Planning, Spyros Markezinis, referred to it: "an American super-government." Another member of the American team likened his role to that of a proconsul. Many years later, Coppock's boss swept aside euphemisms, downplaying the genuine partnerships personified by Packard, Mace, and other missionaries from across the Atlantic. What Greece experi-enced from 1948 until 1951, in John Nuveen's opinion, was "the four-year dictatorship of an American junta," composed of the American Ambassador, the head of JUSMAPG, and ECA's chief of mission. By replacing euphemism with exaggeration, the Chicago investment banker missed a key point. American domination was as much perception as reality, for in truth a tem-porary deal or bargain had been struck. ECA Athens never wielded plenary powers. Instead of usurping authority, desperate Greeks thrust it upon Americans in a national emergency. In the lawful provisions of the bilateral ECA treaty, a member nation diminished its own sovereignty to avoid its own financial disintegration and a Communist takeover. Constantin Tsatsos, a critical Greek government official, was correct: "everything the Americans wanted was given."[23]

As terms of the deal, highly visible Marshall Planners did exercise indi-rect and partial control over exports and imports. They modified prices for major commodities and interest rates on loans. They also oversaw currency and money supply, and ratified bank credits. The American steamroller even ran government bureaus, including finance, foreign trade, and public works. Before Paul R. Porter's tenure as mission chief ended, he had removed all but two Americans overseeing government bureaus. By then, though, considerable damage to Greek pride and self-respect had already been inflicted. The public, as Paul R. Porter once foretold, had not "taken kindly." But the extent of offended sensibilities and ill will can be overstated. Greece had a long history of political intervention by outsiders. "Greece is by her nature a dependent country," observed an American journalist in 1949, "a poorer south Italy without north Italy to draw on." What probably mattered most were the elevated expectations which America's proconsulship instilled in many Greeks. Fulfilling its end of the bargain entailed a new role as godfather, or "nonos," with unspecified future responsibilities for Washington.[24]

In his memoirs Paul R. Porter fondly remembered the remarkable improvements and transformations that occurred during his time in Greece. He also expressed regret that the ECA was guilty of a serious misjudgment. Americans should have been more patient in fostering self-help among Greeks. They did way too much, breaking George Marshall's bedrock rule that "only Europeans can save Europe." No matter what American motives were, a heavy-handedness characterized the treatment of host by guest. Threats of withholding or cutting off Marshall Plan aid actually forced government resignations, toppling Prime Minister Sophocles Venizelos and his cabinet in 1950. In a letter to George Marshall, dating the nadir of Greek-American relations under the Marshall Plan, Queen Frederica accused Ambassador Henry Grady of "imposing" on her people the "unspeakably awful" government of Nikolaos Plastiras as Venizelos's successor.[25]

With the sterling intentions of do-gooders in a hurry, the Athens mission overreached itself, compromising national sovereignty and providing unfriendly Greek politicians with an all-purpose "American card." Thereafter, it could always be played when their chronic failings required a handy scapegoat. Bent on liberating Greeks from economic and political backwardness, as well as ending the rule of a swollen bureaucracy and its bad administration, Marshall Planners eagerly accepted an invitation to rebuild and defend a shattered nation. They hoped to make Greece over "in their own image." Indeed, Greece provided the setting for the most comprehensive effort to Americanize a European nation under Marshall Plan auspices.

But Greek culture strongly resisted American-sponsored change. Its Byzantine politics, for example, was simply unfathomable. Its methods for outfoxing foreign missionaries like John O. Walker and Russell Drake could be ingenious. More Eastern than Western, some Greeks even equated aid with domination, obviating any appreciation on their part. Trying to come to terms for the first time with a country straddling West and East, Marshall Planners unwittingly planted seeds of anti-Americanism. In late 1954 and 1955, when Washington failed to discharge its duties as "nonos" by siding with London on the Cyprus Question, America reaped the whirlwind. Its opposition to a union of Cyprus with Greece, or "enosis," crushed Greek anticipation of a special relationship with the country of the Marshall Planners. Thereafter, a popular sentiment of betrayal exposed, tapped into, and magnified latent resentments. A patron state had entitlements, but to clients in Athens disloyalty was not among them. The Plan's creators had neither wanted nor expected what Will Clayton once belittled as "hosannas of gratitude." But they never imagined the nationalist backlash that swept a society historian William McNeill discovered in the mid-1950s as, supposedly, full of "anarchists and individualists at heart."[26]

"We were guilty," remembered James Warren, "of a little bit of hubris." His open confession is a "bit" of an understatement. Arriving in Greece knowing "very little of Greek society" and almost nothing of the Greek language, Americans still felt that the American Way was the "only acceptable" solution to Greece's problems. A local government specialist in the Athens mission, Harold Alderfer, decided belatedly that "the real Greece cannot be understood in Western terms." As a result, Greek sensitivities about their culture, traditions, and history went frequently unrecognized. In an especially revealing comment in his rich oral history, Warren admitted that Americans were "tied umbilically to our interpreters who were with us in every circumstance." Supposedly to minimize misunderstanding, professional interpreters handled all ECA business. Since the American embassy provided no Greek language training, Marshall Planners who wished to cut the umbilical cord hired tutors at their own expense. Apparently, not many did. Understanding was thus compromised.

A striking weakness of the ECA in Greece was its lack of individual language facility, which elevated local interpreters into wielders of inordinate power. Of necessity, reality was almost always mediated by a third party and seldom experienced directly. One Greek official thought that the Americans were "surrounded too much by [Greeks] who had a language advantage" but were without the best knowledge or good judgment. The same problem surfaced in Turkey. The head of the Turkish Central Statistics Office also commented on the tyranny of English wherever the ECA operated. He detected "a tendency to [hire] very nice fellows speaking English" while the ablest men went unutilized. Badly needed, American clones of Vernon Walters remained in short supply. Genuine appreciation of the characteristics of an older civilization suffered as a result.[27]

Italy

In the Italian case, ECA revealed greater flexibility than it did in Greece, adapting its goals to Italy's priorities and peculiarities. Italy perhaps best illustrated the Marshall Plan's basic heterogeneity. Its ordering of specific objectives varied from recipient to recipient, with their selection depending on each country's distinctiveness. The Procrustean bed into which Greece was tucked proved the exception, for no other Marshall Plan country except West Germany was as acutely vulnerable to a fundamental makeover as was Greece. By contrast, the Italian government, much better able to uphold and defend its sovereignty, tested the limits of America's cooperative spirit. Generally a keen first-hand observer of postwar European affairs, Theodore White did distort an episode in his autobiography, claiming that "Italy was then one of the most docile and obedient partners in the Marshall Plan." Rather, Rome understood fully well that in Washington support for an enthusiastically anti-Communist regime took precedence over unwanted economic reforms. A recent wartime enemy thus received $1,500,000,000 in Marshall Plan aid, 12% of total disbursements, largely on its own terms, not like Greece, as a semiresentful supplicant. Stalemated, the ECA mission did not get very far in pushing its reform agenda in Italy.

Like Greece, Italy's domestic politics and a pervasive fear presented big hurdles that had to be overcome. Alcide de Gasperi's Christian Democrats (DC), the party of a sound lira, financial stability, the Vatican, women, the elderly, and the middle class, greatly feared inflation's destructive power. The country's terrible postwar inflation, when wholesale prices surged to more than fifty times their 1938 levels, was not capped until 1947. The experience left its scars and instilled a dread among centrist politicians equal to their anxiety over internal Communist subversion. As a direct consequence, they were loathe to use counterpart funds for large-scale developmental purposes advocated by ECA. Italian-American disagreement on this subject resided in the marrow of economics. To the ruling Christian Democrats, as well as the International Monetary Fund, the greatest good was in stabilizing the lira, controlling inflation, and regulating money in circulation. Marshall Planners disagreed. Each side regarded the other as taking or advocating serious missteps. Italian historian Vera Zamagni has revealed that ECA Rome "notoriously distrusted the Italian administration" for rejecting reforms tied to Keynesian measures.

Postwar Italian industry provoked a debate about the appropriateness of the Keynesian tools favored by Americans. Surplus capacity coexisted during those years with sluggish production and high unemployment. Surprisingly, World War II had destroyed only about 8% of Italy's industrial plant, sparing Milan, Turin, and Genoa heavy damage and leaving untouched its electric power network. The surviving 92% meant that, unlike other belligerents, its industrial capacity prior to ECA's creation already surpassed 1938 levels by 37%. The rub was that industrial production still remained 43% below prewar output. To ECA's Rome mission, the country's economic problems could never be solved without recourse to Keynesian countermeasures, particularly greater investment in productive industries that raised GNP and reduced worrisome unemployment figures. Amidst excess plant,

*ECA Administrator Paul Hoffman meets with Italian
Prime Minister Alcide de Gasperi, October 1950.*

two million Italians went jobless, 10% of the labor force. "About just as many workers [were] unproductively underemployed" as well, in historian Federico Romero's estimation. At twice its prewar level in October 1948, Marshall Planners tagged unemployment as Italy's Number One Problem.[28] However, to de Gasperi's financial advisers, especially Giuseppe Pella, rapid industrialization, higher wages, and lower unemployment risked another round of uncontrollable inflation. That was unacceptable. In the view of Italian banker and delegate to the OEEC Giovanni Malagodi, ECA policy was wrongheaded and a "mistake," especially in light of Italy's "enormous pressure of population against resources."[29]

Over a barrel, given the Christian Democrats' otherwise impeccably pro-American, anti-Communist credentials, Marshall Planners adjusted and accommodated to Rome's deflationary policies. Faced with an Italian government accepting of high unemployment and stagnant wages, Marshall Planners turned to indirect methods for broadening the country's consumer base and battling unemployment. They pressured, for instance, for the elimination of both gasoline and horsepower taxes. They also encouraged Fiat to develop and market a car for the Italian masses—small and inexpensive. But they were at their most philosophical in encouraging large-scale emigration.

In the early days of the Marshall Plan the Italian government expressed concern about its "surplus population with no opportunities to emigrate," classifying it as a vexation "with no foreseeable solution." By 1949, ECA was publicly defining overpopulation as a "most basic problem in Italian economic life." Galloping population growth in southern Italy produced "too many people for the number of jobs," necessitating emigration on a "mass scale." In deference to Catholic sensibilities on the part of Protestant policymakers and a Jewish Chief of Mission, James D. Zellerbach, birth control as a long-range answer was never discussed.[30]

As promising locations for an Italian exodus, Americans pointed to Argentina and Brazil in South America. The United States, however, never offered itself as a destination. Limits to American generosity and congressional cooperation existed. In solving this particular question, Marshall Planners chose not to get out in front and lead by example, honoring the Plan's purpose to promote European cooperation within a regional framework. Without ECA lobbying, Congress left America's annual immigration quota for Italians at a paltry 5,800, refusing to revise it upwards, despite pressure from the Italian government. Existing legal restrictions on Italian entry into the United States troubled de Gasperi's advisers "very much." Giovanni Malagodi thought the Americans should have increased their quota tenfold, to 50,000 per year. To him, opposition on Capitol Hill was "unjustified." In December 1949 Averell Harriman and Milton Katz met with Finance Minister Guiseppe Pella in Paris to discuss the matter. Pella recommended a bilateral approach, a "Special American-Italian Commission" to study the problem, but was rebuffed. Harriman and Katz wanted instead a strictly European solution worked out at the OEEC rather than a unilateral American one that defeated the Marshall Plan's rationale. They had not forgotten their intention to be "catalytic agents" of change.[31]

Since shipping was then inadequate, and commercial aviation still in its infancy, ECA did agree to fund more Italian shipbuilding to break the bottleneck and help move surplus nationals overseas. Initial results from dumping the jobless abroad were encouraging. Between 1947 and 1949, intercontinental emigration figures trebled, reaching 150,000 in 1949. By 1951, however, an American correspondent in Italy reported that "today no foreign country seems willing to absorb Italian labor." Denied greater access to the American labor market and with the flow of intercontinental emigration peaking in the mid-1950s, the Italian government adopted an intra-European remedy. Italy's single, male, unemployed workers became a source of manpower for nearby construction, mining, and manufacturing industries in France, Belgium, and Switzerland. Sanctioned by bilateral agreements, a system of quotas, temporary contracts, bans on permanent settlement, and unregulated remittances came into existence. Throughout the 1950s Italy's national emigration policy, deemed "a vital necessity," fell consistently short of its goal of 200,000 net emigrants per year. By decade's end, its unemployment problem seemed as intractable as ever, but its predicament had become a regional concern.[32]

For the first two years of the Marshall Plan, an American goal of higher standards of living for the Italian people through economic development was put on hold. To temper the inflationary potential of their primary objectives, Marshall Planners pushed instead for industrial expansion that generated increased foreign trade. Rather than national growth driven by increases in domestic demand and consumption flowing from more employees with higher wages on the American model, boosting GNP would depend on liberalized intra-European trade and greater international demand for competitive Italian products.[33]

Until 1950, when economic growth accelerated, caution and a hard-money policy prevailed. Frustrated by governmental stubbornness and fears about runaway inflation thought to be unreasonable, the ECA substituted words and images for actions in its quest for worker and peasant support. To the average Italian whose standard of living remained largely unchanged during the Marshall Plan's first two years, the Information Division preached a gospel of rising expectations. Unable either to reduce unemployment or to raise wages, ECA elevated hopes instead. To Andrew Berding, a man equal to his task, went the assignment to monetize expectations.

Out of the Rome mission, the forty-six-year-old Berding ran the Marshall Plan's biggest and best propaganda operation, and the one most highly respected by Alfred Friendly, his first boss. Berding came to his position with ideal qualifications. A graduate of Cincinnati's Xavier University, he studied at Oxford for two years, receiving his BA and MA in English literature before moving to Europe, where he lived for the next five years. In 1933, the Associated Press hired him as a correspondent and then as Chief of its Rome bureau, a position he held until 1937. That year he returned to the States as chief Associated Press correspondent covering the State Department.

Before the United States entered World War II, Berding had been a newspaperman for nearly a decade, had lived in England for two years, and on the continent for nine more, including four in Italy where he acquired fluency in Italian. During the war he joined the Office of Strategic Services (OSS), rising to Chief of Counterintelligence in both Italy and Germany with his intelligence duties taking him regularly to London. Experienced in the ways of Europe, Berding quickly set the bar for other information divisions. His innovations included a daily survey of the local press, working arrangements with all media agencies, a documentary film capability, contracts with the national radio network for weekly broadcasts, a mobile film unit, and even a traveling puppet show. With Moscow subsidizing every Communist newspaper in Italy, then roughly 20% of the country's press, and with the Italian Communist Party (PCI) publishing four dailies in Rome alone, Berding's novelties exploited his adversary's weaknesses. David Ellwood has inferred that

Reclaiming land near Svona, Italy, using Marshall Plan–supplied equipment.

the PCI "failed to understand in time that audio-visual mass media [the cinema] possessed capacities of communication and penetration far superior to those of the printed page."[34]

Berding's education, background, language proficiency, and professionalism recommended him as the ideal person to sell the Marshall Plan's messages to the struggling Italian in the village, the factory, and the field. Instead of elites, he targeted workers, women, and children. Knowledgeable about the local culture and people, particularly about pockets of illiteracy among the masses throughout the country, he turned to the visual arts rather than the written word as his most effective medium of persuasion. In a subversive strategy that reached millions at the grassroots, Berding organized a mass program that carried Marshall Plan messages and slogans right to the people and over the heads of those resistant to significant reform—the national government, big businessmen, and large landowners.

Berding commanded a vast arsenal of visual propaganda weapons: the radio (a mighty conjurer of mental images), photographs, posters, newsreels, documentaries, displays, and exhibitions. His most creative instrument was the mobile cinema show with its "fleet of twenty-six mobile projection units" that played Marshall films in the remotest villages. Others included concerts, cartoon strips, puppet shows, and animated films. Beginning with the Bari Fair that stretched over seventeen days in September 1948, the

ECA participated with exhibits in every local fair in Italy. With a million visitors from around Europe, the Milan Fair eclipsed all others in importance. Berding had a special ECA Exhibit housed there in its own pavilion. He invested his greatest faith, however, in conventional documentaries. A disproportionate number of Marshall Plan films were authorized for Italian audiences. Indeed, the largest percentage was made about Italy, the most heavily targeted country in Europe, with forty out of a grand total of three hundred films, or 13%. Subjects ranged, for example, from land reclamation in Apulia to land reform in Calabria; from the reconstruction of shipping, rail lines, and an oil refinery in Trieste to construction of Rome's new railroad station and the reconstruction of Monte Cassino. And regional films highlighted Sicily, Tuscany, Emilia, and Maniago.[35]

Linking much of the subject matter were Berding's themes. Economic prosperity and growth would transform Italians into freer Europeans. The Marshall Plan translated into a higher standard of living, maximum employment, greater production, and a more credible government. By his various methods of communication, Berding estimated that he had reached thirty million Italians after two years of selling the Marshall Plan. By then, 52% of all Italians favored the Plan while only 11% opposed it. Salesman Willy Loman in his prime could not have done much better.[36]

Berding's campaign of outreach was supplemented by the work of the mission's Labor Division, which also swam against a powerful current in Italy. The Labor Division's difficulty was akin to the Information Division's. Without help from the central government, how does one contain or weaken labor radicalism when throughout the Marshall Plan years Italy's jobless remained around two million, averaging over 8.5% annually and the highest rate in Europe?[37] Keeping with larger objectives of enfeebling the Communist-dominated World Federation of Trade Unions (WFTU), regarded as an "instrument of Soviet foreign policy," and creating a new anti-Communist international organization, the strategy adopted was to split the Italian labor movement to isolate the Communists. The Rome mission's euphemism was "special expanded activities." Leading the American effort was a lieutenant colonel in the U.S. Army on loan to ECA and fluent in Italian, Thomas Lane. Averell Harriman thought Lane irreplaceable. In early 1949, he even wrote personally to Secretary of Defense James Forrestal, requesting that Lane's reassignment be rescinded. Forrestal complied and changed his orders; in late 1951 the colonel was still detailed to the Labor Division. By then, he had been promoted to head.[38]

In Italy at the end of World War II, Lane had befriended Giulio Pastore and other anti-Communist trade unionists who he now sought to use to loosen the Communist grip on Italian workers. He needed their help, and they enthusiastically cooperated. In April 1949 Lane and his labor information officer, James Toughill, along with Pastore, Giovanni Canini, and Appio Rocchi, visited the United States for talks with the leadership of the AFL and CIO about the benefits of American labor-management relations. Important contacts were made and, subsequently, American money poured into Pastore's coffers. Lane and Pastore, both devout Catholics, made an effective team and were midwives at the birth of non-Communist, nonpolitical labor organizations that rejected class struggle and embraced collective bargaining.[39]

Using a large budget made possible by the 5% levy on counterpart funds, Toughill attacked Communist unions in his own media offensive. His principal targets for propaganda were industrial workers in Turin and Milan. Every month his staff in Rome published its own trade union journal, while also broadcasting five programs per week over state-run radio. In addition, he released a documentary film every month for commercial distribution around the country in local cinemas. To tout the virtues of greater productivity and assail the vice of class hatred, Toughill's office arranged for visits from American labor leaders and their representatives. People-to-people diplomacy helped to win some converts away from the Red banner, but Communist solidarity generally absorbed the assault.[40]

ECA's efforts on the labor front bore considerable fruit among Catholic workers. At the end of 1948 the Communist-dominated labor organization, the CGIL, had 6 million members, while the non-Communist but sectarian LCGIL had 1.5 million members. After creation of the new non-Communist CISL in May 1950, with Pastore as its general secretary, the former preeminence of the Communist unions weakened into mere dominance of the Italian labor movement. By 1953, the CGIL membership was cut in half, down to 3 million followers while CISL counted 1.75 million supporters. The rank-and-file laborer in Italy was still likely to wave red flags until the end of the 1950s, but an earlier stranglehold had been broken by the Marshall Plan. ECA's partial success, though, owed nothing to the fiscal and labor policies of the Christian Democrats.

In crucial aspects, ECA's labor activities failed. Besides weakening Communists, Marshall Planners aimed to advance industrial democracy in Italy and promote a "New Deal" for its working class. That goal was not realized. Their legacy was not a unified, non-Communist national union, but three separate labor federations, a greatly strengthened big business, and virtually no improvements in traditional labor-management relations. Unintentionally, they ushered in a long era of fragmented, ineffectual unions, together with low wages and the authoritarian management practices that usually accompany them. Italy's chronically large labor surplus only sapped the old vitality of the labor movement further. Between 1950 and 1960, unionization of Italian industry fell from 47% to 19%, which coincided with CGIL's demise. By 1965, the Communist-led union had lost 50% of its 1950 members. Higher company profits, as well as competitive goods in world markets, flowed from labor's loss of power on the shop floor.[41]

Beginning in 1950, the Italian government—prodded at times publicly by Leon Dayton, second Chief of Mission—increasingly utilized its counter-

Italian apartment building developed by Marshall Plan funds.

part funds for major development projects. Indicative of ECA's persistent flexibility, Rome was allowed to make large-scale investments without benefit of the requisite four-year master plan. Back in June 1948 Italian officials had told Harriman in a private meeting that they intended to use the "lira fund" for soil conservation, irrigation in the South, hydroelectric power, shipbuilding, and railroad improvements. Their intentions were never formalized in a coherent plan, as called for in the bilateral agreement. But by the end of the Marshall Plan one-fifth of the fund had been invested in agriculture and one-fourth in modernizing the rail system.[42]

As the Christian Democrats overcame their deep-seated fears of runaway inflation, and undertook some basic reforms long recommended by the Americans, they found themselves whipsawed by the Left and the Right. The ECA had churned up their political lives. Caught in the middle between

The power plant at Lardarello, Italy.

Communists bent on "perpetual unrest" and agitation against the government and the hostility of the "wealthier classes" upset that their "special
interests" were disregarded by reformers and do-gooders, the Christian
Democrats soon understood the high political price of greater social justice.
Especially disturbing was the fact that some of their strident opponents on
the Right controlled Italy's non-Communist newspapers. Harriman regarded
the political fallout stemming from ECA pressure as a "tragedy." In perhaps
a self-congratulatory outburst, the multimillionaire railed against the "short-
sightedness" of wealthier Italians on the Far Right who refused to bear the
financial burden "equitably" and thus lent credibility to Togliatti and the
Communists.[43]

Probably the most controversial of the economic developments was an agrarian reform and regional development program that failed. Initially, Chief of Mission Zellerbach opposed it as worsening Italy's inefficient production. Since half the Italian population engaged in agriculture, an understandably keen interest existed in how the Marshall Plan might improve the lot of farmers and peasants, especially in the country's southern region known as the "Mezzogiorno." The largest chunk of the Food and Agriculture Division's budget went for land reclamation projects, particularly swamp drainage. But a significant amount of the Lire Fund helped to finance creation of an unprecedented public agency whose express purpose was regional development. Its potential impact on village life was enormous. In August 1950, *Cassa per il Mezzogiorno* (CASA, the Southern Fund) was established and given a ten-year assignment to close the economic gap between the industrial North and the poor, agricultural South. An American correspondent described the country's sectional split in the late 1940s thusly: "Northern Italy creates all Italy's wealth [while] Southern Italy parasitically consumes it."[44]

ECA Rome's technicians and economic analysts, particularly a future Chief Economist at the World Bank, Hollis Chenery, played leading roles in planning an end to the Mezzogiorno's poverty, parasitism, and backwardness. Lincoln Gordon had recruited Chenery out of Harvard's doctoral program. His mentor, Wassily Leontief, subsequently won a Nobel Prize in Economics for pioneering the "input-output" method. The thirty-year-old graduate student, who received his Ph.D. while on ECA's payroll, looked upon southern Italy as an ideal place to test his training in input-output analysis. From 1950 until 1952 he expounded a system for how best to invest counterpart funds in development projects that also improved Italy's overall balance of payments situation. To continue his methods, Chenery organized a team of young Italian economists to apply Leontief's principles to economic problems in the Mezzogiorno after his American disciple left Rome.

Wisely, Chenery and his protégés realized that CASA could be no quick fix. Beginning with improvements in infrastructure—roads, water lines, sewers, railroads—it also offered tax incentives and low-interest loans to companies to invest in the South. After six years, CASA had not narrowed the per capita income gap between the two regions. In 1964 the Italian writer Luigi Barzini referred to the Mezzogiorno as "still by far the most miserable region" of Italy. "In spite of the vast sums invested by the government over the past decade," he observed, its poverty was only slightly better than North Africa's. Unfortunately, by the early 1980s the verdict had not changed. CASA had "fail[ed] to solve the unemployment problem in the South," necessitating the safety valve of large-scale emigration to northern Europe. By the 1990s poverty and unemployment rates were both three times those of northern Italy. Not only had the spread in per capita GDP between North and South actually widened, it was greater in fact than the

Repairing the road to Palermo.

separation in the 1950s when Marshall Planners first proferred a remedy for Italy's biggest economic headache. An award-winning theory ultimately flunked its test.

With Marshall Planners pressuring for an expansion in the ranks of small landholders, the Italian parliament passed two laws in May and October 1950 authorizing expropriation, reclamation, and transfer of uncultivated lands. In the Sila Highlands and nearby Ionian territories peasants received land from the breakup and redistribution of big estates by the government. In all, 800,000 acres were expropriated. Roughly 500,000 were resold to peasants who obligated themselves to pay for their acquisitions in thirty year installments. By mid-1956, 100,000 Italian peasants had been allotted small holdings linked together in a network of marketing cooperatives.[45]

In hindsight, the Marshall Plan constructed both intentionally and accidentally a strong foundation for Italy's subsequent economic prosperity. Though the Rome mission thought the Italian government's fear of hyperinflation unrealistic, prices were stabilized and inflation was successfully contained from 1947 until 1952. Italian budget deficits were shrunk. In the crucial first year of its existence, the Marshall Plan paid for 40% of Italy's imports, releasing funds for other purposes. Well before its Greek counterpart, the drachma, the lira gained respect and bank deposits grew after 1947. By committing itself to trade liberalization, mainly abolition of quotas with other EPU countries, and upholding thereby the Marshall Plan principle of multilateralism, Italy promoted its own economic growth through expanded exports. Between 1951 and 1962 Italy's annual rate of growth surprised almost everyone, reaching 6%.

During the Marshall Plan, Italy imported American technology in its oil, automobile, and textile industries. With Fiat, the country's largest employer, in the lead, industrial production doubled between 1938 and 1953. Car production, in fact, broke all records. New American-style industrial practices, especially conveyor-belt technology, spurred productivity, which, according to Anthony Carew, "rose faster in Italy in the 1950s than in almost any other Western economy." Then again, breaking with a sluggish past had its downside. Increased productivity and profits were not accompanied by either higher salaries, increased domestic consumption, or lower tariffs. Italian mass production and mass consumption were not yet in tandem. With 15% unemployment in metal working and big layoffs in the steel industry, and with workers' wages lagging behind, foreign sales drove the economy. These were imbalances that post–Marshall Plan policymakers needed to address.[46]

America's promotion of increased productivity and economic growth did not translate into an automatic embrace of American attitudes and values by Italians. The Marshall Plan in Italy was a partnership of expedience rather than genuine preference. A Stalinist menace and a shared anticommunism muted serious reservations that Christian Democrats held about American ideas. As Pope Pius XII's "political arm" and beholden to an authoritarian church, the DC's attachment to American-style democracy was questionable. When critics referred to it as the "American Party," they used words more for their emotive than their descriptive power. Cultural and religious tensions often unsettled Italian-American relations. Like the Greeks, Italians were ambivalent about the gospel of the American missionaries. Like the hierarchy of France's Catholic Church, Italian bishops scorned capitalism, considering its materialism as un-Christian.

Guided by the teachings of a Catholic Church as suspicious of Protestant America and its liberal, secular culture as it was of Soviet communism, Italians generally resisted what they regarded as Hollywood values. The Vatican believed that "a godless ideology" shaped the American Way. Indeed, the Italian writer Luigi Barzini could yet remark in the mid-1960s that "the contemporary capitalistic world is still almost incomprehensible to most Italians" even though they seemed reconciled to it by then. Beneath ECA fanfare the Christian Democrats of Alcide de Gasperi, a former Vatican librarian, were committed primarily to traditional Catholic values and teachings, and to a Catholic "Third Way," an alternative to Moscow and Washington. During the Marshall Plan years much about American culture was unwelcome in Italy, a country that exhibited no shortage of un-American traits. Consider, for example, just two: ridiculing Catholicism or publicly insulting the Pope were then crimes in Italy, and Protestant evangelicals, especially members of the Church of Christ, were persecuted for their faith by authorities. Italian authorities did gratefully accept $1,500,000,000 in American assistance, 94% of it in grants, but they also kept Americanization at bay as long as they could.[47]

Turkey

After World War II, the Soviet Union demanded bases and privileges from Turkey. Sharing both the Black Sea and its eastern border with the Russians, Ankara refused to be intimidated. Throughout 1946 the Turkish Army mobilized for war because of recurring threats to its eastern provinces. To bolster resistance, "interim" American military and economic aid, authorized under the Truman Doctrine, arrived the following year. As in Greece, when the Marshall Plan commenced operations in Turkey in mid-1948, it was a tack-on to an existing aid program. In fact, an American military commission had already begun a $5,000,000 road construction project for purely defensive reasons.

Unlike Italy and Greece, American fears that led to Turkey's inclusion in the Marshall Plan were aroused solely by an external Communist threat. Foreign Minister Necmeddin Sadak informed Washington officials throughout the late 1940s that domestic communism posed no significant internal danger. While Socialist parties were outlawed in late 1946, a politically stable Turkey imposed no similar ban on Communist Party activities. "In Turkey," a visiting American noted, "it was not and is not safe to be known as a Communist." More than Islam, Turkish nationalism provided a powerful social adhesive, and a labor force near full employment also acted as a deterrent to Communist inroads. A Department of State "Policy Statement" in May 1949 described Turkey as the "only country" in the area in which communism "has made no headway." Turkey's general suspiciousness of outsiders, and its opposition to too many foreigners in residence, were cultural facts of life to which Marshall Planners had to adapt.[48]

When Russell Dorr, a New York lawyer, member of the Council on Foreign Relations, and diplomat took up residence in Ankara for a nearly four-year appointment as Chief of the ECA's fifty-man mission, OSR in Paris expected that Turkey would not require much economic aid. As George Harris has noted, "the Marshall Plan was not designed to deal with Turkey's particular situation." After all, no "recovery" or "reconstruction" of wartime damage was needed. Unlike Western Europe, Turkey struggled with neither a balance of payments problem nor a dollar gap. Ankara, however, strongly disagreed. Latter-day disciples of Kemal Ataturk did not want to squander an opportunity for Westernization which promised creation of a unified home market.

Despite over 40,000 villages tied to a subsistence economy and 60% of its population still illiterate—weak foundations to support either economic development or democratization—Turkish officials had great expectations. Insisting that their costly position in the Cold War's front lines warranted substantial American subsidies and technical assistance, leading politicians and newspapers soon established a pattern that persisted for the life of the Marshall Plan. On July 1, 1948, President Ismet Inonu told C. L. Sulzberger of the *New York Times* that his country was "getting a very stingy allotment under the Marshall Plan."[49] With the amount of ECA aid as well as its apportionment, the Turks were chronically disappointed. In their initial dealings with Turkish authorities, Marshall Planners operated under a major constraint: all neutrals in World War II were ineligible for grants. It was a "clear rule" of policy that Washington revised in later years to accommodate the Turks. Nevertheless, the Istanbul press served up allegations of American stinginess as common fare. Its general unhappiness intensified after Ankara dispatched combat units to Korea, a brigade of 4,500 men that suffered large casualties.

Because a typical aid package was 90 to 10, grants-to-loans, and because loans generated no counterpart, Turkey received considerably less economic stimulus per dollar than nearly all other OEEC members. Only Ireland's and Portugal's packages were less attractive. (See Appendix D.) In the Marshall Plan's first year, for instance, instead of outright grants—the American stock-in-trade—Turkey received 100% of its $35,000,000 in loans carrying a 2.5% interest rate. In the second year its allocation more than doubled, with 50% in the form of loans. Aid for the third year amounted to $50,000,000, and the percentage of loans continued to drop, down to 33%. Much of Turkey's grant money was also conditional, requiring negotiation of drawing rights with western European exporters. Thus, notwithstanding receipt of over $225,000,000 in aid by June 1952, 62% in grants, Ankara always felt shortchanged by Washington. In truth, they were treated differently. From their point of view, they were entitled to see themselves as second-class participants in the Marshall Plan.[50]

Towards the end of his long tour of duty, a perplexed Russell Dorr looked back and described the Marshall Plan in Turkey as the target of a "continuous campaign of belittling" and "ignoring [its] very real benefits." He even condemned some editorial attacks as "insidious." The principal complainers had been the Turkish press and high-ranking government officials, particularly Prime Minister Adnan Menderes and Foreign Minister Fatin Zorlu. Son of a trustee of Istanbul's Robert College, who implanted in him a love of the country, Dorr never supposed that as an agent of its modernization his task would be a largely thankless one.[51]

As a result of Turkey's unusual circumstances, Dorr presided over a development program mainly consisting of capital goods, with primary emphasis on modernizing agriculture. He adopted different criteria for determining success, with economic "viability"—in all its ambiguity—high on his list. Means to its attainment were cultivation of new lands; development of mining and mineral resources, particularly strategic metals like chromium; promotion of private enterprise and foreign investment for manufacturing; and new farming methods and machinery, along with easy credit for farmers. This is what the Ankara Mission meant by a more balanced, diversified, productive Turkish economy. Initially, $35,000,000 were earmarked for a broad range of improvements, a figure that grew under constant Turkish complaints to over $225,000,000 before MSA absorbed ECA.[52]

Fortunately, Dorr and Turkish authorities did agree that agriculture deserved highest priority in the aid program. In 1948–49, 50% of ECA's allocation went for agricultural machinery. Between 1948 and 1952, agriculture obtained 60% of all assistance. The reason was fairly obvious. Farmers comprised 80% of the nation's population and their habits and techniques were centuries old. Their three to four months of idle time, as well as ox carts and wooden plows dating to the Hittites, mystified Americans. Dorr's top-level understanding conveniently ratified ECA's fundamental thinking about how to integrate Turkey into the larger western European economy. OSR Paris expected Ankara to target farm commodities and raw materials for export to other Marshall Plan countries. Turkey's economy, in other words, was to be "complementary," a policy predicated on the classical liberal concept of comparative advantage. Heavy emphasis on agriculture and raw material exploitation fostered the impression by some Turks, particularly in the press, that the United States wished to confine Turkey to a mercantilist system, a mere producer of foodstuffs and minerals for an industrialized western Europe. Over the years, criticism mounted that mercantilism had returned under a new name. Their country, some nationalists claimed, still served as an economic colony for a western European metropolis. Such oversimplifications appealed to many Turks unable to forget the so-called Ottoman capitulations to the European powers.[53]

In its agricultural work, the Ankara mission went straight to the grass-roots, where raising and diversifying output per man and per acre competed strenuously. But its overriding aim was to dramatically increase total agricultural supply through various means. New and reclaimed lands, principally marginal areas in the dry central Anatolian plateau, were brought under wheat cultivation. For the first time on record Turkey harvested an exportable surplus of wheat. In the Marshall Plan's second year it also produced the largest cotton crop in its history, and increases in cotton production were labeled "phenomenal."[54]

One mission official attributed the remarkable gains "almost wholly to the increased land" being farmed. For better harvests, however, consider-

*Explaining new equipment to Turkish farmers
at Ankara Agricultural School.*

able credit must go to the adoption for the first time of farm machinery. Marshall Plan tractors played their role in expanding wheat output. By 1950, Turkey had imported from the United States over 4,000 tractors, 2,000 disc harrows, and around 500 combines. Another 400 tractors originated in England and Germany. Under the Plan's auspices the number of tractors increased from 2,200 in 1948 to 26,000 in early 1952, more than one for every two villages. A significant turning point occurred in early 1949 when Turkish officials also asked for American technical assistance and training. They, too, proved valuable. Russell Dorr later extolled ECA's agricultural program as a great success, as did most Turkish politicians. In fact, according to Dorr, "in a way [it was] too successful," because the host government allegedly went on to overextend the objectives of Marshall Planners. Dorr's praise calls for other qualifications. His own program, it should be admitted, was as much Potemkin Village as it was agricultural miracle.[55]

Ironically, before the country team invested broadly in Turkish agriculture, two published reports already circulated in early 1949 with warnings of potential dangers. The Twentieth Century Fund had commissioned an extensive economic survey of Turkey by a team of American specialists headed by Max Thornburg, a no-nonsense oilman in charge of Standard Oil of

California's Middle East operations. Among his many pointed observations, Thornburg reminded would-be agricultural reformers about the "heavy costs of mistaken planning" in Turkey's past. Back in 1946, for example, "thousands of tons of cereals had to be left rotting in the central plateau" because railroads gave priority to coal and ore shipments at farmers' expense. The Ankara mission also had available its very own country study which spotlighted past inefficiencies in Turkish agriculture, particularly in marketing cereals. ECA's research had revealed that waste and spoilage often consumed an astounding 50% of total output in years of good harvests. It identified two principal culprits: a primitive transportation network, with which Thornburg agreed, and an inferior system for grading, packing, and storing grains. Silos and grain elevators had also been in short supply. Both reports clearly implied that any major push for greater yield, expanded irrigation, and mechanization among grain farmers carried big risks unless Marshall Planners carefully coordinated their separate projects.[56]

Forewarned, ECA decided to hang its reputation on the many agricultural technical assistance programs that proliferated in Turkey. By the end of 1952, twenty such projects were still underway with the "Big Story" being the acclaimed work of internationally famous Elmer A. Starch, Chief of the Agricultural Advisory Group at the Ankara Mission, and his team of eight agricultural specialists. Before the farm economist with the perfect Dickensian name headed off for his Turkish assignment, he had established himself in the United States as an expert on the semiarid American West, acquiring within the U.S. Department of Agriculture the nickname "Mr. Great Plains." Arriving in February 1950 as one of the country team's highest paid members, Starch worked out of the "Technical Assistance Division," which stood apart from the "Food and Agriculture Division." In a radio and television address in early March 1952, President Harry Truman spoke of a "veritable agricultural revolution" that had occurred in Turkey during the previous three years. Grain production, the President boasted, had risen by over 50% and cotton yield had tripled. Truman lionized a homespun miracle worker as simply "Elmer Starch of Lincoln, Nebraska." The President's was a deft, understated riposte to fellow Nebraskans Howard Buffett and Kenneth Wherry, who had earlier condemned ECA in Congress as "Operation Rathole." While certainly priceless publicity for the Marshall Plan in Turkey, the White House reference was also highly selective in its disclosures.[57]

Amidst recollections of his years in Turkey as American Ambassador, George McGhee made a point that Turkish farm experts contributed in equally important ways to the agricultural revolution. He especially remembered the Turkish cotton specialist as more knowledgeable than his American counterpart. And he cautioned, as if providing a belated rejoinder to President Truman's 1952 televised speech, that Americans must "avoid exaggeration" in talking about the exploits of Nebraska's Elmer Starch and his team of reputed revolutionaries. His was excellent advice.[58]

What actually happened during the "agricultural revolution" was more complicated than President Truman's radio and television audience realized. There was, to be sure, an increase of four million tons of wheat, but as an inducement to greater production the Turkish government had set and paid a price well above the world market rate. Worse, a baffling and abysmal lack of coordination by the Ankara mission caused great waste. Increases in grain production, in Brice Mace's informed view, were "nothing more or less than the utilization of hitherto unexploited fertile and abundant agricultural lands." Putting plow to virgin soil was the central feature of the success story. An equally significant aspect—what President Truman omitted and Ambassador McGhee hinted at—was that in new wheat regions that were opened up, a disturbing amount of what was harvested never made it to the consumer. Neither the road system nor the available trucks could handle greatly expanded output. What managed to get to market found inadequate storage facilities. The result was a debacle: a perishable commodity stored in Ankara's unfinished Parliament building, buried underground, or else deposited behind false partitions at railroad depots. A national transportation infrastructure of roads and rail lines was not yet finished when bumper crops made their appearance. Turkey could not distribute and market much of what it now grew in abundance: 1946 had repeated itself. That next round of waste and spoilage that Max Thornburg and ECA Ankara once feared eventually materialized. Turkish agricultural progress thus had its illusory quality.

Apparently, the legendary Professor Starch—he chaired Montana State University's Economics Department in the 1930s—and his band of experts operated outside the Ankara mission's strict control and without any sense of *déjà vu*. A "unique situation" was allowed to develop. The celebrated "Starch Group" affiliated itself in effect with Turkey's Ministry of Agriculture, undertaking projects financed by counterpart funds. With a nose for lemons as well as grains, Brice Mace has described him as "the perfect absent-minded professor." The maverick director's administrative skills were so poor that he "never knew from one day to the next what his group was up to." Starch earned high marks from Mace only in the art of self-promotion and for his considerable accomplishments in self-dramatization back at ECA Washington.

The final component of Mace's critique involved the trade-offs that accompanied modernizing Turkish farming. In his report to the Twentieth Century Fund, Max Thornburg had also cautioned about the risks of both mechanization and losing sight of crucial bottlenecks. "The use of tractors," he explained, "requires facilities for their repair, which are to be found nowhere in Turkey today." Instead of buying tractors, Turkey needed, first and foremost, to develop reliable transportation and communication systems. Thornburg's caveat constituted a second instance of prophecy spurned. By mid-1951, Turkish farmers operated around 10,000 tractors. Of those, Turkey imported 136 different makes, for which there then existed in

Paul Hoffman (right) confers with Turkey's Minister of Agriculture, Ankara, October 1950.

the entire country commercial service for just 4 models, and nationwide maintenance for only two foreign manufacturers. After four years of the Marshall Plan, Turkey experienced acute imbalances in the agricultural sector of its economy, despite the Plan's original purpose to promote balanced economies in recipient nations. Agricultural production had raced ahead of infrastructure, even though road building was a definite ECA priority. A "Road Revolution" simply failed to keep pace with an "Agricultural Revolution." Consumption of farm machinery had also outpaced its service and maintenance.[59]

In 1948, with fewer than 380 miles of asphalt roads and the rest impassable after rain, Turkey really had no state roadway system. Its highway to the future started practically from scratch. Launched for military purposes the prior year as part of the Interim Aid package, Turkey's "Road Revolution" was the handiwork of American civil engineers and Turkish laborers. The U.S. Public Roads Group designed new roads, and road-building machinery purchased in the United States was essential to their construction. Under the Marshall Plan, road building was regarded as absolutely vital to homegrown economic development. Ultimately, 20% of all dollar aid to Turkey went into expanding, improving, and linking roads. They were perceived as liberators of farmers, arteries by which their improved crop yields flowed into a single national market and their purchasing power multiplied. Not only did all-weather highways increase to around 10,000 miles, but the entire network of roads expanded from just 1,500 miles to between 25,000 and 30,000 miles under Marshall Plan direction. Committed to sustaining such physical improvements, Turkish authorities sent many of the nation's best engineering students to the United States under the technical assistance program to study road-building methods. The editor of the Istanbul newspaper *Vatan* thought that "the road program made a country" out of Turkey.[60]

The Marshall Plan pushed industrialization in Turkey on a smaller scale than in most recipient countries and only on condition that it "contribute to general European recovery." Regionalism and multilateralism certainly operated as Dorr's guiding principles. But with two large-scale white elephants, Turkey possessed disincentives all its own. In the giant Zonguldak coal complex and Karabuk steel plant the Ankara mission encountered ill-advised industrial installations dating from before World War II. An inefficient layout, absurdly high production costs, wasteful management, and domestic subsidies left Zonguldak an economic mess producing coal unable to compete in the world market. After inspecting Karabuk, the country's only steel mill, Max Thornburg called it an "economic monstrosity" and "industrial moloch." Under the circumstances, ECA Ankara seems to have struck a compromise about industrial development: help salvage Zonguldak, put Karabuk basically off-limits, and promote small projects on their prospects for "assist[ing] the other participating countries."

Except for Zonguldak, the litmus test for American approval was whether projects were advantageous for Turkey as well as "directly or indirectly helpful" to other Marshall Plan nations. Though Turkish officials wanted better steel mills as much as better harvests, ECA extended only token aid to Karabuk. To help with local construction projects, ECA did fund, for example, a new cement plant in Izmir and expanded an old one in Istanbul. But for many other projects, Harriman referred the Turks to the World Bank, recommending that they make "full use" of its services. Prior to the outbreak of the Korean War, however, the World Bank turned down loan requests from the Turkish government because it refused to put up its gold reserves as collateral. Without gold backing, bank officials invoked their own catch-22, deeming any loan as too risky because of Turkey's proximity to the Soviet Union. More promising, Harriman suggested that a favorable investment climate would attract private American capital.[61]

In mining, the Ankara mission made some notable exceptions. Plagued by cost overruns, its big-ticket items involved modernizing and improving productivity at Turkish mines through joint Turkish-American ventures. Because Turkey was an aberration in the Middle East, without a single producing oil field, coal remained the nation's monarch of energy. Consequently, for improvements in equipment, port facilities, and washeries the Marshall Plan invested $16,000,000 in the government-run Zonguldak mining complex on the shores of the Black Sea. Americans paid $12,000,000 of the $55,000,000 cost for upgrading the nation's biggest coal mines and $4,000,000 of the $9,000,000 for improving its harbor installations. According to a World Bank report, salvaging Zonguldak ranked as "probably the largest investment project ever undertaken in Turkey." Iron ore and lignite mines attracted additional American investment, while ECA money funded oil drilling in south-central Turkey.

Public power never acquired the prominence on ECA's agenda in Turkey that it did in neighboring Greece, even though in the late 1940s Turkey had a per capita use of electricity lower than Greece and Bulgaria. In all, roughly $25,000,000, or one-fourth Greek expenditures, went for power-related developments. Russell Dorr considered as "essential" a major long-range project, the Sariyar Dam and hydroelectric power station on the Sakarya River. With transmission lines to Istanbul and Ankara, its 80,000 kilowatts of electricity promised accelerated economic growth in northwest Anatolia.

To the projected final cost of $47,000,000, ECA contributed $27,000,000, or 57%. Although hampered by frustrating delays, with its date of completion rescheduled from 1953 to 1955, the six-year Sariyar Project served as centerpiece and symbol of Turkey's ambitious plans for Western-style development and as the envy of nationalists throughout the Middle East.[62]

Long before the Korean War, Averell Harriman justified Marshall Plan aid to Turkey on the grounds that by strengthening its economy, Ankara could support a large military establishment. He wanted a more prosperous Turkey as an "effective deterrent to Soviet aggression." "They must expand their economy to support their Army," Harriman insisted in early 1949, "principally in agriculture and mining."[63] But what was acceptable expansion? When Turkish authorities submitted an overly ambitious investment program to Chief of Mission Dorr a year later, one that threatened to unbalance the government's budget, Dorr exercised his veto on the counterpart fund to restrain them from expanding their economy too quickly. Frustrated, the Turkish government grumbled, and its sense of mistreatment simmered.[64]

On the front lines of the Cold War, Turkey in the late 1940s and early 1950s spent around half its national budget on defense and was sensitive to the special burden it alone carried. Very much aware that other Marshall Plan countries not bordering the Soviet Union appropriated considerably less for their security than Turkey did, Turkish officials fully expected economic rewards commensurate with their sacrifices. Foreign Minister Sadak bluntly informed Averell Harriman and Paul Hoffman at the Turkish Embassy in Paris in February 1950 that Belgium spent only 8% of its budget on national defense and France around 18%, far less than did Turkey. For fiscal year 1950–51, Italy spent 4.4% on defense; the U.K., 7.5%; and the Netherlands, 10%. All twelve NATO countries spent, on average, 6.6%. Turkey was not only at the head of the ECA class, it was clearly in a class by itself. In early 1951, with its press again attacking the supposed close-fistedness of Marshall Planners, Turkey requested $100,000,000 in additional economic aid. Russell Dorr in Ankara approved $75,000,000, but ECA Washington refused at first to support more than $30,000,000 for fiscal year 1951–52. Ultimately, Turkey received $70,000,000. Its self-image guaranteed disappointment and resentment whenever Washington provided less than they felt they deserved. Instead of forming a "bond" between Turkey and the United States, the Marshall Plan turned into a point of "grievance and misunderstanding."[65]

Unlike Greece, where political life approached the pathological, Turkey was a country of political stability throughout the Marshall Plan years. Dictatorship was Turkey's long political tradition rather than an excess of democracy. Turkey faced and weathered its toughest political test in May 1950 when, after a revision in election laws, the political party of the revered Kemal Ataturk, the People's Party, lost in the national election for the first time since 1923. The incumbent President, Ismet Inonu, was ousted in an unexpected landslide that put a new party, the Democratic Party, in control. The peaceful transfer of power staggered Russell Dorr. "The only case I know in history," he declared, "where a dictatorship has voluntarily accepted a transition to democracy."[66]

According to Leon Dayton, Dorr's replacement as Chief of Mission, it was really the Marshall Plan that made possible the victory of the darkhorse challenger. Its candidates had put ECA programs to good advantage, promoting policies impossible without American aid. The ECA's Information Division in Ankara took a low-key approach to the demise of the Inonu dictatorship. "We [didn't] want to be over-dramatic toward building up democracy," the division head later explained. When the new party came into office, its leaders enlarged the Marshall Plan's benefits to the Turkish people. When the ECA first arrived in Turkey, most businesses were state-owned. The victorious Democratic Party promoted private enterprise and improved the climate for foreign investment. The Marshall Plan's influence on Turkey's political culture remains one of the lesser-known by-products of using economic aid to deter Soviet ambitions.[67]

Narrowly interpreted, the Marshall Plan as "catalyst" was a great economic success in Turkey. GNP surged, increasing 7% annually, on average, and jumping 21% from 1948 until 1951, and 40% from 1950 until 1952. By then, cotton had replaced tobacco as the nation's most valuable export, and Turkey promised to supplant eastern Europe as western Europe's breadbasket. With ECA help, imports also grew 45%.[68] Prior to the Marshall Plan, Turkey's economy was a curious blend of state socialism and free enterprise, with a great income gap between the far western part of the country and other regions. Afterwards, more free enterprise, greater free trade, and a more prosperous agriculture could be detected. Like Italy, the sectional disparity persisted. Perhaps the administration of national government underwent the most exceptional changes. Permanent legacies of the four-year ECA presence were six new government bureaus: Bureau of Reclamation, Market Research Agency, Ports Administration Authority, Public Roads Bureau, Agricultural Extension Service, and the emblem of modernity, the Central Statistics Bureau.[69]

Along with the latest IBM equipment and reliable censuses, Marshall Planners left behind new values that undermined a traditional society. According to the head of Turkey's Central Statistics in the 1950s, Sefik Bilkur, they taught Turks to be "data-minded" and "statistics-minded." To preserve a new approach to governance, the Marshall Plan paid for Turkish students in statistical fields to study in the United States. The Westernization of Turkey, the true legacies of Kemal Ataturk and the Marshall Plan, would be a continuous process. Between 1948 and 1952 America's first serious encounter with a Middle Eastern state aspiring to be Western revealed just how easily mutual misunderstanding afflicted good intentions. In March 1950, an old Turkish friend told an American journalist on his visit to Ankara that "the Americans were not too popular" is his country. If past is prologue, then gratitude was the improbable reward awaiting future outside agents of macroeconomic change in Turkey and disagreement the probable essence of Turkish-American relations.[70]

Bizonia and West Germany

In contrast to Turkey, an undamaged wartime neutral devoid of guilt, West Germany's ascent from postwar hopelessness to economic dynamo left its politicians and people profoundly grateful for the Marshall Plan's contribution to their remarkable turnaround. Indeed, it might be argued that, both then and ever since, Germans have overwhelmed their American partners in recovery with an appreciation nearly as puzzling as the underwhelming thankfulness of the Turks. More so than other recipients, West Germany's state of mind during the Marshall Plan years was paramount. Hence, the Federal Republic's leaders in Bonn grasped the economic, political, and psychological nature of George C. Marshall's countervision, judging its political and psychological aspects as its most valuable assets. How different mentalities and perceptions were in Adana and Istanbul. Turkey's elite approached the Marshall Plan as essentially a glorified bazaar.

For three years after its unconditional surrender, a vanquished Germany paid an additional grievous price for its military failure. Although students of Greece's postwar misery might object, the historian Michael Hogan has reckoned economic conditions in Germany "the worst in Europe."[71] Dismemberment and partition into four zones of Allied military occupation—American, British, and French in the west and Soviet in the east—traced out a victors' harsh peace. Poland received German land east of the Oder and Western Neisse rivers, an amputation of the nation's traditional breadbasket that imposed great hardship. In all, Germany lost one-fourth of its former territory, compelling the western zones to import 40% of their food requirements.

As domestic markets stopped working, normal food distribution broke down. Shortages and undernourishment became commonplace. As millions of refugees and expellees flooded into a truncated country, homelessness taxed resources as well. Thanks chiefly to GARIOA, Government and Relief in Occupied Areas, a relief fund set up by Congress in 1946 and administered by the War Department, the wolf of starvation was barely kept in the wild. Prior to arrival of Marshall Plan aid in mid-1948, GARIOA provided $840,000,000 in food, medicine and fuel for the hungry, sick, and needy. In fact, America's first safety net for the German people cost $1,600,000,000 by 1950, exceeding ECA aid of $1,500,000,000 by 1952.[72]

Primitive conditions of barter, hoarding, and black markets also spread widely after the surrender. And because the Soviets debased a loser's currency by printing mountains of virtually worthless reichsmarks in their zone, a modern absurdity humiliated a proud people: cigarettes substituted for legal tender. With its monetary system in shambles, its inflation terrible, its economy debilitated and makeshift, its governance segmented, and its mood grimly fatalistic, Germany's problems and demoralization seemed insoluble. As long as the dire situation persisted, it encouraged Josef Stalin's belief that he might split the West over Germany. A first halting step towards recovery and reconstruction finally occurred on January 1, 1947, when British and American zones merged into Bizonia, a single economic area with forty million people. The following year, the French zone incorporated itself economically into Bizonia. Not until June 20, 1948, however, was a true turning point reached, at last. On that day western Germany crossed a "demarcation line." Once on the other side the German people positioned themselves to use Marshall Plan aid effectively.[73]

Placed in charge of Bizonia was the commander of American forces in Europe, head of OMGUS (Office of Military Government, U.S.) and former military governor of the American zone, General Lucius Clay. As an Army engineer, the military's most political branch, Clay understood how Congress worked. His appointment surely attested to one individual's importance in history and to just how much personalities count. Milton Katz, who had known him since their days together at the War Production Board, once attempted to take the measure of the professional soldier. The general struck him as an exceptional public servant with a first-rate mind but also a "fiery man who sometimes seemed to run an emotional temperature of 104." "Resolved on a course of action," Lincoln Gordon later marveled, "he was like a D-8 bulldozer."[74]

A career officer with wartime experience in supply and logistics, but not combat, Lucius Clay operated without any helpful precedents. Before 1945, America had never occupied a defeated world power whose central government had simply dissolved. The military governor also discharged his duties without benefit, in his own words, of "a clear definition of policy," leaving voids which he filled. His was a broad mandate from the War Department. Consequently, and by his own admission, Bizonia emerged as largely his "show," a constant challenge to his powers of improvisation and his sense of right and wrong. On his economic chief, Major General William Draper, he came to depend heavily. Wielding enormous discretionary authority, at least the equal of General of the Army Douglas MacArthur's in occupied Japan, General Clay found himself in the middle of chronic interagency conflicts as well as inter-Allied feuds in exercising his powers.

In hindsight, OMGUS's assignment was infinitely more difficult than MacArthur's in Japan. Three tributaries fed a river of friction and quarrels that regularly jumped its banks in postwar Germany. The first originated in Clay's discordant instructions formulated in and forwarded from Washington. Truman's administrators refused to speak with one voice on how to deal with a prostrate Germany. The source of the second was the intolerable conduct of a one-time ally carrying out Josef Stalin's nonnegotiable orders about how to treat a fallen enemy. The third stream sprang from undiminished hatred for Germany in European countries overrun, subjugated, and brutalized by Hitler's armed forces and Gestapo. They opposed rebuilding an aggressor, fearing German revanchism.

Until his showdown with Averell Harriman in early 1949, Clay's official guidelines for administering postwar Germany embroiled him in recurring military-civilian controversy. His boss, the U.S. Army, and its State Department rival disagreed fundamentally about his priorities, rendering JCS 1067 a divisive blueprint for its executor. Clay understood his top responsibilities to be his zone's rapid restoration to economic self-sufficiency and elimination of the financial burden on American taxpayers as soon as possible. Unfortunately, his original charge was conceived in theories that later ran aground of unforeseen

At the Deutsche Werft Shipyard in Hamburg, a shipyard worker shades his eyes as he uses a welding tool. In the background are two new ships under construction.

European realities. If applied literally, they threatened to undermine the multilateralism and regional planning on which the Marshall Plan was based. OMGUS and the State Department battled specifically over how long and at what cost Americans should prop up Bizonia. By relaxing the cap imposed on German output so as to expand their revenue-generating exports, Clay felt he was doing what was best for both Germans and Americans. Western Europe was simply not his worry. In this spirit, he instituted in August 1947 a new "level of industry" plan, lifting Bizonia's industrial production ceiling from 50% to 75% of prewar levels while cutting the number of plants to be dismantled from 1,800 to 858. Clay's order exposed a profound dilemma in American foreign policy.[75]

Unlike Clay, State Department officials worried chiefly about how best to devise a peaceful future for a western Europe with western Germany its peaceful economic powerhouse. Especially did they dread an unpunished

Deutsche Werft Shipyard was reconditioned with the help of Marshall Plan aid.

and unbowed industrial phoenix rising quickly from war's ashes, threatening once again its neighbors. Ultra-sensitive to French anxiety over her postwar security and economic ambitions, concerns enmeshed with Paris's domestic political tensions, they perceived a hasty German revival as strengthening a growing Communist movement inside France. As Prime Minister Georges Bidault liked to educate his listeners that "we have 180 Communists in the French Parliament who say 'the Marshall Plan means Germany First.'" French sensibilities could be easily bruised on the subject of Germany. Thus, in 1947 and again in 1948 General Clay received explicit directives that the German standard of living could not exceed France's.[76]

State wanted protections in place, and a "level of industry" restraint, which Clay proposed to scrap entirely, was its most trusted safeguard. Besides, economic improvement in Germany had to wait its turn behind political reform. Ironically, the decision to reshape the former enemy's political culture from the bottom up was Clay's. On his own authority, and *sans* guidance from Washington, he turned over villages, towns, and cities under his control almost immediately to local citizens to elect their own officials. State and national elections required more preparation. The State Department preferred more time for seeds of democratic governance which OMGUS itself had planted to germinate and root securely. At that point they then expected economic growth to solidify political gains. Denazification and supplanting totalitarian institutions with democratic ones took precedence and time. Traditional political parties, like the Christian Democratic Union (CDU) and the Social Democratic Party (SPD), had to be revived. A whole new national system had to develop from the grassroots. State's Charles Kindleberger, who worked on German affairs after World War II, condensed his department's policy towards defeated Germany, identifying its "first objective" as "building a solid base for political democracy." For its proponents, only economic measures politically acceptable to other Europeans should be adopted in Frankfurt by OMGUS. In a rush, Clay had other constituents, ideas, and problems to worry about.[77]

Clay's troubles with the Russians sped up his "chipping away" at State's alternate German policy. Moscow simply ignored provisions in the Potsdam Conference accords, refusing to play by the rules of summitry. In seizing reparations from their eastern zone, the Soviets not only dismantled and removed plants and machinery without any accounting, as required, but they also demanded immediate transfer of their share from the western zones, regardless of consequences for German recovery. In Clay's view, Stalin had transformed reparations gathering into plundering. On his own authority, in mid-1946 he stopped shipments out of his zone to the East of all new commitments while continuing the old ones. Avoiding public confrontation was never his personal style.

When arguments with his own State Department and Soviet authorities were not bedeviling Clay's staff, Bizonia's economic woes were. From war's end until mid-1948 western Germany needed desperately a sound currency. In June, OMGUS gambled on a socially risky experiment, resorting to a "drastic contraction of the money supply": 93.5% of the old currency was withdrawn from circulation. Brainchild of Edward Tenenbaum, a brilliant twenty-five-year-old lieutenant in the Army Air Forces and Special Assistant to OMGUS's Finance Adviser, the switch from reichsmark to deutschmark involved slashing bank deposits and personal savings accounts to 6.5% of their original value. Especially hard hit, workers who had entrusted their savings to safekeeping had them wiped out in a changeover that seemed to offer a choice between national prosperity and social equality. In truth, only those Germans foolish enough to have kept savings in paper currency rather than goods suffered. Moreover, although the changeover briefly raised real prices, it greatly aided the poor by wiping out inflation, an extra tax on all their purchases.

More in theory than in practice, the effect of reform appeared fundamentally unfair because "it took away liquid assets" while treating more considerately factory owners and large real estate owners with illiquid assets. Their personal sacrifices were, in fact, minimal. For a larger good, some Germans did voluntarily empty their pockets and further tightened their belts in the short run only to benefit in the long run. One can perhaps date West Germany's economic resurgence from the moment Bizonia's trade unions under Hans Boeckler's leadership made peace with a necessary but radical measure. The remarkable success of currency reform owed much to the absence of a militant response by labor.[78]

Despite its inequities, currency reform had an immediate "tonic effect." The deutschmark, after all, had purchasing power. Black markets and hoarding largely ceased. Industrial output and supplies of retail goods rose dramatically. Such rapid improvements resulted in part because OMGUS had the good economic sense to time its hardening of the currency with a much larger liberalization program masterminded by Ludwig Erhard, then head of Bizonia's economic administration and a virtual one-man trauma team from

Bavaria. To their mutual benefit, "a purely American measure" combined with an unconventional German economist's wide array of reforms. Together, they set in motion forces accelerated by the Marshall Plan and culminating in the 1950s in West Germany's "economic miracle." Returning to classical liberal ideas about how markets function, Erhard, who never attended college, rejected Keynesian orthodoxy for *laissez faire* doctrines. In agreement with General Clay, he emphasized limiting government's role in the marketplace.[79]

Some of Erhard's most important non-Keynesian methods included freer trade, reductions in individual and corporate income taxes, abolition of price controls and rationing, tax incentives to boost savings and wring greater production out of existing capabilities, lower tax rates on reinvested profits, and a credit freeze to fight inflation. His incentives generated the predicted surge in levels of private investment. Of course, the supreme irony in this homespun package of economic reforms was, according to German historian Holger Wolf, that its German author "favored supply-side policies that often were the direct antithesis of the postwar Keynesian recipe for rapid growth," an orthodoxy prevailing among Marshall Plan economists in Washington and Paris.

It would be a big mistake, however, to attribute the subsequent "economic miracle" exclusively to the admixture of OMGUS's monetary reform and supply-side economics, albeit in an extra-large dose. Each made its heavy contribution as inspired jolts to an ailing economy. Each was essential preparation for the Marshall Plan's constructive impact, establishing the requisite stable economic foundation on which it built. The "miracle" was, in truth, a compelling example of polygenesis. Internal and external determinants were many. Holger Wolf has even suggested that fortuitous events, both inside and outside Germany, were vital contemporaries of those celebrated reforms, one external stimulant being ECA after mid-1948. Amalgamated, they all steadily boosted West German industrial production: to 51% of prewar levels in 1948; 72% in 1949; 94% in 1950, and 167% by 1955.[80]

Maybe the luckiest occurrences from which Erhard's policies benefited were supply-and-demand shocks that complicate judgments about the efficacy of a purely supply-side cure for West Germany's economic malaise. In the first place, a painful but valuable transfer of human capital took place during the late 1940s. Ten million refugees and released prisoners of war flooded into the western zones. Czechoslovakia expelled a few million Sudetens. Hungary kicked out their Swabians. Also pouring in were East Prussians, Pomeranians, Upper Silesians, and East Germans. Among the millions of displaced workers filling Bizonia's manpower pool, an estimated twenty thousand newcomers were highly trained engineers and technicians. Exactly when their production took off, industrialists had available a surplus of skilled and motivated laborers with an ethic of hard work and a demand for a high standard of living. With their productivity outpacing their real wages for the next few years, workers energized national recovery.

Moreover, the bulging labor market, with its chronically high unemployment rates, helped to suppress trade union militancy. The years 1948 to 1952 were marked by wage moderation, acquiescent union behavior, and a deemphasis of the Social Democrats' redistribution schemes, all of which further encouraged business investment. Unlike in France, relatively peaceful labor-management relations characterized the era. Thus, a serious potential for instability and extremism manifested instead as a boon, indeed a godsend, for German industry.[81]

General Clay's decision to extend the new deutschmark to West Berlin provoked Josef Stalin into another ill-advised Cold War escalation that unified his squabbling adversaries. With Stalin's timely antics, and American C-54s taking off from its airport every three minutes, who needed the German-born Lothar Wolff and his creative Documentary Film Division at Frankfurt's ECA headquarters? The best propaganda for the Marshall Plan now filled morning newspapers in Munich and Cologne. A Soviet military blockade of West Berlin, and the lengthy American and British airlift, lasting from June 1948 until May 1949 and involving over 275,000 flights, not only convinced the German people of America's seriousness of purpose but, in a symbolic sense, terminated their pariah status in the eyes of their former western European victims. Whereas currency reform hardened Germany's legal tender, the Berlin Blockade hardened its anticommunism while at the same time softening anti-German feelings in the West. As General Clay remembered the crisis, hardly a western German was brave enough to be a Communist in public after the Soviet siege.[82] Enhanced American credibility translated into a more resolute German political will to reconstruct on democratic foundations. Another upshot was a greater readiness on the part of the French and British to put the painful recent past to rest. In their dealings with West Germany, both proved more cooperative thereafter. About a year after Stalin ended his futile gambit, the Korean War erupted. Its outbreak sped up rearmament in NATO countries, ultimately triggering in West Germany an export boom which absorbed excess manufacturing capacity. Afterwards, a Cold War–driven movement to defend the West boosted demand for German finished goods even further.[83]

The final major assurance of the long-term success of currency reform and Erhard's supply-side innovations was the Marshall Plan itself. Like paddles to an arrhythmic heart, OMGUS and Erhardian stimuli restored Bizonia's heartbeat to near normal. The Marshall Plan then improved the patient's health in several ways. From his perspective as Counselor at the Marshall Plan Ministry in Bonn, Hans-Georg Sachs believed that currency reform risked stillbirth had it not taken place on the eve of ECA assistance. The two, he argued, reinforced one another. As a supporter of the polygenetic interpretation, Sachs shares company with numerous economic historians and economists.[84]

When the Marshall Plan finally arrived in the summer of 1948, its implementers also inherited two unenviable predicaments: how to reconcile

Above: *Entire families form crews of builders working on an ECA-aided block of apartments in Berlin.* Below: *Housing under construction in Nürnberg.*

OMGUS and State Department versions of America's German policy and, excepting Moscow and its satellites, how to reconcile Germany's wartime enemies to a new democratic West Germany. For fifteen months, until General Clay and OMGUS turned their authority over to a civilian organization, the U.S. High Commission for Germany, or HICOG, in the summer of 1949, ECA's search for solutions to its twin dilemmas produced for a time one last interagency clash in occupied Germany, noisily pitting OMGUS against ECA.

The overlap of OMGUS and ECA witnessed a messy organizational overload. "At first," Milton Katz observed," relations were "confused and muddled and full of tensions." The two agencies labored until early 1949 at cross-purposes, with General Clay bent, foremost, on "liquidating World War II" by reducing the "dollar load" on his occupation administration. In vintage Harvard law professor diction, Katz classified the bureaucratic tangle as "an intricate problem of interrelationship." More plainly put, a cantankerous military governor, used to getting his way, resented civilian interlopers telling him how to run his European command post. To defend his authority, he treated ECA personnel heavy-handedly, resisted their separate mission and policies, and often seemed more foe than friend or fellow American.

Because Clay resented ECA's presence in Bizonia, he demanded the impossible: that Averell Harriman serve as Chief of Mission in Frankfurt. Refusing to leave OSR, Paris, Harriman sent instead a representative, Norman Harvey Collisson, to run ECA operations as *de facto* head of mission. For many months, Collisson endured Clay's displeasure and lack of cooperation, forced to conduct business without administrative support staff. Denied independent means of communications, his cables passed through OMGUS headquarters. He was also barred from formulating zonal policies, being consulted only after their establishment. Nor was Harriman's man permitted contact with German officials. Collisson was, in other words, hamstrung in conducting Marshall Plan affairs.[85]

After humiliating their delegate, General Clay embarrassed Harriman and Hoffman in the eyes of their European partners. Such conduct should have come as no surprise, since the military governor had already rebuffed the CEEC's attempt to review Bizonia's recovery plans. In August 1948, amidst the tense Berlin Blockade, Clay refused to accept OEEC's proposed allocation of $364,000,000 to Bizonia. According to Lincoln Gordon, "he raised the roof" over the amount. Grumbling about its inadequacy and unfairness, he accused the organization's member countries of "still look[ing] upon Germany as an enemy." Like the Soviets in their confrontation with Clay, the OEEC blinked too, upping his share another $50,000,000. Unlike Stalin, the general had important friends and supporters in the Pentagon and on Capitol Hill. Perhaps they instilled an overconfidence because he soon overreached himself, lecturing Harriman that Europeans were content to let Uncle Sam "support Germany indefinitely," an attitude he refused to abide. As a result of Clay's misbehavior, the comment that "the least cooperative member of the OEEC was the US occupation zone in Germany" circulated widely in official Washington.[86]

As historian Thomas Schwartz has pointed out, Clay regulated economic affairs in his occupation zone in such a way as to "sharply discourage European trade with Germany." This was anathema to OSR Paris. The general wanted to receive payment in dollars, raise export prices, and limit dollar expenditures to "essentials," undermining thereby the broader purpose of promoting intra-European dependency. ECA was always more troubled by the total dollar load in western Europe. Before 1948 ended, Clay and the ECA clashed over two more issues: East-West trade and the price of Bizonian coal. ECA policy, established in November, called for restrictions on trade between Marshall Plan recipients and eastern Europe countries. When Clay ignored ECA by entering into agreements with several Communist countries in violation of the "permissible volume" stricture, Harriman erupted. The two squared off in a test of wills. Prickly and defensive, Clay responded to Harriman's attack on his independence with pointed reminders. His first retaliatory blow was that Bizonia was not Europe's "whipping post" solely because Clay would not permit it. The second, a most powerful counterpunch that rocked a pillar of the Marshall Plan, was that he took his orders from the Secretary of the Army, not ECA.[87]

During the holiday season Clay further blackened Harriman's mood by depositing an overpriced lump of coal in his Christmas stocking. Their dispute over pricing German coal exports brought matters to a head. It spotlighted how Marshall Planners always walked a tightrope strung across Europe. For some time Clay had been "disgusted" with ECA over its attitude towards both the Ruhr Authority and the conversion of sterling balances. In turn, Harriman simmered over the fact that Clay wanted German coal exported throughout Europe for dollars instead of for local currencies. But since the coal sold at the low price of ten to fifteen dollars per ton, Harriman bit the bullet. In late December, however, he swallowed the cartridge. That month an increase of five dollars per ton in the price of coal, authorized by the Secretary of the Army and scheduled to take effect on New Year's Day, was announced by Clay as a purported means to reduce OMGUS's costs of occupation. Projections indicated that the price rise would generate an additional $80–100,000,000 annually in Bizonian revenues.

The central problem with Clay's coal policy was its conflict with ECA's policy that low-priced Ruhr exports would facilitate a greater western European recovery. Whereas Clay wanted Bizonians and American taxpayers to benefit from German production, Harriman's interests were not nearly so narrow. A higher German price came at the expense of France, Luxembourg, the Netherlands, Italy, and Austria. In Harriman's view, it guaranteed a "devastating effect." Why? Because the cost of steel and transportation throughout western Europe would then jump, triggering a general inflation as well as undercutting ECA's efforts to lower the price of coal in the United Kingdom. In addition, OMGUS had tossed political dynamite westward, lending plausibility to Allied charges of favoritism—that the United States put recovery of World War II's perpetrator ahead of its victims. With so much emotion churning, Harriman advised Secretary of State Marshall during his last days in office that ECA planned to reduce aid to Bizonia the exact amount that the price rise generated as well as increase aid to coal-importing countries, like France, as compensation for their added costs. The net result would be yet another American payment to France for not obstructing German recovery.[88]

As his next countermove in his struggle with Clay, Harriman appealed to Marshall's right-hand man, Robert Lovett, for redress of grievance. Complaining that Washington had allowed Bizonia's "economic management" to get out of sync with ECA's overall European design, he called for limitations on Clay's powers and responsibilities. Eventually, the showdown ended with Harriman victorious and private German management running mines in the Ruhr. After Harriman's old friend and World Bank president, John J. McCloy, was chosen in June 1949 as U.S. High Commissioner in Germany, and agreed to wear two hats in Bonn, doubling as ECA's Chief of Mission, peace and cooperation at long last marked interagency relations in West Germany. Economic difficulties did not disappear, however. Akin to the Italian workplace, the most intractable problem faced by McCloy's staff until late 1950 was mass unemployment. The jobless rate shot up in late 1948 in the aftermath of the Erhardian reforms and the huge influx of refugees. From 4.5% it climbed inexorably to its zenith of 12% in March 1950, dropping to 11% at year's end. At one point, a troubled McCloy even threatened Chancellor Konrad Adenauer and Economics Minister Ludwig Erhard with suspension of Marshall Plan aid unless they modified their laissez faire policies to lower their unemployment figures. In 1951, West Germany's surging export economy started absorbing surplus workers. The jobless rate then steadily plunged until 1960, when it reached 1.3%. Erhard's non-Keynesian faith was vindicated.[89]

In its very first country study in February 1949, after the donnybrook with OMGUS, ECA Washington publicly described its purposes in "Western Germany" as, in order, "avoid[ing] the political dangers which might well resolve from economic distress" and "enabl[ing] it to become economically self-supporting."[90] Seldom have institutional aims so grand in conception been so blandly represented. Germany, in fact, occupied the nucleus of Hoffman's and Harriman's thinking about postwar Europe. Harriman confided to Ludwig Erhard that his government attached "great importance" to German economic integration into western Europe because its success meant that there was a good chance that political integration would follow. Marshall Planners envisioned a reconstructed West Germany as "workshop for Europe's recovery." They wanted revitalization of its economy in order to substitute West Germany for the United States as "main supplier of the capital goods needed for [European] recovery." Besides lifting the onus from

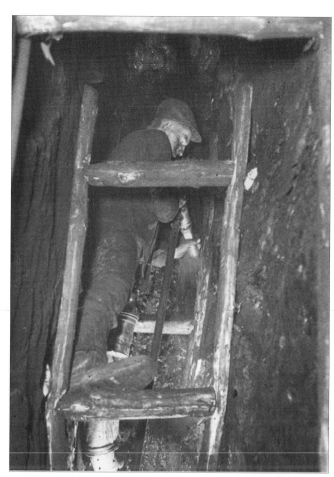

These German coal miners were a key link in West Europe's energy economy.

the American taxpayer, a German rebound meant that America no longer had to supply "food to Germany, capital goods to Western Europe, and dollars to all of them." Their strategy's linchpin was encouragement to industrialists to give exports primacy in the marketplace. The workings of the Plan then "enabled Germany to commit itself to free trade and to stick to this commitment." In myriad ways, in fact, the Marshall Plan functioned as the Great Enabler in West Germany's revival, which in turn made possible western Europe's economic self-sufficiency and political stability.[91]

The Marshall Plan moved Bizonian revival along in several stages. It first targeted the "food bottleneck" and near starvation. After the war the daily diet in the American and British zones averaged only 1,300 to 1,400 calories per person, even less in the French zone. German nutrition had improved but little by the time the inaugural shipments of grain, canned beef, and potatoes arrived in June 1949. By year's end, 78% of all ECA exports—valued at $478,000,000—were food. Raising per capita caloric intake above the danger level was the Frankfurt mission's overriding humane concern. By joining GARIOA in relief efforts, ECA immediately reduced hunger and malnutrition while removing one obstacle to greater worker productivity. Because of essential food purchases, Bizonia under OMGUS had run a large trade deficit with the Western Hemisphere. ECA food imports helped to balance dollar accounts. Only later in the year did deliveries of vital raw materials, like cotton, swell the flow of imported commodities. Overall, the Marshall Plan impacted western Germany's economy with $1,400,000,000 in commodities and services and another $1,350,000,000 in counterpart funds. The initial release of counterpart followed the emergence in September 1949 of the Federal Republic of Germany with Konrad Adenauer, a Christian Democrat, as Chancellor. In 1949, counterpart constituted 5.8% of West Germany's aggregate fixed investment, rising to 7.8% the following year before dropping back to 4.1% in 1951. The infusions proved invaluable to a robust national recovery.[92]

Ten million refugees in a population of forty-seven million constituted a second humanitarian crisis in need of full attention. In early 1950, at a dinner with Averell Harriman and Vernon Walters, Vice Chancellor Franz Blücher referred to their "present misery" as a "tremendous" problem which threatened his country's social and political stability and was therefore "very serious for all of Europe." He advised Harriman that expanded domestic production in Germany was the best permanent solution to the unfortunate situation. In response, OSR, Paris pursued both short-term relief and long-run remedies.[93]

To reduce human suffering, refugee assistance commanded a considerable slice of both regular and counterpart monies. Resettlement and housing construction, particularly in Schleswig-Holstein, Lower Saxony, and Bavaria, were heavily subsidized. In the February 1949 country study, Marshall Planners had already identified housing as the German people's "most acute need." In all, ECA funds built 125,000 dwellings throughout

West Germany. Marshall Plan officials also created a "refugee bank" for providing credits and loans with 127,000,000 deutschmark in counterpart. The rest of the counterpart fund was directed into investment rather than debt payment. Americans focused on West Germany's transportation and communication infrastructure, along with its industrial plant. But their biggest, most ambitious, and wisest investment went into electric generating capacity, the "power bottleneck" limiting future industrial expansion and which was beyond the capability of private capital markets to break. Eighteen percent of the over $1,000,000,000 in counterpart, or around $240,000,000, ultimately financed power development. With its most publicized in West Berlin, ECA sponsored energy projects nationwide. They encompassed sixty-seven new power stations supplying nearly one-fourth of the country's electricity requirements. Railroad reconstruction and coal mines in the Ruhr were two other specific beneficiaries. Railway transport received over 1,500 new locomotives and 70,000 freight cars. Improvements in mining depended on nearly 10% of counterpart funds. All answered, in effect, Blücher's call for expanded domestic output. According to the head of Kreditanstalt bank, the Marshall Plan also enabled West Germany "to negotiate its debts, including both the pre-war debts . . . and the postwar debts."[94]

Surprisingly, West Germany received more Marshall Plan aid in proportion to GDP than did Great Britain. Such a statistic can be misleading. Because Germany's economic recovery was already underway (an industrial plant, like Italy's, less damaged than imagined), and because of the relatively modest amount of assistance—annual percentage of national income ranged from a high of 5.3% in 1948 to a low of 1.6% in 1951—the Plan's direct economic impact was probably minor. At least one significant indirect benefit spurred economic growth. Holger Wolf has concluded that "by prodding more interventionist governments towards liberalization," Marshall Planners "increased the payoff to the liberal policies adopted by Germany" in advance of ECA programs.[95] Decisive political and psychological antecedents to the "economic miracle" of 8% annual growth, on average, throughout the 1950s can be traced straight to the Marshall Plan. Leading German public officials have thought so. Soon after the Plan expired, Vice Chancellor Franz Blücher dwelled on the interrelatedness of economic and political factors. Besides permitting West Germany to purchase badly needed raw materials while directing counterpart into productive investments, ECA had rechanneled an outcast nation back into the European mainstream. Apparently, international respectability, especially the West's reacceptance of the German people, rivaled currency reform as a national "demarcation line."[96]

Twelve years later, former Information Officer at the Marshall Plan Ministry in Bonn, Gustav Sonnenhol, and former Chancellor Konrad Adenauer underscored Blücher's final point. Sonnenhol stressed the great psychological value of the Federal Republic's first postwar diplomatic missions—to the

OEEC in Paris and the ECA in Washington—and its first postwar treaty, a 1949 bilateral agreement with ECA. Adenauer noted his countrymen's improvements in mood and morale that followed, telling an interviewer that ERP supplied "hope" along with "provisions." In his estimation, "extension of the Marshall Plan to Germany was first of all a deed of extremely great political significance" because "in spite of her past, Germany was placed . . . on an equal footing with other suffering countries." Equality of treatment had an "extraordinarily good psychological effect." The clearest evidence of a new "European solidarity," according to Karl Albrecht of the Marshall Plan Ministry, was the "$120 million in credits . . . granted to Germany by the European countries [EPU in 1950] without US participation." The Marshall Plan had returned a nation's self-respect, a precondition for the economic achievements, extraordinary prosperity, and a new European order that ensued.[97]

Marshall Planners succeeded politically and psychologically in their German policy. By situating West Germany within a framework of western European economic cooperation, interdependence, and mutual benefit, they diluted anti-German feelings and tamed French security fears. Generous Marshall Plan aid to both France and Britain also staunched a hemorrhaging Bizonian economy, eliminating a powerful disincentive to rebuild by helping to silence demands for a continuation of war reparations.[98] In belatedly unleashing German industrial might within an existing regional system of mutual assistance, most clearly demonstrated in the enlightened policies of the OEEC and European Payments Union during Bonn's balance of payments crisis of 1950–51, and with some unintentional help from Josef Stalin, they solved the difficult "German Question." What had poisoned relations between OMGUS and the State Department, and among the western Allies, lost its potency. The antidote was the Marshall Plan.

PART TWO: A CONTINGENT AND RELEVANT PAST

V

An Unusable Marshall Plan?

Is the Marshall Plan, designed and engineered primarily for western Europe in the late 1940s and early 1950s, still a realistic, useful model for postwar reconstruction and stabilization today and in the future? Can George Marshall's successful experiment serve as forerunner of other favorable outcomes for policymakers, an inspiration to other experiments tailored to new conditions? Are the principles, values, methods, and practices around which the Marshall Plan was once constructed still relevant? How might they benefit the process of contemporary decision making? In search for history's utility, the place to start is with an awareness of the siren song often composed by the past, a place where false or facile analogies, wrong lessons, and valuable insights coexist. And where the unusable does proliferate in abundance.

As original and creative statesmanship, George C. Marshall's inspiration relied on three factors for its attainments: good fortune, conducive conditions, and purposeful planning. Luck was definitely a Marshall Plan hallmark, teaching an important lesson about history's texture as well as about how acutely, on occasion, outside or external events influence achievement of public policy goals. Historical actors cannot receive all the credit for a favorable result. While the Marshall Plan itself is best understood as either the necessary or sufficient variable in the successful reconstruction of western Europe, chance's contribution to that happy outcome demands recognition. The importance of good timing, unplanned occurrences, and unintended consequences in the fortunes of the Marshall Plan should not be underrated. The most thoughtful preparations, without uncontrollable circumstances playing into the hands of the planners, might not have had the same impact. In the lingo of poker, Marshall Planners caught some breaks. A summary of the most significant historical contingencies effecting the approval, implementation, and outcome of their masterpiece numbers, of course, seven.

Historical Contingency

The Czech coup in February 1948 elevated popular fears of communism, disarmed the ERP's lingering opponents, and clinched its passage by

American lawmakers. By December, a flood of over ten thousand Czechs pouring out of their country served as a constant reminder of totalitarianism's westward movement.[1] While perhaps not the single biggest reason for the favorable result, Stalin's open break with Tito and the latter's expulsion from the Cominform in late June 1948 did assure a Communist insurgency's defeat in Greece by sundering the KKE leadership and denying sanctuary and support in Yugoslavia for Greek rebels. So, too, did the blunder by Greek Communist leaders in calling for an independent nation of Macedonia, putting themselves on the wrong side of Greek nationalism and dissipating popular sympathies. Both simplified considerably the military problems faced by the American-backed Greek National Army, no matter what General Van Fleet and Field Marshal Papagos argued to the contrary.

An unprecedented call-to-arms in 1948 by the Vatican, which endorsed Christian Democrats and mobilized at the grass roots an electorate, conveniently 99% Catholic, to save its soul by turning its back on Communist politicians, altered the course of postwar politics in Italy. The Catholic Church's organizational might—parish priests and the militant lay organization Catholic Action especially—determined the defeat of the Communists at a time when more than 70% of Italians regularly attended Sunday mass. Without Pius XII's decisive intervention, the valuable work of the ECA mission in Rome would have been impossible.[2] A Soviet attempt in the summer of 1948 to intimidate the people of West Germany, especially 2,250,000 West Berliners, backfired as a Cold War tactic into a public relations coup for the West. The dramatic Berlin Airlift and a resulting surge in pro-American sentiment among Germans proved a godsend as well. Paul Hoffman and others, quite correctly, called it a "moral defeat" for the Soviet Union. As Dean Acheson once summarized the postwar years, "We were fortunate in our opponents."[3] Yet another miscalculation by Stalin, the Korean War, after an initial inflationary shock to western Europe's economies, stimulated the region's economic growth in ways that helped to usher in the continent's "economic miracle" of the 1950s. A dramatic jump in demand for western European goods and raw materials provided an unplanned, potent boost.[4]

The seventh and last contingency is perhaps least appreciated because European contributions to the Marshall Plan's effective administration have long lingered in the historical shadows in American accounts, even though ultimate success depended as much on the attributes of Europe's leadership as on America's role. As such, the selection of Robert Marjolin, a respected French economist, as OEEC's Secretary General may have been the most fortunate of all fortuitous events between 1948 and 1952. The Belgian Chairman of the OEEC Council during its first two years, Baron Jean-Charles Snoy, has remarked that "the situation of the West in 1948 was so grave that everybody in every country sent his best people to OEEC and to ECA." Marjolin may have been the cadre's very finest. The head of the

Robert Marjolin (left) en route to the United States with British representatives at the OEEC. To his left are Edmund Hall-Patch, Harry Lintott, and Eric Roll.

Swedish Mission to the OEEC felt he was "as good as anybody you could find" and a "genuine international civil servant." His European colleagues referred to him as "The Brain."[5]

Because Averell Harriman wanted an honored elder statesman, preferably an aristocrat like himself, to run OEEC day-to-day and provide the critical coordination, he actually opposed Marjolin's nomination. Regarding him as "capable" yet not of the "highest caliber," Harriman was initially disgruntled over his selection. Young, by Harriman's standards, at thirty-seven, boyish-looking, and without a senior statesman's prestige, the upholsterer's son possessed nonetheless a special blend of character, determination, experience, skill, and empathy that few Europeans could have brought to his position.[6]

Much as it troubled some American colleagues, the demon of World War I's failed peace haunted Marjolin. Bad memories supplied him with a power-

Unloading Marshall Plan–funded coal in the Netherlands.

ful compulsion to learn from the past. The Frenchman also knew well and respected both Americans and Englishmen, being "as much at home in Britain and America as he was in his own country." Indeed, a Dutch friend regarded him as "one of the very few Frenchmen who had an open eye for the Anglo-Saxon world."[7] There were good reasons. In 1940, he had joined Charles de Gaulle's Free French movement, spending the early part of World War II in London. In 1943, though, de Gaulle dispatched him to the United States to assist Jean Monnet, who was heading France's Purchasing Mission. For two years, he worked and lived in Washington; there he also married an American. This was his second extended stay in the States. Back in 1932 and 1933, he pursued graduate studies at Yale University thanks to a Rockefeller Foundation grant. After the war, Marjolin returned to his homeland as the pro-American Monnet's protégé, serving as his deputy on the so-called Monnet Plan, an ambitious government program for "Modernization and Equipment" that preceded the Marshall Plan. Marjolin's executive leadership on the CEEC staff also recommended him to the OEEC's members, who "universally accepted [him] as objective and fair," in the estimation of Sir Eric Roll, a British delegate. Being bilingual and speaking fluently the only languages permitted in the organization's official business—French and English—were added bonuses.

Marjolin's sympathy for Americans, as well as old ties born of years studying and living in the United States and working with Monnet, plus his distaste for the French Left, made him ECA's ideal European liaison, as Harriman finally realized. No one worked harder at Anglo-French-American cooperation and harmony than did Marjolin. His personal leadership, and the unity for which it was responsible, were essential for a satisfactory resolution of the difficult "German Problem" that OEEC faced. With Marjolin officiating, a European marriage of sorts took place without need of a shotgun. Every month, overcoming limited formal powers as Secretary General, he met secretly with fellow Yalie Richard Bissell and two high- ranking Englishmen, Roll and Edmund Hall-Patch, at a Paris restaurant. There, they coordinated policy and ironed out differences. Their friendships obliterated cultural preconceptions and stereotypes. Moreover, as Lincoln Gordon has stressed, another of Marjolin's many assets was "empathy with both southern and northern European cultures." Knowing how to deal with diverse peoples was his special gift. His personality and skills lubricated Marshall Plan wheels, allowing them to run more smoothly than expected.[8]

The Seven Contingencies illustrate the limitations of the purposeful planning poured into the Marshall Plan. They refresh our memory of how appeals to historical authority can be deceptive. There might be, moreover, an even greater disadvantage to the Plan. It has to do with conducive conditions. The near-universal sentiment of those who were once directly connected with its conception and/or execution, as well as scholars, like Stanley Hoffmann and Charles Maier, who have studied carefully its historical record, is that chances for a remake are unpromising. Walt Rostow, Richard Bissell, Ted Geiger, Jacob Kaplan, and Jacques Reinstein all agree with Helmut Schmidt that the conditions that prevailed in western Europe from 1948 until 1952 are unlikely ever to recur elsewhere. The Marshall Plan was arguably a workable arrangement only in western Europe, and only because American and western European interests coincided. In all probability, they imply, its seeds would fall on barren ground in the contemporary developing worlds of Russia, Africa, and the Middle East. The devil, it turns out, may be in the setting, not the details. The Marshall Plan's environment perhaps equaled or exceeded in importance its personnel and methods. If so, then replicating that context is rather improbable.

Institutional preconditions crucial for success were many and possibly uniquely interrelated. Besides a working legal system, a respect for private property rights, and good, democratic governance, the mandatory prerequisites for a second Marshall Plan should include, first, a modern market-based economy with a "long-standing entrepreneurial heritage"; second, skilled, motivated, and educated managers and workers; and, third, technical know-how, especially engineering capabilities. It would also require an educational infrastructure in place and functioning, guided by principles of academic freedom. In short, presupposing an Enlightenment and Industrial Revolution when extending large-scale aid to non-Western countries could very well guarantee disillusionment.[9]

What western Europe had before the first Marshall Plan cargo ship or country mission arrived were, in Richard Bissell's concise version, "skills, habits, motivations, customs, and procedures required for the operation of a modern economy." When they were lacking or deficient in another region or country, attempting a second Marshall Plan made no sense whatsoever to him.[10] Maybe another worthwhile way to think about all considered claims as to the Marshall Plan's contemporary irrelevance is a comparison with Mikhail Gorbachev's failed policy of "perestroika," introduced in the Soviet Union in the mid-1980s. By means of a batch of economic and governmental reforms, Gorbachev similarly attempted to restructure a vast, failing economy. In effect, ECA anticipated Gorbachev, trying forty years before to revitalize western European capitalism while changing internal behaviors. Yes, the Marshall Plan was a successful precursor of "perestroika," but principally because western European institutions were compatible with major reforms. The West's democratic and legal traditions, in particular, were strong enough to accommodate pressures for basic economic change. The Soviet Union's collapse seems to prove that the politics of good intentions is never enough.

The Disservice of the Marshall Plan

At least three Marshall Plan veterans have issued identical caveats about its subsequent misuses by American foreign and domestic policymakers. Walt Rostow, Richard Bissell, and C. Tyler Wood have lamented the "false hopes" the Plan aroused in Third World countries, inner cities, and post-Communist East Europe that quick and dramatic successes could be achieved outside of West Europe with a mass infusion of capital. All eventually affirmed what a principal formulator of the Marshall Plan wrote in July 1947. At its very inception, George Kennan had warned that "there was no reason to believe that the approaches here applied to Europe will find any wide application elsewhere." One of the masterminds of the Marshall Plan's inspired programming, Bissell regretted its "unfortunate heritage" and "disservice" in propagating various myths: of rapid results, of the power of enthusiasm combined with huge resources, and that "economic and political problems could somehow be separated."

A British auto—manufactured with copper for wiring, nickel for steel, and zinc for die-casting supplied by the ECA—is loaded for export at a London dock. Helped by credit and raw materials from the U.S., the U.K. increased car production 36% between 1947 and 1950.

119

Wood, who served ECA as Assistant Deputy Administrator for Operations prior to a long government career in foreign aid, learned the hard way that "if you stir up a traditional society and give people all sorts of expectations of a better life," the results are "tension, problems and dissatisfaction." For Wood, a mass infusion of capital was "absolutely essential" in western Europe, yet it turned out to be a mistake in underdeveloped areas. American policymakers, in Wood's emphatic judgment, "rushed to the conclusion that you can do the same thing with a backward country, and you just can't do it." Probably with the wayward Alliance for Progress in his thoughts, the old Marshall Planner offered his own memorial: "our success in the Marshall Plan led a lot of people astray."[11]

Economists Speak

Some economists also deny that any repetition of the Marshall Plan can happen because the American government has lost its former preeminence in financial markets. They stress the remarkable role-reversal experienced by the United States ever since those Marshall Plan days. The "universal emporium" with huge trade surpluses everywhere in the world now struggles with enormous trade deficits. Other economists, Barry Eichengreen in particular, regard another Marshall Plan as "inconceivable today" because flush private capital markets render a redux as "superfluous" and the "response developed by Marshall and his colleagues" as "no longer appropriate." International capital markets, currently full and flourishing, have changed profoundly the context of the late 1940s. To Eichengreen, private streams of capital have supplanted public flows. Individual and corporate investors and lenders worldwide can be expected to meet the needs of countries or regions invoking, misguidedly in his estimation, the hallowed name of George C. Marshall.[12]

An implication of Eichengreen's analysis is that, in the face of economic crises and human misery comparable to western Europe's after World War II, private banks and companies will serve in the foreseeable future as reliable instruments of public policy. Profit-driven investments will substitute for the Marshall Plan's governmental grants, counterpart funds, and Keynesian management. Being up to a liquidity challenge is a quite different matter, however, than being a faithful implementer of the national interest. Will private capital really move into sub-Saharan Africa on its own? Is borrowing in the private sector the long-term equivalent of national grants? When China finances America's deficits and holds dollar reserves—thanks to its giant trade differential with the United States—fast approaching $1,000,000,000,000, just how private are those vaunted capital flows? Eichengreen also chooses to overlook the historical clash, especially in the 1920s, between public policy and private power that, for the most part, was suspended during the Marshall Plan. In fact, another of the Plan's legacies is its implicit warning about the danger of confusing and equating private and public goals, something to which Hoffman, Harriman, and Bissell were especially attuned.

The Marshall Plan never had the unanimous backing of American businessmen. In the run-up to passage of the Foreign Assistance Act, corporate executives expressed opposing views about what their government's embrace of internationalism ought to mean. What appeared consensual in April 1948, the result of a general attitude of watchful waiting, turned contentious by 1950. An initial split widened, separating on one side business liberals who had joined the Committee for Economic Development or National Planning Association and, on the other side, business conservatives and protectionists more at home in the National Association of Manufacturers or the National Foreign Trade Council. While liberals like Philip Reed, head of General Electric, remained steadfast in their support, conservatives grew more unsympathetic towards and critical of the ECA. They wanted the Marshall Plan to expand their sales overseas rather than enlarge European consumer markets and intra-European trade. They preferred that Washington create more opportunities abroad for them.

Instead, the Marshall Plan in operation actually undercut America's exports to Europe. Because ECA provided French, Dutch, and Belgian businessmen with tutelage in the latest American production methods and technology, many conservatives regarded their future profits at risk. Technology transfers especially worried them. Increasingly, they found themselves "at odds with federal agencies over policies that revived [former] competitors overseas . . . and limited market development worldwide." They came to resent Marshall Planners who supposedly sacrificed short-term business self-interest to a grand government theory. Blowing on embers from the Yalta Conference, their congressional allies even accused the ECA of "selling out" their interests in Europe.[13]

Nearly always, in appropriation battles waged annually inside Congress, Marshall Planners prevented special interests from transforming a foreign aid program with strategic objectives into governmental favoritism and provisions for private businesses with powerful lobbies and an oversupply of products. There were, to be sure, some accommodations and a few notable exceptions. All added unnecessarily to taxpayers' expense. For example, in the shape of a 50% rule tied to strategic arguments, preferential treatment was afforded to the shipping industry and organized labor for transporting ECA commodities. Flour millers obtained, for a time, a favorable quota for wheat shipments, and tobacco growers were permitted to export 40,000 tons of a crop that Europe did not want.[14]

But as a rule political meddling was rebuked and political enemies accumulated. With his European perspective, Robert Marjolin found decisions made by ECA's leaders prior to the Korean War to be driven exclusively by calculations of the long-term public good. That they almost never ran interference for American businessmen impressed him greatly. Indeed, he marveled that "their interest was not American trade, American exports or things of that sort." A Norwegian Marshall Plan official, Knut Getz Wold, remembered that "the object was to discriminate to the maximum extent possible against the exports of United States products. That this was . . . positively encouraged by the U.S. authorities . . . is really a measure of the degree to which the immediate self-interests were subordinated to the interests of European economic recovery."[15]

Marjolin and Getz Wold almost got it right. While Hoffman and Harriman refused to curry favor with powerful Senators, hiring none of their relatives to positions in the Marshall Plan, and while they adamantly opposed subsidies to ailing lumbermen and other businessmen by steering European buyers their way, they did compromise their own principles when it came to oil. Years before Dwight Eisenhower's Secretary of Defense, Charles Wilson, equated America's national interest with General Motors' corporate interest, Marshall Planners treated the interests of the country and the oil industry interchangeably. ECA's relationship with America's oil companies provides, in one sense, a cautionary tale about entrusting the private sector to do what is best for the nation as a whole. Put simply, the private objectives of oilmen could not be reconciled with the ECA's announced national goal of self-sustainable western European recovery and growth in four years. Their public relationship was marked, accordingly, by a lack of cooperation along with a serious falling out over crude oil prices. But, in private, matters were quite different.

Walter Levy, an OSS oil analyst during World War II and Chief of ECA's Petroleum Branch in 1948 and 1949, eventually concluded that "the mere dollar saving approach is too narrow in the case of oil." The United States could not, in his expert opinion, sacrifice a "vital national interest" in order to comply with guidelines for aiding western Europe. What was perfectly appropriate for lumber and aluminum was inappropriate for oil. As the premature absorption of ECA by MSA indicated most forcefully, the strategic argument overpowered all others. Levy's superiors in Washington agreed that oil deserved to be in the forefront of strategic calculations. Although Levy did have the pricing convention used for twenty years by the multinationals modified, in the end ECA advanced Big Oil's interests at the expense of European recovery by deliberately restricting the European oil industry's economic growth. The act qualified as the unselfish Marshall Plan's most selfish.[16]

After World War II, western Europe's massive dollar shortage had a variety of causes. A large contributor to that shortfall was oil imported from American companies operating overseas, primarily in the Middle East. Europe paid for half its consumption in dollars to American suppliers. While coal still met around 90% of the continent's energy needs (down to 75% by 1950), cars, trucks, tractors, and planes could not move without gasoline. Moreover, King Coal was in the process of being dethroned. In 1949, ECA spent $600,000,000 for petroleum products, while estimates for the following year of $800–900,000,000 amounted to 20% of total expenditures.

Overall, in excess of 10% of ECA commodity assistance went for purchasing oil, more than on any other commodity.

Before long, Marshall Planners realized that if western Europe reduced its oil imports, they could shrink the dollar gap appreciably, especially since the price of crude more than doubled—from $1.05 to $2.22 per barrel—between war's end and the spring of 1948. Aggravating the situation was the fact that for a time America's oil giants, acting in collusion, overcharged ECA for deliveries to western Europe. Their prices reflected production costs in the United States rather than the Middle East. Eventually rolled back, the price illegally charged ECA still exceeded the price American customers paid. The differential was, in fact, sizable—$0.32 per barrel. Squabbling eventually led to litigation. In 1952, the oil companies were taken to federal court.

ECA understood well that another way to save dollars in western Europe, besides curtailing the influx of petroleum, involved expansion of Europe's refinery capacity, particularly since refined products were more expensive than crude oil. This was the alternative, however, that Walter Levy and ECA Washington rejected because it would simultaneously hurt the overseas business of American oil companies and American strategic aims. ECA opted to finance refinery improvements and expansion only to replace imports of some dollar-denominated products. According to business historian David Painter, Marshall Planners "would not finance projects that threatened to compete with US companies." So, they ended up funding "very few refinery projects." In all, the $24,000,000 the Plan invested in refineries contrasted with $1,200,000,000 in oil purchases from American firms.[17]

Oilmen's special needs, like those of shippers, took priority over the general interest of lasting European recovery. Guided by their own agenda of costs and profits, private oil companies served as poor instruments of a specific public policy, even as detriments to its timely achievement. Perhaps on all counts they merited preferential treatment, given the subsequently vital role which cheap, unlimited oil played in western Europe's unprecedented economic growth in the 1950s along with oil's strategic importance in the Cold War. Yet the Marshall Plan's oil tangle does draw into sharp relief the overriding question of primacy: whenever incompatible, should long-term public planning or short-term private interests determine America's approach to postwar reconstruction? Though not unequivocally, the Marshall Plan came down on the side of the former. The two prominent exceptions of the shipping and oil industries aside, governmental interests and business interests were, to Marshall Planners, distinguishable and divisible. Their separation qualifies, in fact, as one of many keys to the ERP's success bearing directly on the challenges of postwar reconstruction today. All validate the Marshall Plan as a prime example of a usable past.

Hamburg, Germany: Mönckebergstrasse in the business district, 1945 vs. 1950

VI

A Usable Marshall Plan

If governmental agencies, Keynesian methods of demand management, trade surpluses, and reliance on the public sector are now out-dated and obsolete—or suffer from a fatal loss of confidence—and unregulated global markets rule, then it might seem that the time for another Marshall Plan is assuredly past. If so, the Marshall Plan can remind us in such altered domestic and international contexts still not to forget what once informed its formulation and implementation, namely, that economics, politics, and psychology are inseparable in building support at home and in rebuilding other nations abroad.

What also needs to be learned from the Marshall Plan, a lesson that belongs to the category of the "avoidable past," is its failure to heed Sun Tzu, the ancient Chinese military strategist and philosopher, to take full measure of the Communist threat. As a former military man, Secretary of State Marshall understood the difference between Stalin's strategy and tactics, recognizing that the Soviet leader masked his revolutionary purposes with short-term, reformist, "front" governments in West Europe. The general knew *maskirovka*. The moderation of Communists in the West was classic "cover and deception" for the ultimate goal of domination by Moscow. For his clear-eyed reading of Stalin's conduct, Marshall deserves high marks. Yet, surprisingly, the ECA's analysis of the roots of indigenous communism that Stalin manipulated in West Europe lacked sophistication. Marshall Planners adopted the "myth of belly communism" and settled for half-truths. They recognized a mass murderer's disguise, yet were disinclined to learn as much as they could about the enemy. Theirs was a mistake which shapers of antiterrorism strategy today need to study, lest they commit their own variant.

Know Well Thy Enemy (and Thy Self)

The myth purported that poverty, hunger, unemployment, and misery were responsible for Communist popularity. Its cognate notion was that chaos and despair bred and fed totalitarianism. But did bad economic and social conditions necessarily constitute fertile ground for the spread of communism? The answer is that the causes and sources of its appeal were misunderstood in the late 1940s and, hence, its strength both conceived too narrowly as well as overrated. Some further telling Gallic evidence must suffice.

From November 1947 until 1949, the French Minister of Interior, reviled by French Communists as the "Assassin," was Jules Moch. Those were years, of course, when France heaved with violent strikes, revolutionary rhetoric, and widespread civil unrest. In a good position to pass judgment, Moch felt that the Americans blew up the Communist threat into something much bigger than it actually was. His assessment, later shared with an interviewer from the Truman Library, was that "the danger was not so great" and "always overestimated in America." To illustrate his point he cited the richest village in a wine-growing department in southern France where Communists commanded 100% of the vote. Even landowners with very prosperous vineyards supported the party of Marx, Lenin, and Stalin. Moch explained such communal solidarity and Leftist politics as a local tradition that went back a century or more. "Ideologically," he insisted, "they were nothing." In fact, the former Interior Minister calculated that a large percentage of his countrymen who voted Communist in the late 1940s did not know its ideology.[1]

Oversimplifications nonetheless underwrote fear of Communist expansion and the zeal with which many Marshall Planners discharged their duties. They exaggerated what they truly had control over, giving too great an emphasis to materialistic explanations of Communist motivation and falling short of Sun Tzu's standard. They did not know their enemy very well. As a secular religion, like nazism, communism was as much about people's "souls" and spiritual needs as their material wants. A faith with its own catechism and dogmas, its appeal went beyond the proletariat. Moreover, the global ideological battle between democracy and totalitarianism turned on many axes: one rotated in the Kremlin, where Stalin's penchant for discrediting Communist movements through misjudgments and misadventures played itself out (and where in 1956 his successors preserved his blundering ways by invading Hungary). Stalin's behavior, in fact, validated key assumptions on which George F. Kennan erected America's containment policy. Kennan knew the Soviet enemy well enough. His grand strategy worked, forcing Moscow to regularly expose its immorality.

Since the proper prescription for western Europe's political woes presupposed the proper diagnosis of the problem, the Marshall Plan's remedy was deficient. American-sponsored economic renewal was insufficient to undermine the lure of communism in France, Italy, and Greece. Such a shortcoming serves as a caveat to contemporary policymakers responsible for postwar reconstruction in the larger and very likely context of another totalitarian threat to Western values. Their programs must not be structured on oversimplifications of the root causes of Islamic fundamentalism, a more traditional religion than communism. Neither the educated, middle-class intellectuals and merchants in France and Italy who threw in their lots with Maurice Thorez and Palmiro Togliatti, nor Mohammed Atta who accepted a fateful suicide mission for al-Qaeda, had blue collars or empty bellies.

The Relevant Past

To help contemporary policymakers answer the call for informed planning for postwar reconstruction, the Marshall Plan provides ample additional guidance that is usable. What worked once in a bygone era should not be forgotten. While luck was their companion, Marshall Planners did not triumph because they were luckier than other practitioners of American policy over the last sixty years. And success surely was not the offspring of Stalin's blunders. Neither randomness nor destiny had much to do with the ERP's final outcome. What mattered decisively was that George C. Marshall's followers put their breaks to wise use. Benefiting from "accidents of history," they also created optimum conditions for attaining their goals. Superbly equipped to profit from their good fortune, they conceived a strategy based on sound principles of statecraft and leadership. Their script had structural integrity, and they improvised brilliantly when circumstances required.

Though an old conception, the Marshall Plan's distilled essence yields fundamental lessons that override the historical contingencies and context of 1947–51 and still pertain in changed circumstances. Elements of strength that existed in the original have application today. Indeed, the higher the resolution of the historian's photograph of the Marshall Plan, the greater the pertinence of those elements. At the head of any list of general requirements for success as revealed in ECA operations are four prerequisites: national selflessness, the self-help of beneficiaries, a multilateral approach to problem solving, and an understanding of leadership. All were wisely prescribed by the Plan's architects who shared a healthy respect for their own past as a valuable teacher.

The Marshall Plan's soul, never out-of-date, was the same personal sense of public purpose and sacrifice summoned earlier by the New Deal and World War II. Over a span of forty-five months a generous nation transferred 1.2% of its GNP (2% in 1948) and 6–9% of the federal budget into Europe's recovery, reconstruction, and reform. To put such a substantial shift of resources into perspective, $13,000,000,000 equates to $100,000,000,000 in today's dollars, or less than 1% of today's GNP and 4% of the 2005 federal budget. The percentages of 1948–52 now translate into $144,000,000,000 of GNP and a $180,000,000,000 slice of the federal budget. Although the scale of American help was extraordinary, without the self-help of recipient nations billions of dollars in assistance were fated to descend down Congressman Howard Buffett's "rathole." "We believed with the Marshall Plan's leaders," remembered Henry Reuss, "that our role was not to direct the Europeans but to help them to help themselves."

In all countries bent on self-renewal, but most prominently in the Netherlands and West Germany, the Marshall Plan showcased the superiority of human and social capital over physical assets. Industrious, educated Europeans, determined to rebuild and better themselves, surpassed in importance the wherewithal made available to them by Americans. Not confusing aid with charity constituted a critical insight with perpetual utilization, as did an insistence on self-investment which took most obvious shape in the counterpart fund, at least partly an emblem of national self-help.[2]

By refusing to be seduced after World War II by their own preponderance of economic and military power into fashioning a unilateral solution to West Europe's predicament, George C. Marshall and his advisers comprehended the dangers of national arrogance, as well as the value of a cooperative effort with friends and allies. They understood well what the editor of *Die Zeit* recently reemphasized: "multilateralsim is not muddleheaded idealism, but part of realpolitik."[3] They rejected unilateralism as a dead-end, backing instead an arrangement which fostered habits of cooperation that matured into even greater achievements, like NATO. As a virtue, humility eventually fell from grace in American culture but surely warrants retrieval. It once informed Secretary Marshall's expectation that good works in the national interest did not necessitate gratitude and should not be expected. He advised Congress accordingly. He preferred West Europe's consent over America's popularity and its confidence over its affection. His forewarning eventually cushioned Italian resistance, along with Greek and Turkish resentments.

Unappreciated by isolationists, fortifying America's friends meant strengthening America's security, which Republican Senator Henry Cabot Lodge, Jr., of Massachusetts liked to point out. Likewise, ignoring the nation's European allies, as was also the case with unilateral action, courted disaster. Winston Churchill's quip—that the only thing worse than fighting a war with allies was fighting one without them—has always been a valuable piece of advice. Realists like Secretary Marshall, who grasped the limits of American influence, knew what, on their own, they were equipped and unequipped to solve beyond the nation's borders. They entertained no illusions of omniscience or omnipotence.

Helping others save themselves in the short run while saving oneself in the long run defines enlightened self-interest in foreign policy, another aspect of the Marshall Plan having universal relevance. Henry Reuss has described such statecraft differently, as "a happy amalgam" of softheartedness and hardheadedness. With Clio, the Muse of History, whispering in their ears and with broad vision, his fellow Marshall Planners prodded Europeans to help one another while promoting stronger European interconnections as the best deterrent to the twentieth century's third continental war. They insisted on treating western Europe as a unit, fully expecting that it would "behave as a unit." The Plan marked perhaps the finest hour, in peacetime, of an Atlantic civilization, with America's and western Europe's best combining in a synergy that bequethed a benchmark for future policymakers. Despite a subsequent outbreak of amnesia in the 1960s, when the Alliance for Progress drew up its development plans on a national basis and *sans* a Latin American OEEC, the principle of regionalizing markets through coordinated multinational effort ought to continue to inspire policymakers today. A collective regional approach that targeted West Germany, the region's natural economic power-house, for inclusion and integration certainly accelerated postwar recovery, leaving in Thomas Schelling's view a model of "successful multinational cooperation to achieve a common goal" as a lasting legacy.[4]

Probably the most helpful tutelage the Marshall Plan can provide is about how most decisively to approach policymaking itself. For an expensive, innovative foreign aid program to fulfill its promise, the American people and their congressional representatives had to understand the reasons for its existence. In first mastering the machinery of domestic politics as well as the arts of persuasion in order to undertake grand strategy, formulators of the Marshall Plan achieved a near-perfect score. They obtained bipartisan backing and great popularity. With a publicity and public relations blitz that lasted nearly six months, they patiently provided the public, press, and Congress with a wealth of facts, figures, and arguments that assured its creation and retention. Thus, Secretary Marshall and his cohorts built a consensus and committed their nation prior to committing its resources and manpower.

As the Founding Fathers imagined, the American people started on a historical departure with eyes wide open. Next, Marshall Planners assiduously cultivated domestic, public, and congressional opinion to guarantee support throughout its four-year life. "In one year," Paul Hoffman's biographer has revealed, ECA's Administrator "personally made about 150 speeches," one nearly every two days, extolling the Marshall Plan's value for America's security and prosperity.[5] In western Europe the planners skillfully exploited a range of media in a vast, innovative propaganda war with the Cominform. Their campaign was directed by high-caliber professionals from the working media with the most advanced celluloid weapons a big part of their arsenal. Their results were consistently high approval ratings for the ERP at home and abroad. Marshall Planners authored, in other words, the classic text on the proper mechanics of making policy, particularly on the centrality of communication and the effective dissemination of information. It deserves, therefore, the closest reading by contemporary shapers of America's foreign relations.

Even if the Marshall Plan's specific design and engineering cannot be replicated precisely or approximately, America's human and intellectual capital—in Clark Clifford's words, those full of "professionalism, daring, inventiveness and sacrifice"—which the Plan drew down on with great profit for nearly four years, can certainly be reconstituted and reinvested. Recruiting the right people means, quite simply, duplicating what the Marshall Plan once prized and frowned upon in its hiring practices. Its stringent regulations resulted in exceptionally low turnover in personnel, with two years a standard tour of service which probably constituted a minimum commitment for success. (See Appendix C.) The resulting continuity of personnel, with Greece's chief of mission one glaring exception to the rule, assured deeper personal relations with foreign counterparts and increased effectiveness in problem solving.

In a highly selective process ECA's leadership preferred, identified, and enlisted a battalion of Phi Beta Kappas, ex-valedictorians, Ph.D.s, former Rhodes Scholars, budding Nobel Laureates and college presidents, future heads of professional associations, masters of business administration, and one-time law review editors to staff its projects. (See Appendix B.) With their objective a meritocracy, credentials absolutely mattered. Qualifications overruled all other considerations. Smart, educated people were essential to success abroad, as were cosmopolites. Those worldly bilingual and multilingual folk who understood Europe well, providing great strength to the ECA's Information Divisions, also taught other valuable lessons: their adopted nation's multiculturalism can be an incomparable asset, America's diversity has always constituted a potent force to be capitalized upon in a foreign crisis, and mastery of foreign languages can neutralize local interpreters while enriching cultural interactions.

Organizers of the Marshall Plan opted for a blend of dedicated civil servants, corporate executives, and public-spirited professionals from the private sector. They proved to be an ideal mix. By also placing a premium on transferable experience, for instance, prior employment in a government mobilization agency, recruiters merged theoretical and practical knowledge into a winning team. Moreover, they administered no political or ideological tests for employment while imposing a nonnegotiable ban on relatives, cronies, amateurs, dilettantes, and political appointees. Political loyalists and administration favorites received no special consideration whatsoever. The stakes were too high then and certainly even more so today in the war on terrorism for a partisan pickup team with White House connections to be in charge of postwar reconstruction.

In their collective memoirs, Marshall Planners suggested that the ways they elaborated their assignments should remain highly instructive. In fact, they remind advocates of future initiatives in large-scale foreign assistance of how interwoven the original experiment actually was. Besides being an approach to foreign policymaking, the Plan's layers included a decision-making process, a problem-solving method, and a management style. Each presupposed consensus, a continual synergy between donor and recipients, and a constant wariness of "purist dogmatism" in pursuit of the coveted new European order. Knowledge of one's own deficits in knowledge was critical. Alan Valentine's Dutch experience taught him three lessons with contemporary applications. First, it was "a mistake to be doctrinaire about economics"; second, "different postwar conditions [in Europe] called for different treatments" rather than "rigid uniformity"; and, third, Dutch experts "understood the economy of the Netherlands better than the American specialists understood it."

Whether greater productivity, less protectionism, currency convertibility, or increased intra-European trade was the specific, limited goal, Marshall Planners accepted other nations as not necessarily seeing matters as they did. Because they constructed a framework within which those committed to a "new Europe" could debate those willing to be rebuilt or reformed, the critical hinge was always a recipient's readiness to change. The essence of their process, method, and style was, however grudging at times, mutual trust and understanding. In the Marshall Planners' exercise of American power, national and political differences were almost always respected. In the case of Greece, where that rule and a few others went to pieces, considerable frustration and disappointment awaited them. There, promotion of public works succeeded while furtherance of American-style democracy ran aground. An official with more than two years of service in the six-man Civil Government Division in Athens later pinpointed ECA's mistake. According to C. William Kontos, its "total approach [in Greece] was much too bold."

Openness was another telltale ECA trait, and more productive than boldness. Tolerance for variety helped to advance an anti-Communist agenda: Socialists, Catholics, and Muslims enlisted as crucial allies in battling Communist influence and stemming its growth. Likewise, it furthered negotiations with Europeans. Since most nations, including the United States, regard themselves as superior, the Marshall Plan method simply amounted to conversations among officials who styled their nations to be exceptional. No overbearing American sense of exceptionalism suffocated their exchanges. The typical Marshall Planner's mindset embraced long-term thinking, pragmatism, transparency, compromise, and coaxing. It eschewed short-term as well as black-and-white thinking, secrecy, self-righteousness, and bullying.

Unquestionably, ECA preferred certain courses of action and on occasion sermonized. At no time, however, did it imitate Stalin's coercion in East Europe. Marshall Planners grasped the crux of leadership. They knew how to forge a bond between a leader and followers. Their means were mutual respect and collaboration. For Paul Hoffman, "the essence of genuine leadership" was "to share power with people rather than display power over people." In dealings with both Americans and Europeans, he practiced what he preached. Alan Valentine has noted in his autobiography that "Hoffman's policy was to pick men he thought had good ability and judgment and turn them lose." According to a knowledgeable Dutch official, Americans so entrusted provided assistance "without in any way imposing their will." To him "this was the key to the way that it could work so well." The CEEC's English chairman, Sir Oliver Franks, paid the Marshall Plan an identical compliment. The Frenchman Robert Marjolin echoed their sentiments, lauding the unwillingness of his American collaborators to attempt "to make the Europeans behave in a manner contrary to their fundamental interests." The genius of the Marshall Plan method, another yardstick for future measurement, was its balance of economic might with political restraint.[6]

A union of American largesse with Washington's respect for the recipients of that generosity bonded seventeen European nations to America's leadership. Such "bonding," in Josef Joffe's estimation, necessitated "an eye for the common interest and a commitment to cooperation" and a willingness to construct "an order that . . . advance[d] American interests by serving those of others." The outcome, in West German Chancellor Konrad Adenauer's opinion, was that in the late 1940s "the Americans are the best Europeans." Much like a gifted and devoted impresario, Marshall Planners conducted, in effect, the first-ever West European Philharmonic in which seventeen former soloists followed a single, American-made baton. Only the conductor's dedication to the well-being of the orchestra earned such acceptance, trust, and collective achievement. Occasional discord was therefore expected.[7]

Tempered by politics, applied economics turned out to be more art than science in the European Recovery Program. Economic theories were at times either inappropriate or ineffectual, as witnessed in Italy's Mezzogiorno especially. Indeed, the task in developing regions like Greece, Turkey, and southern Italy, in contrast to merely recovering regions like West Germany and northern Italy, was a far greater challenge. Neither "pure market forces" nor Keynesian doctrines always operated as forecast. The ECA's work validated practical experience, flexibility, and—after considerable American reluctance—deference to local knowledge and priorities, particularly in the diverse management of seventeen counterpart funds. Indeed, if one voice can be heard throughout the ECA's flexible elaboration of its structured programs, it is George Kennan's upstaging in effect Woodrow Wilson's: West Europe must be made safe for diversity, totalitarians excluded of course. A greater American readiness to accept Europe's variety than to proselytize on behalf of America's real, imagined, or exaggerated distinctiveness prevailed, notwithstanding the counterclaims of some prominent historians. Frequently, in fact, Europeans treated Washington's preferences as irrelevant. The Marshall Plan's rejection of a "one-size-fits-all approach to recovery programs" offers wise and useful counsel to present-day specialists in postwar reconstruction in other parts of the world.

As proof of their characteristic adjustability, which contrasted with the rigidity of Stalin's Five-Year Plans for the East, Marshall Planners cooperated with governments of the Center as well as the Far Right in Greece, the Center-Right in Italy and West Germany, and the Left in Great Britain, Norway, and elsewhere. Some have forgotten that Belgium's Paul-Henri Spaak, chairman of the OEEC Council, was himself a Socialist who believed that "the only answer to Communism is Socialism." Others overlook Averell Harriman's admiration for the "Socialist government in England" because of its ability "to distribute funds received from the Marshall Plan on a more just basis—giving the workers a greater cut—than had been the case in France and Germany." Americans even dealt with secular authoritarianism in Turkey.

Though many latter-day New Dealers were in their ranks, with their American-style liberal ideas about proper relations between capital and labor, Marshall Planners still partnered with Christian Democrats and royalists, along with Socialists and Labourites. In West Germany, avowed Keynesians allied with supply-siders committed to competitive, unregulated markets. In Great Britain, France, and Norway they made common cause with Socialists pledged to nationalize industries. In fact, after World War II British and French governments nationalized big chunks of their private sector—banks, mines, and utilities—with France putting 20% of its industry under state control by mid-1946. As Marshall Planners arrived at their missions in 1948, recipient governments throughout West Europe were enlarging their welfare systems, including national health care. Thus, an estimable trait of those who answered George Marshall's summons was that they seldom preferred, above all else, to be right, a double entendre to be sure. In Italy, West Germany, and Turkey a collision of economic creeds invariably took place, yet American egotism never amounted to an insurmountable hurdle. Today's architects of policy should take note of the zigzagging required for arriving at the ultimate destination.[8]

Some critically important virtues of the Marshall Plan can provide other guidelines worthy of re-creation. In light of the pathologies that of late beset many foreign aid programs, especially the serious problem faced by the World Bank, adopting ECA's principles might prevent a subculture of corruption and scandal. Of the "four great lessons" Paul Hoffman drew from his oversight of the Marshall Plan, two pertained to eliminating waste. The first was that "We Must Use Guided Dollars" that joined a "detailed program of needs" by recipients with "end-use checks" by the donor. The second was that "A Hardheaded Administration of Aid is Necessary" with a premium on "tightfistedness." Wherever ECA operated, accountability was demanded and received. Its anticorruption mentality meant rigorous accounting controls and a disbursement system that minimized, through PAs primarily, the flow of dollars out of the United States and across the Atlantic. Disincentives to skimming and embezzlement of funds extended to a veto wielded over the use of counterpart locally as well as ECA's retention in American banks of its contributions to the European Payments Union. A $13,000,000,000 foreign aid program virtually free of scandal qualifies as the touchstone for all future reconstruction efforts.[9]

In hindsight, the Marshall Plan's structure serviced its strategies extremely well. Its decentralized theater command, for instance, advanced its purposes and was yet another source of organizational strength. Few features, however, exceeded in overall value the manner in which ECA itself was set up. A small, independent, elite, and well-run government agency, burdened with as little bureaucracy as possible, to handle future initiatives in postwar reconstruction has its compelling historical precedent in the Economic Cooperation Administration. Selecting the "Ad Hoc Option," rather than elevating either the State or Defense Department to the role of lead agency in such an eventuality, is a lesson embedded in the past. Avoidance of officialism, with its excessive rules, regulations, and red tape, assured ECA's effectiveness. A human scale and autonomy were crucial to more than just the morale and esprit of Marshall Planners; they also fostered innovation while keeping the albatross of careerism flying far away.

How can the State Department with thirty thousand employees, or even the World Bank with more than ten tnousand employees worldwide, achieve the same rapid response, creativity, and efficiencies that ECA once did? There is, of course, nothing magical about improvisation. After all, what is one to make of the Coalition Provisional Authority in Iraq, or CPA, which undertook postwar reconstruction in a single Middle Eastern country with a cumbersome force of fifteen hundred employees at its peak continually rotating in and out of Baghdad's Green Zone? The answer: probably no one in authority cared much about extracting history's lessons beforehand.

With considerable congressional nudging, Marshall Planners also incorporated a psychology of human nature into their programs. Their insights contributed critically to realizing their objectives. First, they guaranteed West European recipients assistance for the duration of four years rather than for either a year or as an open-ended commitment. They predicated their sunset provision and specific timetable on the assumption that lasting recovery required time, yet too much time was counterproductive to achieving that goal. Second, they made all aid conditional and conditionality mandatory. They clearly understood that incentives to compliance, particularly concerning pledges of financial and budgetary reforms, were crucial. Failure to uphold provisions in bilateral contracts could mean sanctions or loss of funding. Realistically, the donor attached strings, or *quid pro quos,* and then spelled them out in formal treaties. In light of its good effect, this portion of the ECA contract ought not to be tampered with or discarded by the next organization of postwar region builders.

A Final Rumination

Twenty years ago that indispensable European, Robert Marjolin, called the Marshall Plan "the most dazzling political and economic success in the history of the western world since 1914."[10] Since then, not every economic historian or economist has espoused his view. Chiefly in European academic circles where multivariate regression analysis, counterfactual simulations, and input-output methods rate highly, Marjolin's superlative has encountered dissent and skepticism. To being a Marjolinite I confess, though I also admit doubts as to whether a reproduction of that "dazzling success" can grace the twenty-first century. In order to weigh the odds for that actually happening, some day, the consequence of one factor, relative to other determinants, needs highlighting—lest history reproach this author unmercifully.

That quintessential American, Ralph Waldo Emerson, once avowed, "character is higher than intellect." Too infrequently quoted since the passing of

George Catlett Marshall and his generation, Emerson's aphorism penetrates to the heart of the Marshall Plan. Compared to the dominant role of character in the self-image of ECA's leaders and staffers, everything else wanes in significance. In at least one vital way, Marshall Planners are reminiscent of the nation's Founding Fathers. They were avatars in that, like Washington, Jefferson, and Madison, they clung to a conviction: power and influence derived from personal merit. Despite flaws in their nature, they nonetheless rechanneled their energies, talents, reputations, and personal ambitions into the "service of benevolence." They believed that curtailing special interests and doing the public good were, in fact, instruments for achieving individual greatness.[11]

The character possessed by most Marshall Planners, surely inspired by George C. Marshall's life of selfless service, lends itself poorly to quantification. When General Marshall served as Army Chief of Staff, he was, in his own words, "always on the lookout for the real performers who are self-effacing."[12] Somehow, Paul Hoffman and Averell Harriman managed to find those American hybrids in abundance. Today, character seems in much shorter supply than in the late 1940s. But if force of character were reinvigorated in American culture, and Emerson's truth widely reembraced, another Marshall Plan would become more feasible. Americans of character and intelligence, free of hubris, mindful of history's warnings, equipped with realistic objectives, proven methods, and proper procedures, might then be equal to the uncertainties, mysteries, and imponderables implicit in a "new" or "second" or "present day" Marshall Plan. When they are committed to Marshall's prescription of trading "sacrifices today" for "security and peace tomorrow," the outlook brightens even further.[13] When America's best once again see themselves as national servants, in the image of George C. Marshall, the time will have arrived to entertain that prospect seriously.

Appendix A

Wartime Government Service of Selected Marshall Planners

BUREAU OF THE BUDGET
Bartlett Harvey
Thomas C. Schelling
Donald C. Stone

OFFICE OF PRICE ADMINISTRATION (OPA)
William R. Auman
Vincent M. Barnett
Leland Barrows
Alice Bourneuf
Henry Reuss

OFFICE OF STRATEGIC SERVICES (OSS)
Andrew Berding
David Bruce
Jean Cattier
John H. F. Haskell
Milton Katz
Charles Kindleberger
Walter Levy
Arthur Schlesinger
Stuart Schulberg
Samuel van Hyning

OFFICE OF WAR INFORMATION (OWI)
Dowsley Clark
Sidney Fine

WAR PRODUCTION BOARD (WPB)
Vincent M. Barnett
William L. Batt
Thomas Blaisdell

WAR PRODUCTION BOARD (WPB) *(continued)*

Walker Cisler
Lucius Clay
Norman H. Collisson
John O. Coppock
Theodore Geiger
Lincoln Gordon
Hubert Havlik
Paul A. Jenkins
Milton Katz
Shaw Livermore
John Nuveen
Paul R. Porter
Augustus Eugene Staley
Harold Stein
C. Tyler Wood

WAR SHIPPING ADMINISTRATION (WSA)

Richard M. Bissell
Lewis Douglas
Samuel van Hyning

Appendix B

Educational and Professional Achievements of Selected Marshall Planners

Ph.D. DEGREES

Vincent M. Barnett
Richard M. Bissell
Alice Bourneuf
Hollis Chenery
Howard Cottam
Theodore Geiger
Huntington Gilchrist
Lincoln Gordon
Hubert Havlik
Charles Kindleberger
Shaw Livermore
Thomas C. Schelling
Irving Swerdlow
Henry Tasca
Henry W. Wiens

RHODES SCHOLARS

Harlan Cleveland, Princeton University, 1938
Lincoln Gordon, Harvard University, 1933
John McNaughton, DePauw University, 1942
Waldemar Nielsen, University of Missouri, 1939
Norman S. Taber, Brown University, 1913
Lane Timmons, University of Georgia, 1938
Alan Valentine, Swarthmore College, 1921

COLLEGE DEANS AND PRESIDENTS

Vincent M. Barnett, President, Colgate University, 1963–69
Kingman Brewster, President, Yale University, 1963–77
McGeorge Bundy, Dean, Faculty of Arts & Sciences,
Harvard University, 1953–60
Joseph E. Carrigan, Dean, School of Agriculture, University of
Vermont, 1942–48
Harlan Cleveland, Dean, Maxwell School, Syracuse University, 1957–61;
President, University of Hawaii, 1969–74

Lincoln Gordon, President, Johns Hopkins University, 1967–71
Shaw Livermore, Dean, University of Arizona Business School
Donald C. Stone, President, Springfield College, 1953–57; Dean, School of
International Affairs, University of Pittsburgh, 1957–69
Alan Valentine, President, University of Rochester, 1935–48

NOBEL LAUREATES
Henry R. Labouisse and UNICEF, Nobel Peace Prize, 1965
Thomas C. Schelling, Nobel Prize in Economics, 2005

PULITZER PRIZE WINNERS
Alfred Friendly
Arthur Schlesinger, Jr.

AMBASSADORS
Kingman Brewster, United Kingdom, 1977–81
David Bruce, France, 1949–52; Federal Republic of Germany,
1957–59; United Kingdom, 1961–69; NATO, 1974–75
Howard Cottam, Kuwait, 1963–69
Harlan Cleveland, NATO, 1965–69
Thomas Finletter, NATO, 1961–65
Lincoln Gordon, Brazil, 1961–66
C. William Kontos, Sudan, 1980–83
Henry R. Labouisse, Greece, 1962–65
James E. Lowenstein, Luxembourg, 1977–81
Henry Tasca, Greece, 1969–74
Lane Timmons, Haiti, 1963–67
James David Zellerbach, Italy, 1956–61

EXECUTIVE DIRECTOR OF UNICEF
Henry R. Labouisse, 1965–79

Appendix C

Length of Service of Selected Marshall Planners

William R. Auman (OSR, Paris; Denmark) 1948–52: 4 years

Vincent M. Barnett (Italy) 1948–50: 2 years

Andrew Berding (Italy) 1948–50: 2 years

Philip W. Bonsal (OSR, Paris) 1948–50: 2 years

Kingman Brewster (OSR, Paris) 1948–49: 1 year

Hollis Chenery (OSR, Paris; Italy) 1949–52: 3 years

Harlan Cleveland (ECA Washington) 1949–50: 1 year

Russell Dorr (Turkey) 1948–52: 4 years

Russell Drake (Greece) 1948–52: 4 years

Roscoe Drummond (OSR, Paris) 1949–51: 2 years

Thomas Flanagan (OSR, Paris; Turkey) 1949–52: 3 years

Alfred Friendly (OSR, Paris) 1948–49: 1 year

Robert Hanes (Belgium, W. Germany) 1949–51: 2 years

Hubert Havlik (OSR, Paris) 1948–52: 4 years

Paul Hoffman (ECA Washington) 1948–50: 2.5 years

Milton Katz (OSR, Paris) 1948–51: 3 years

Shaw Livermore (OSR, Paris) 1948–51: 3 years

John McNaughton (OSR, Paris) 1949–51: 2 years

Robert R. Mullen (ECA Washington) 1949–52: 3 years

John Nuveen (Greece, Belgium) 1948–50: 2 years

F. Taylor Ostrander (OSR, Paris) 1948–51: 3.5 years

Paul R. Porter (Greece; OSR, Paris) 1949–51: 2 years

Henry S. Reuss (OSR, Paris) 1948–50: 14 months

Thomas C. Schelling (OSR, Paris; Denmark) 1948–50: 2 years

Arthur Schlesinger (OSR, Paris) 1948: 2–3 months

Donald C. Stone (ECA Washington) 1948–52: 4 years

Alan Valentine (Netherlands) 1948–49: 1 year

Vernon Walters (OSR, Paris) 1948–50: 2 years

Henry W. Wiens (Turkey) 1948–52: 4 years

Appendix D

U.S. Economic Assistance to Europe, 1945–52

(amounts in millions of dollars; years are U.S. government fiscal: July 1 to June 30)

	Pre-Mar. Plan[a] July 1, 1945–April 2, 1948	Marshall Plan[b] 1948[c] Total	1949 Total	1950 Total	1951 Total	1952 Total	Total	1948–52 Grants	Loans
Austria	289.3	38.6	235.4	168.8	118.6	116.3	677.7	677.7	0
Belgium-Luxembourg	31.4	0	261.0	225.2	59.8	9.2	555.2	491.2	68.0
Denmark	1.0	9.8	116.3	83.5	49.3	14.2	273.1	239.8	33.3
France	503.0	206.1	1,107.2	702.0	436.4	262.1	2,713.8	2,488.2	225.6
Germany	1,280.2	64.2	541.8	290.0	402.5	92.0	1,390.5	1,173.6	216.9
Greece	478.5	32.0	161.8	177.1	156.5	179.3	706.7	706.7	0
Iceland	0	2.3	6.0	7.1	8.4	5.5	29.3	24.0	5.3
Ireland	0	0	85.6	45.3	16.5	0	147.4	19.2	128.2
Italy	1,060.4	110.6	573.5	402.3	262.7	159.5	1,508.6	1,413.0	95.6
Netherlands	36.0	43.0	461.8	269.0	107.8	100.5	982.1	832.6	149.5
Norway	25.0	5.8	94.7	95.4	41.9	17.4	255.2	216.0	39.2
Portugal	0	0	0	31.5	19.7	0.1	51.3	15.2	36.1
Sweden	0.5	0	45.2	51.6	21.7	-11.3	107.2	86.8	20.4
Turkey	12.2	0	33.8	71.9	49.8	69.6	225.1	140.1	85.0
United Kingdom	3,610.8	226.1	1,387.6	957.3	267.1	351.8	3,189.9	2,805.1	384.8
Europe (Regional)[d]	0	0	0	1.9	352.2	52.9	407.0	407.0	0
TOTALS	7,328.3	738.5	5,111.7	3,579.9	2,370.9	1,419.1	13,224.1	11,736.2	1,487.9
U.S. Gross Natl. Prod.[e]		194,284	258,229	286,826	329,822	347,956	1,417,117		
Mar. Plan $ as % of GNP		0.38	1.98	1.25	0.72	0.41	0.93		

Notes:

a. The numbers in this column may be found in the U.S. Agency for International Development statistics in the 2001 "Green Book," pp. 190–211 (see www.dec.org/pdf_docs/PNACR900.pdf). Since the time periods overlap by three months in 1948, the amount of Marshall Plan aid for April through June of that year has to be subtracted from the total.

b. The numbers in these columns are from U.S. Agency for International Development, *U.S. Economic Assistance Programs Administered by the Agency for International Development and Predecessor Agencies, April 3, 1948–June 30, 1970* (Washington, D.C.: AID Office of Statistics and Reports, June 1971), pp. 16, 22, 68–77.

c. President Truman signed the Economic Recovery Act on April 3, 1948, so this column shows the funding for April 3–June 30 of FY 1948.

d. Switzerland received no grants or loans during this period.

e. GNP figures are in U.S. Bureau of the Census, *Statistical Abstract of the United States, 1954* (Washington, D.C.: GPO, 1954), p. 299.

Notes

Preface

1. Ernst van der Beugel, head of the Marshall Plan division within the Dutch Ministry of Foreign Affairs, quoted London's *Economist* in comments on a speech delivered by Sir Oliver Franks at a Marshall Plan 30th Commemorative Conference held in Paris, June 1977. Text of the speech and commentaries are in Box 1, Folder 9, ERP Commemoratives Collection, George C. Marshall Library, Lexington, Virginia (hereafter cited as GCML).

2. Interview with Paul R. Porter, Harry B. Price Papers, GCML; Constantine C. Menges, ed., *The Marshall Plan from Those Who Made It Succeed* (Lanham, Md., 1999), 3, 7.

3. See Charles Cerami, *Marshall Plan for the 1990s* (New York, 1989); and Wojciech Kostrzewa et al., "A Marshall Plan for Middle and Eastern Europe?" *World Economy* 13 (March 1990): 27–50. For some recent invocations of the Marshall Plan as a silver bullet, consult U.S. House of Representatives, Committee on International Relations, *Hearing*, "Economic Development and Integration as a Catalyst for Peace: A Marshall Plan for the Middle East" (107th Cong., 2nd sess.), July 24, 2002; John A. Merkwan, "Balkan Stability and the 'Second Marshall Plan,'" *Strategy Research Project*, U.S. Army War College (2000); Philip Dimitrov, "To Ensure Peace in the Balkans, A New Marshall Plan," *Boston Globe*, June 26, 1999; Francine Kiefer, "Will A New Marshall Plan Work in Balkans?" *Christian Science Monitor*, July 30, 1999; George Melloan, "Europe's Balkan 'Marshall Plan' Has Many Pitfalls," *Wall Street Journal*, June 15, 1999. Of late, there is Robert Evans, "U.N. Urges Trade 'Marshall Plan' for Poor States," *Washington Post*, June 14, 2005; Ibrahim al-Jaafari, "A New Marshall Plan for Iraq," *Times* (London), June 27, 2005; Doug Smith and Borzou Daragahi, "Marshall Plan for Iraq Fades," *Los Angeles Times*, January 15, 2006; and Michael R. Auslin, "North Korea's Marshall Plan," *Asian Wall Street Journal*, August 15, 2006, 13. Al-Jaafari, Iraq's former Prime Minister, claims that today's dollar equivalent of Marshall Plan aid, 1948–52, is $500,000,000,000, a grossly inflated figure and more on the order of $90–100,000,000,000.

Chapter I: Conceptualizing the Marshall Plan

1. Tony Judt, *Postwar: A History of Europe Since 1945* (New York, 2005), 116; Lincoln Gordon Oral History (July 17, 1975), 66, Harry S. Truman Library, Independence, Missouri (hereafter cited as HSTL); George W. Ball, *The Past Has Another Pattern: Memoirs* (New York, 1982), 77; Robert J. Donovan, *The Second Victory: The Marshall Plan and Postwar Revival of Europe* (Lanham, Md., 1987), 20; Robert Marjolin, *Architect of European Unity: Memoirs, 1911–1986* (London, 1989), 180. Norway imposed tight rationing on consumer goods until 1951. See Halvard M. Lange Oral History, 7, HSTL.

2. Scholarly disagreement has the U.K.'s Official Cabinet Historian, Alan Milward, on one side. In his *The Reconstruction of Western Europe, 1945–1951* (Berkeley, Calif., 1984); "Was the Marshall Plan Necessary?" *Diplomatic History* 13 (1989): 231–53, and "Europe and the Marshall Plan: 50 Years On," in John Agnew and J. Nicholas Entrikin, eds., *The Marshall Plan Today: Model and Metaphor* (London, 2004), 58–81, the leading revisionist Milward developed his complex case against the Marshall Plan playing a crucial or very significant role in restoring West Europe back to health. The dissenters on the other side are American diplomatic historian Michael Hogan, *The Marshall Plan: America, Britain, and the Reconstruction*

of Western Europe, 1947–1952 (Cambridge, 1987), and American economists Barry Eichengreen, Marc Uzan, and J. Bradford DeLong. See Eichengreen and Uzan, "The Marshall Plan: Economic Effects and Implications for Eastern Europe and the Soviet Union," *Economic Policy* 14 (April 1992): 13–75; DeLong and Eichengreen, "The Marshall Plan: History's Most Successful Structural Adjustment Program," in Rudiger Dornbusch et al., eds., *Postwar Economic Reconstruction and Lessons for the East Today* (Cambridge, Mass., 1993), 189–230; DeLong, "Post–World War II Western European Exceptionalism: The Economic Dimension," in Agnew and Entrikin, eds., *The Marshall Plan Today,* 25–57. Kathleen Burk has persuasively criticized Milward's analysis as "relentlessly economic" and Hogan's as "relentlessly political." See her "The Marshall Plan from the European Perspective," The 1995 Sir Alec Cairncross Lecture, St. Peter's College, Oxford, England, September 22, 1995. Eichengreen and Uzan draw a distinction between the Marshall Plan's direct and indirect impact on West European economic growth. Both sides have gathered followers and defenders.

3. Paul Hoffman, "The Marshall Plan: Peace Building—Its Price and Its Profits," *Foreign Service Journal* 44 (June 1967): 20; Paul G. Hoffman Oral History (October 1964), 8, HSTL. Hoffman authored the "Only the Europeans Can Save Europe" line.

4. Oliver Franks, "Lessons of the Marshall Plan Experience," June 1977, in Box 1, Folder 9, ERP Commemoratives Collection, GCML. France underwent some arm-twisting over her initial postwar policy towards Germany. See Milward, *The Reconstruction of Western Europe,* Chapter 4.

5. Imanuel Wexler, *The Marshall Plan Revisited: The European Recovery Program in Economic Perspective* (Westport, Conn., 1983), 14. Hoffman oversaw the Marshall Plan until his resignation in August 1950, when he was replaced by William C. Foster, another industrialist.

6. Charles L. Mee, *The Marshall Plan: The Launching of the Pax Americana* (New York, 1984), 117, 208; Joseph M. Jones, *The Fifteen Weeks* (New York, 1955), 263; Kathleen Burk, "The Marshall Plan: Filling in Some of the Blanks," *Contemporary European History* 10 (2001): 267–94; David Ellwood, "From 'Re-education' to the Selling of the Marshall Plan in Italy," in Nicholas Pronay and Keith Wilson, eds., *The Political Re-education of Germany and Her Allies After World War II* (Totowa, N.J., 1985), 223–24. Professor Luciano Segreto, University of Florence, has concluded from Italian sources that "Togliatti . . . did not want any revolution at all in Italy." Segreto to author, June 20, 2006.

7. Diane B. Kunz, "The Marshall Plan Reconsidered," *Foreign Affairs* 76 (May-June 1997): 165. In a revealing interview at Communist Party headquarters in Paris on February 6, 1948, Maurice Thorez lectured the chief foreign correspondent for the *New York Times* that U.S. policy was hurtling the world toward war "within a relatively short time" and that "a grave economic crisis" would soon plunge the United States into another depression that would spread worldwide. See C. L. Sulzberger, *A Long Row of Candles: Memoirs and Diaries, 1934–1954* (New York, 1969), 377–79.

8. Melvyn P. Leffler, "The United States and the Strategic Dimensions of the Marshall Plan," *Diplomatic History* 12 (Summer 1988): 277–81.

9. Averell Harriman Oral History (1971), HSTL; Theodore H. White, *In Search of History: A Personal Adventure* (New York, 1978), 277. "That Western Europe would have 'gone Communist' without the ERP" the historian Charles S. Maier finds "unlikely." See Maier, "The Marshall Plan and the Division of Europe," *Journal of Cold War Studies* 7, no. 1 (2005): 173.

10. Stanley Hoffmann and Charles Maier, eds., *The Marshall Plan: A Retrospective* (London, 1984), 66; Milton Katz Oral History (July 1975), HSTL.

11. Thomas C. Schelling, "The Marshall Plan: A Model for What?" in Agnew and Entrikin, eds., *The Marshall Plan Today,* 236; Curt Tarnoff, "The Marshall Plan: Design,

Accomplishments, and Relevance to the Present," in Menges, ed., *The Marshall Plan from Those Who Made It Succeed,* 362, 365; Milward, *The Reconstruction of Western Europe,* 94–95. Like many students of the Marshall Plan, Tarnoff and Milward disagree about the amount of the nonloan component of American aid. Whether Tarnoff's $12,840,000,000, or Milward's $11,900,000,000, assistance did take three forms. Milward's breakdown is: outright grant ($9.2 billion), conditional grant ($1,540,000,000), and loan ($1,140,000,000). In his calculations Tarnoff lumps the two different grants together. ECA loans, about whose dollar value Tarnoff and Milward agree, were administered through the Export-Import Bank, generally carrying an interest rate of 2.5% on thirty-five-year notes.

12. David Reynolds, "The European Response," *Foreign Affairs* 76 (May-June 1997): 177; Charles S. Maier, "From Plan to Practice: The Context and Consequences of the Marshall Plan," *Harvard Magazine* 99 (May-June 1997): 42–43.

13. Lincoln Gordon to Harry B. Price, November 12, 1954; Van Cleveland to Harry B. Price, July 30, 1954, with 4-page attachment, Box 1, Price Papers, GCML.

14. Albert O. Hirschman, *Crossing Boundaries* (Cambridge, Mass., 1998), 35–39; John Killick, *The United States and European Reconstruction, 1945–1960* (Edinburgh, 1997), 10; Hoffmann and Maier, eds., *The Marshall Plan,* 11; Maier, "From Plan to Practice," *Harvard Magazine,* 43. Robert Marjolin, who became a Keynesian himself before World War II after reading *The General Theory,* found every American economist cooperating with the CEEC in the summer of 1947 to be a fellow Keynesian. See his memoirs in translation, *Architect of European Unity,* 120–21, 185.

15. Hoffman, "The Marshall Plan."

16. David Ellwood, "The Marshall Plan and the Politics of Growth," in Peter Stirk and David Willis, eds., *Shaping Postwar Europe: European Unity and Disunity, 1945–1957* (New York, 1991), 17, 26. Conventionally, Hoffman's speech to the OEEC Council in Paris on October 31, 1949, in which he promoted the cause of regional integration, dates the shift in ECA's priorities.

17. With persistence, James Warren has pointed out to me that the only change occurring on December 31, 1951, was the issuance of new stationery with a new letterhead.

Chapter II: Selling the Marshall Plan

1. Harold L. Hitchens, "Influences on the Congressional Decision to Pass the Marshall Plan," *Western Political Quarterly* 21 (March 1968): 60, 67.

2. *Congressional Record* (80th Cong., 1st Sess.) December 8, 1947, 11: 150–56; Evan Thomas and Walter Isaacson, *The Wise Men: Six Friends and the World They Made* (New York, 1986), 427; Will Clayton, "Is the Marshall Plan 'Operation Rathole'?" *Saturday Evening Post* 222 (November 29, 1947): 26–27, 137–38. Commonplace among doubters, skeptics, and critics, the caustic expression "Operation Rathole" apparently originated with Republican Senator Kenneth Wherry of Nebraska. Other strident congressional opponents of the Marshall Plan were Representative Harold Knutson of Minnesota, Representative George Bender of Ohio, Senator William Langer of North Dakota, and Senator George Malone of Nevada.

3. The most informative biography of Robert R. McCormick is Richard Norton Smith, *The Colonel: The Life and Legend of Robert R. McCormick* (Boston, Mass., 1997).

4. Charles P. Kindleberger, "In the Halls of the Capitol: A Memoir," *Foreign Affairs* 76 (May-June 1997): 186–87; Lincoln Gordon to Harry Price, November 12, 1954, Box 1, Price Papers, GCML; "Outline of Remarks by Paul G. Hoffman," June 5, 1967, Box 1, Folder 4, ERP Commemoratives Collection, GCML.

5. Hitchens, "Influences on the Congressional Decision," 65; Hoffmann and Maier, eds., *The Marshall Plan*, 15–17.

6. Richard Bissell Oral History (July 1971), HSTL; Bissell, *Reflections of a Cold Warrior* (New Haven, Conn., 1996), 36–37.

7. Menges, ed., *The Marshall Plan from Those Who Made It Succeed*, 89, 197–98. The noted Harvard historian Arthur Schlesinger, Jr., who spent the summer of 1948 as Harriman's assistant at OSR, Paris, with "special responsibility for his public appearances," has recollected that "in those days he was an inveterate mumbler." See Schlesinger, *A Life in the Twentieth Century: Innocent Beginnings, 1917–1950* (Boston, 2000), 471.

8. Shaw Livermore Oral History (March 1974), HSTL.

9. Gunther Harkort Oral History (November 1970), HSTL; J. Bradford DeLong and Barry Eichengreen, "The Marshall Plan," in Dornbusch et al., eds., *Postwar Economic Reconstruction and Lessons For the East Today*, 218.

10. Larry I. Bland, ed., *George C. Marshall Interviews and Reminiscences for Forrest C. Pogue*, 3d ed. (Lexington, Va., 1996), 556–60; Forrest C. Pogue, *George C. Marshall: Statesman, 1945–1959* (New York, 1987), 244–57; Ed Cray, *General of the Army: George C. Marshall, Soldier and Statesman* (New York, 1990), 620; Federico Romero, *The United States and the European Trade Union Movement, 1944–1951* (Chapel Hill, N.C., 1992), 109.

11. Michael Wala, "Selling the Marshall Plan at Home," *Diplomatic History* 10 (Summer 1986): 258–59, 262; John Bledsoe Bonds, *Bipartisan Strategy: Selling the Marshall Plan* (Westport, Conn., 2002), 79–87; Dean Acheson, *Present at the Creation: My Years in the State Department* (New York, 1969), 240–41. On CCMP, also consult Michael Wala, *The Council on American Foreign Relations and American Foreign Policy in the Early Cold War* (Providence, R.I., 1994), 181–216.

12. Hitchens, "Influences on the Congressional Decision," 51.

13. Allen W. Dulles, *The Marshall Plan* (Providence, R.I., 1993), 33, 95.

14. Hitchens, "Influences on the Congressional Decision," 51–52, 52 n. 3, 59; Mildred Strunk, "The Quarter's Polls," *Public Opinion Quarterly* 12 (Summer 1948): 365–67. For reverberations on Capitol Hill from the Czech coup, see Bonds, *Bipartisan Strategy*, 155–57, 161–64, 171–73, 177–86, 200–201.

15. Paul G. Hoffman, *Peace Can Be Won* (Garden City, N.Y., 1951), 91; Wala, "Selling the Marshall Plan at Home," 264.

16. Richard Bissell Oral History (July 1971), HSTL.

17. Wala, "Selling the Marshall Plan at Home," 264.

18. David Ellwood, "You Too Can Be Like Us: Selling the Marshall Plan," *History Today* 48 (October 1998): 33–39; Ellwood, "The Marshall Plan and the Politics of Growth," 18.

19. Robert R. Mullen to Harry Price, July 27, 1954, Box 2, Price Papers, GCML; Sulzberger, *A Long Row of Candles*, 361.

20. David Ellwood, in Nicholas Pronay and Keith Wilson, eds., *The Political Re-education of Germany and Her Allies After World War II* (Totowa, N.J., 1985), 225; Judt, *Postwar*, 96. Twenty years later, in the student uprising of May 1968, children of the 1948 generation were still hostile to market forces and still bent on creating a socialist society in France.

21. Andrew Berding to Harry Price, June 8, 1954, Box 1, Price Papers, GCML.

22. Mark Wyatt Oral History, February 1996, National Security Archive, George Washington University, Washington, D.C. (hereafter cited as NSA, GWU).

23. Interview with Richard Bissell, Price Papers, GCML; Sallie Pisani, *The CIA and the Marshall Plan* (Lawrence, Kans., 1991), 129.

24. John N. Hutchinson to Harry Price, June 3, 1954, Box 2; interview with Thomas Flanagan and Lawrence Hall, Price Papers, GCML.

25. Berding to Price, June 8, 1954, Box 1, Price Papers, GCML; Hoffman, *Peace Can Be Won,* 143–44.

26. Alfred Friendly Obituary by Martin Weil, *Washington Post,* November 8, 1983. On Waldemar (Wally) Nielsen, see Wolfgang Saxon, "Waldemar Nielsen, Expert on Philanthropy, Dies at 88," *New York Times,* November 4, 2005; Menges, ed., *The Marshall Plan from Those Who Made It Succeed,* 198–200.

27. Alfred Friendly to Harry Price, May 29, 1954, Box 1, Price Papers, GCML; Chiarella Esposito, *America's Feeble Weapon: Funding the Marshall Plan in France and Italy, 1948–1950* (Westport, Conn., 1994), 95, 98–99; Theodore H. White, *In Search of History: A Personal Adventure* (New York, 1978), 273. ECA's information budget ultimately reached $17,000,000 in counterpart, according to Paul Hoffman. See *Peace Can Be Won,* 144.

28. Mullen to Price, December 3, 1954, Box 2, Price Papers, GCML; W. John Kenney Oral History (November 1971), HSTL; Menges, ed., *The Marshall Plan from Those Who Made It Succeed,* 106, 200; Martin Schain, ed., *The Marshall Plan: Fifty Years After* (New York, 2001), 269.

29. Linda R. Christenson, "Marshall Plan Filmography" (2000) at www.marshallfilms.org; Albert Hemsing, "The Marshall Plan's European Film Unit, 1948–1955: A Memoir and Filmography," *Historical Journal of Film, Radio and Television* 14 (August 1994): 279–97; Thomas Doherty, "A Symposium on the Marshall Plan Films in New York City," *Historical Journal of Film, Radio and Television* 25 (March 2005): 151–54. In 1946 nearly 90% of Italian box office receipts went for foreign films, mostly American. The following year French movie studios produced just forty films while importing from the United States more than eight times that number. See Judt, *Postwar,* 231. The most recent public screenings of "Films of the Marshall Plan," twenty-four in number, took place at National Archives, Washington, D.C., October 17–20, 2006. Preceding them was a Panel Discussion with Charles Maier, Lincoln Gordon, Amy Garrett, and Sandra Schulberg.

30. Stuart Schulberg, "Making Marshall Plan Movies," *Film News* (September 1951): 10, 19, as quoted in Sandra Schulberg and Richard Pena, *Selling Democracy: Films of the Marshall Plan, 1948–1953* (New York, 2004). Also at www.sellingdemocracy.org.

31. "The Men Behind the Marshall Plan Films," in Schulberg and Pena, *Selling Democracy*; David Culbert, "Albert E. Hemsing, 1921–1997," *Historical Journal of Film, Radio and Television* 17 (August 1997): 401–2; Hemsing, "The Marshall Plan's European Film Unit," 269–78.

32. Hutchinson to Price, June 3, 1954, Box 2, Price Papers, GCML.

33. Anthony B. Carew, *Labour Under the Marshall Plan: The Politics of Productivity and the Marketing of Managerial Science* (Detroit, Mich., 1987), 223, 240, 249–50.

34. Friendly to Price, May 29, 1954, Box 1, Price Papers, GCML.

35. Ellwood, "You Too Can Be Like Us"; Schain, ed., *The Marshall Plan,* 286; Pisani, *The CIA and the Marshall Plan,* 104.

Chapter III: Analyzing the Marshall Plan

1. Donovan, *The Second Victory*, Preface; Agnew and Entrikin, eds., *The Marshall Plan Today,* 191.

2. Dafne C. Reymen, "The Economic Effects of the Marshall Plan Revisited," in Agnew and Entrikin, eds., *The Marshall Plan Today,* 82.

3. Dirk U. Stikker Oral History (April 1964), 2, HSTL; Oliver Franks, "Lessons of the Marshall Plan Experience," Box 1, Folder 9, ERP Commemoratives Collection, GCML.

4. Hogan, *The Marshall Plan,* 337, 415; Robin W. Winks, *The Marshall Plan and the American Economy* (New York, 1960), 45; Wexler, *The Marshall Plan Revisited,* 250–52; Eichengreen and Uzan, "The Marshall Plan," 202, 204–5; DeLong and Eichengreen, "The Marshall Plan," 219; Menges, ed., *The Marshall Plan from Those Who Made It Succeed,* 369–70.

5 Imanuel Wexler, "The Marshall Plan in Economic Perspective: Goals and Accomplishments," in Schain, ed., *The Marshall Plan,* 147–51.

6. Schain, ed., *The Marshall Plan,* 6–7; Judt, *Postwar,* 97; Vernon Walters, "The Marshall Plan and Harriman," in Walters, *Silent Missions* (Garden City, N.Y., 1978), 187–88; Chiarella Esposito, "Influencing Aid Recipients: Marshall Plan Lessons For Contemporary Aid Donors," in Barry Eichengreen, ed, *Europe's Postwar Recovery* (Cambridge, U.K., 1995), 68, 77, 84–86, 88.

7. Charles P. Kindleberger, *Marshall Plan Days* (Boston, 1987), 74, 88, 90, 246; Agnew and Entrikin, eds., *The Marshall Plan Today,* 84.

8. Menges, ed., *The Marshall Plan from Those Who Made It Succeed,* 367; Agnew and Entrikin, eds., *The Marshall Plan Today,* 234; DeLong and Eichengreen, "The Marshall Plan," 191; Eichengreen and Uzan, "The Marshall Plan," 227, 230–33, 238.

9. Interview with Harold Stein, Price Papers, GCML; Shaw Livermore Oral History (March 1974), HSTL; William Pfaff, "Expanding Headaches," *International Herald Tribune,* June 24–25, 2006, 6.

10. Hoffmann and Maier, eds., *The Marshall Plan,* 51, 77, 80; C. A. Munkman, *American Aid to Greece: A Report on the First Ten Years* (New York, 1958), 273; Milton Katz Oral History (July 1975), HSTL.

11. Menges, ed., *The Marshall Plan from Those Who Made It Succeed,* 188.

12. Interview with Russell Dorr, Price Papers, GCML.

13. William Parks Oral History, November 1988, Foreign Affairs Oral History Project (hereafter cited as FAOHP), Georgetown University, Washington, D.C.; Richard Bissell Oral History (July 1971), HSTL; Lincoln Gordon, "ERP in Operation," *Harvard Business Review* 27 (March 1949): 132; Hadley Arkes, *Bureaucracy, the Marshall Plan, and the National Interest* (Princeton, N.J., 1972), 245, 290–91; Theodore H. White, *Fire in the Ashes: Europe in Midcentury* (New York, 1953), 61–62.

14. Melbourne Spector Oral History, December 1988, FAOHP, Georgetown University; interview with Sam Board, Price Papers, GCML.

15. Comments by Miriam Camps on Speech by Oliver Franks, Paris, June 1977, Box 1, Folder 9, ERP Commemoratives Collection, GCML.

16. Kunz, "The Marshall Plan Reconsidered," 167; interview with Richard Bissell, Price Papers, GCML. In his autobiography Theodore White actually comments favorably on the size of OSR, Paris. "At its peak," he declares, "the Paris headquarters . . . held *only* 587 people on payroll, and another 839 all across Europe" [italics added]. White's figures approximate Bissell's, but they describe a different distribution of personnel. See *In Search of History,* 302; William Parks Oral History, November 1988, FAOHP, Georgetown University.

17. Leland Barrows Oral History (January 1971), HSTL.

18. Melbourne Spector, "A Transcendent Experience," in Menges, ed., *The Marshall Plan from Those Who Made It Succeed,* 84; William Parks Oral History, FAOHP, Georgetown University; W. John Kenney Oral History (November 1971), 65, HSTL; Alan Valentine, *Trial Balance: The Education of an American* (New York, 1956), 165. Henry Reuss praised ECA's

operational leadership—Hoffman, Harriman, and Foster—as an "inspiration" and thought that "one reason Marshall Planners were a happy breed was that we admired our bosses." See his autobiography, *When Government Was Good: Memories of a Life in Politics* (Madison, Wisc., 1999), 30–31.

19. Interview with Sam Board, Price Papers, GCML; Theodore Geiger Oral History (February 1996), NSA, GWU; Forrest Pogue, "George C. Marshall and the Marshall Plan," 65, in Charles Maier and Gunter Bischof, eds., *The Marshall Plan and Germany* (New York, 1991); Lincoln Gordon, "Recollections of a Marshall Planner," *Journal of International Affairs* 41 (Summer 1988): 237; Lincoln Gordon Oral History (July 22, 1975), 119, HSTL; Alan Raucher, *Paul G. Hoffman: Architect of Foreign Aid* (Lexington, Ky., 1985), 61, 65.

20. Paul G. Hoffman Oral History (October 1964), HSTL; interview with Paul Hoffman, Price Papers, GCML; Gordon, "Recollections of a Marshall Planner," 238; interview with Sam Board, Price Papers, GCML; Gordon, "ERP in Operation," 132; Valentine, *Trial Balance,* 169–73; Melbourne Spector Oral History, December 1988, FAOHP, Georgetown University; Richard Bissell Oral History (July 1971), HSTL.

21. Leland Barrows Oral History (January 1971), Paul R. Porter Oral History (November 1971), HSTL; Paul Porter to Harry Price, September 15, 1954, Box 2, Price Papers, GCML; Carolyn Eisenberg, "Working Class Politics and the Cold War: American Intervention in the German Labor Movement, 1945–1949," *Diplomatic History* 7 (Fall 1983): 284–85 n.10.

22. Spector, "A Transcendent Experience," in Menges, ed., *The Marshall Plan from Those Who Made It Succeed,* 78.

23 Hatch to Donald Stone, May 19, 1948; Stone to Harriman, June 10, 1948, Box 267, W. Averell Harriman Papers, Library of Congress, Washington, D.C. (hereafter cited as LC). In Menges, ed., *The Marshall Plan from Those Who Made It Succeed,* 83, Melbourne Spector erroneously refers to Maurice Moore as Hoffman's brother-in-law. Hiring Michael Forrestal may have been more nepotism than cronyism. Note the observation by Arthur Schlesinger, Jr., on the relationship between the Forrestal and Harriman families. "Because of his mother's alcoholism and his father's preoccupations," Michael Forrestal was "largely reared by the Harrimans." See *A Life in the Twentieth Century,* 471.

24. Leland Barrows Oral History (January 1971); Hubert Havlik Oral History (June 1973), 141, 156–61, HSTL; William Parks Oral History, FAOHP, Georgetown University. While attached to the U.S. Embassy in Paris as a Foreign Service Officer, Philip Bonsal also served as Harriman's Political Adviser at OSR, 1948–50.

25. Raucher, *Paul G. Hoffman,* 43–50, 61; Hoffmann and Maier, eds., *The Marshall Plan,* 68; Menges, ed., *The Marshall Plan from Those Who Made It Succeed,* 242; Reuss, *When Government Was Good,* 30–31.

26. Gunther Harkort Oral History (November 1970); Ernst H. van der Beugel Oral History (June 1964), HSTL. The Secretary-General for Administration of the Marshall Plan in Belgium appraised the ECA mission in Brussels as comprised of "first-class people" and "really the top." Roger Ockrent Oral History (July 1971), 18–19, HSTL.

27. Menges, ed., *The Marshall Plan from Those Who Made It Succeed,* 304–5.

28. Lincoln Gordon Oral History, January 1988, FAOHP, Georgetown University; Lincoln Gordon Oral History (July 17, 1975), 67, HSTL; Paul Nitze, *From Hiroshima to Glasnost: At the Center of Decision, a Memoir* (New York, 1989), 52.

29. Primary sources for much of the following discussion of ECA innovations are Theodore Geiger, "The Innovations of the Marshall Plan," in Menges, ed., *The Marshall Plan from Those Who Made It Succeed,* 303–6; and Theodore Geiger Oral History (February 1996), NSA, GWU. Geiger served in ECA Washington as Richard Bissell's right-hand man and has apparently described standard procedures. Chief of the Import Program Office, Athens,

James C. Warren, experienced a different mechanism. In some European countries less funneling through Washington occurred. In Warren's version, the sequence of steps for importing ECA commodities omitted a government purchasing mission in Washington and bypassed governmental ownership of American exports right up to their delivery in Europe. Importers deposited local currency in local banks *to purchase foreign exchange* to pay for dollar-denominated goods, instead of buying them from the local government. Warren to author, February 8, 2006. Warren's memory is supported by A. F. Freris in *The Greek Economy in the Twentieth Century* (New York, 1986), 133.

30. Theodore A. Wilson, *The Marshall Plan, 1947–1951* (New York, 1977), 42.

31. Curt Tarnoff, "The Marshall Plan," in Menges, ed., *The Marshall Plan from Those Who Made It Succeed,* 373; Bonds, *Bipartisan Strategy,* 98–99. Consult, also, the Marshall Plan film *Your Eighty Dollars* (1952)

32. Lincoln Gordon Oral History, January 1988, FAOHP, Georgetown University; Lincoln Gordon Oral History (July 22, 1975), 125, HSTL; Clarke to Price, September 21, 1954, Box 1, Price Papers, GCML; White, *In Search of History,* 278.

33. Agnew and Entrikin, eds., *The Marshall Plan Today,* 100. According to Hadley Arkes, UNRRA had first introduced an unrefined form of counterpart, and interim aid continued the practice. See *Bureaucracy, the Marshall Plan, and the National Interest,* 156–57.

34. Etienne Hirsch Oral History (June 1970), HSTL; Judt, *Postwar,* 96; Killick, *The United States and European Reconstruction,* 102; Menges, ed., *The Marshall Plan from Those Who Made It Succeed,* 363, 365. Robert Marjolin put the amount of counterpart released by ECA at $7,600,000,000. See Marjolin, *Architect of European Unity,* 226.

35. Theodore Christides Oral History (July 1970), HSTL; Marjolin, *Architect of European Unity,* 198–99. The key institution for the functioning of "drawing rights" was the Bank for International Settlements (BIS) in Basel, Switzerland, which served as OEEC's fiscal agent. There a monthly settlement of current balances of member central banks took place. Hubert Havlik Oral History (June 1973), HSTL.

36. Bissell, *Reflections of a Cold Warrior,* 57, 61–62, 64; Arkes, *Bureaucracy, the Marshall Plan, and the National Interest,* 363; Wexler, *The Marshall Plan Revisited,* 153–59; Lucrezia Reichlin, "The Marshall Plan Reconsidered," 52–53, in Barry Eichengreen, ed., *Europe's Postwar Recovery* (Cambridge, U.K., 1995); Alexander Cairncross Oral History (June 1970), HSTL. The most comprehensive treatment of the EPU is Jacob J. Kaplan and Gunther Schleimenger, *The European Payments Union: Financial Diplomacy in the 1950s* (Oxford, U.K., 1989).

37. Agnew and Entrikin, eds., *The Marshall Plan Today,* 176–77; Helge Berger and Albrecht Ritschl, "Germany and the Political Economy of the Marshall Plan, 1947–52: A Re-revisionist View," in Eichengreen, ed., *Europe's Postwar Recovery,* 228–41. Maximizing leverage, ECA retained its EPU contribution in Washington, releasing funds as needed instead of depositing a lump sum in an EPU account at BIS in Basel. Hubert Havlik Oral History (June 1973), 180, HSTL.

38. Hirschman, *Crossing Boundaries,* 41–42.

39. Frank Schipper, "You Too Can Be Like Us: Americanizing European (Road) Transport After World War II," paper delivered at the T2M Conference, York, England, October 6–9, 2005; Curt Tarnoff, "The Marshall Plan: Design, Accomplishments and Relevance to the Present," 364, in Menges, ed., *The Marshall Plan from Those Who Made It Succeed*; Kathleen Burk, "The Marshall Plan: Filling in Some of the Blanks," *Contemporary European History* 10 (2001): 274.

40. Matthias Kipping and Ove Bjarner, eds., *The Americanisation of European Business: The Marshall Plan and the Transfer of US Management Models* (London, 1998), 129, 197;

Lucrezia Reichlin, "The Marshall Plan Reconsidered," 44, in Eichengreen, ed., *Europe's Postwar Recovery*; Tarnoff, "The Marshall Plan," 364–65.

41. Kipping and Bjarner, eds., *The Americanisation of European Business,* 14; Jacqueline McGlade, "From Business Reform Programme to Production Drive," 18–34, in Kipping and Bjarner; McGlade, "A Single Path for European Recovery?" 192–95, in Schain, ed., *The Marshall Plan*; McGlade, "Confronting the Marshall Plan: US Business and European Recovery," 177–78, in John Agnew and J. Nicholas Entrikin, eds., *The Marshall Plan Today: Model and Metaphor* (London, 2004). Also consult Solidelle F. Wasser and Michael L. Dolfman, "BLS and the Marshall Plan: The Forgotten Story," *Monthly Labor Review* 128 (June 2005): 44–52.

42. Charles Kindleberger Oral History (July 1973), HSTL; Ernst H. van der Beugel Oral History (June 1964), HSTL; Nitze, *From Hiroshima to Glasnost,* 55, 59; Marjolin, *Architect of European Unity,* 185, and *Le Travail d'Une Vie* (Paris, 1986), 186–87, as cited in William Diebold, "The Marshall Plan in Retrospect: A Review of Recent Scholarship," *Journal of International Affairs* 41 (Summer 1988): 431; ECA, *Italy: Country Study* (1949), 44, 50; Vera Zamagni, "Betting on the Future: The Reconstruction of Italian Industry, 1946–1952," 287–88, in Josef Becker and Franz Knipping, eds., *Power in Europe?* (Berlin, 1986); David Reynolds, "The European Response," *Foreign Affairs* 76 (May-June 1997): 177; Wilson, *The Marshall Plan,* 26–27.

43. Interviews with Harlan Cleveland, Helene Granby, Herbert Rees, and Robert Marjolin, Price Papers, GCML; Randall B. Woods, *The Marshall Plan: A Forty Year Perspective* (Washington, D.C., 1987), 23.

44. Kindleberger, *Marshall Plan Days,* 127; Apostolos Vetsopoulos, "The Economic Dimensions of the Marshall Plan in Greece, 1947–1952" (Ph.D. diss., University College London, 2002), 358.

45. Interview with MacDonald Salter, Price Papers, GCML; Richard Bissell Oral History (July 1971), HSTL; Sulzberger, *A Long Row of Candles,* 577.

46. On the Grady-Nuveen Feud, see Vetsopoulos, "The Economic Dimensions of the Marshall Plan in Greece," 101, 114–26, 358. On the Dunn-Gervasi Tussle, see Milton Katz to William C. Foster, April 24, 1951; Foster to Katz, May 1, 1951 (draft); Foster to Katz, May 2, 1951, Box 4, Folder 15, C. Tyler Wood Papers, GCML.

47. Hoffmann and Maier, eds., *The Marshall Plan,* 51; Averell Harriman Oral History (1971); Richard Bissell Oral History (July 1971); Lincoln Gordon Oral History (July 22, 1975), 95–98, HSTL; Bissell, *Reflections,* 64; Hirschman, *Crossing Boundaries,* 33–44. GATT was later renamed the World Trade Organization, or WTO.

48. Leffler, "The United States and the Strategic Dimensions of the Marshall Plan"; Memorandum by Harriman, November 11, 1948, Box 272, Averell Harriman Papers, LC.

49. Interview with Walter C. McAdoo, Price Papers, GCML; Clarke to Price, September 21, 1954, Box 1, Price Papers, GCML; Menges, ed., *The Marshall Plan from Those Who Made It Succeed,* 372, 386 n. 27.

50. Knut Getz Wold Oral History (May 1964), 24; Erling Wikborg Oral History (May 1964), 30; Per Haekkerup Oral History (May 1964), 13, HSTL; Judt, *Postwar,* 79.

51. Leffler, "The United States and the Strategic Dimensions of the Marshall Plan," 281.

52. Armand Clesse and Archie Epps, eds., *Present at the Creation* (New York, 1990), 111; Pronay and Wilson, eds., *The Political Re-education of Germany and Her Allies After World War II,* 226; Sulzberger, *A Long Row of Candles,* 379. Christian Democrats did make inroads into some working-class strongholds. CBS's Chief European Correspondent covered the April elections in Milan where one industrial suburb, referred to as "Little Stalingrad" because of its "solid pro-Communist vote in the past," turned dramatically away from the

Left. In the Turin suburb of Fiat, de Gasperi's party received a majority of the votes. See Smith, *The State of Europe,* 203.

53. Pisani, *The CIA and the Marshall Plan,* 112.

54. Maier and Bischof, eds., *The Marshall Plan and Germany,* 220; James Lowenstein to author, June 20, 2006. Lowenstein worked at OSR, Paris in 1950 and 1951; *New York Times,* February 23, 1949, 1.

55. William H. McNeill, *Greece: American Aid in Action, 1946–1956* (New York, 1957), 199–201.

56. David Ellwood, "The Limits of Americanization and the Emergence of an Alternative Model," in Kipping and Bjarnar, eds., *The Americanisation of European Business,* 149–66.

57. Ellwood, "You Too Can Be Like Us"; Pronay and Wilson, *The Political Re-education of Germany and Her Allies,* 220.

58. Interviews with Helene Granby and Averell Harriman, Price Papers, GCML.

59. William F. Sanford, "The Marshall Plan: Origins and Implementation," *U.S. Department of State Bulletin* 82 (June 1982): 10; Richard Bissell, "Foreign Aid: What Sort? How Much? How Long?" *Foreign Affairs* 31 (October 1952): 24; Jones, *The Fifteen Weeks,* 84.

60. *Congressional Record* (80th Cong., 1st Sess.), December 8, 1947, 11,150–56.

61. Interviews with John Lindeman, Shaw Livermore, Donald Stone, and Samuel van Hyning, Price Papers, GCML.

62. Marianne De Bouzy Oral History, NSA, GWU.

63. Schlesinger, *A Life in the Twentieth Century,* 476.

Chapter IV: Implementing the Marshall Plan

1. Paul R. Porter, "Greece's Vital Role in The Triumph of the Democracies," 170, in Eugene T. Rossides, ed., *The Truman Doctrine of Aid to Greece: A Fifty-Year Retrospective* (New York and Washington, D.C., 1998); James Warren Oral History, NSA, GWU; C. A. Munkman, *American Aid to Greece: A Report on the First Ten Years* (New York, 1958), 275.

2. E. N. Holmgren to Harry Price, August 9, 1954, Box 2, Price Papers, GCML; John Nuveen, "Answering the Greek Tragedians," 1237; ECA Mission to Greece, Information Division, "Morning Press Headlines," August 3 and 18, 1948, Box 52, Folder 24, James A. Van Fleet Papers, GCML. For AMAG's organization and personnel, see George C. McGhee, "Implementation of the Aid Program," in Rossides, ed., *The Truman Doctrine of Aid to Greece,* 64–65.

3. Constantinos Doxiadis Oral History (May 1964), HSTL.

4. Jones, *The Fifteen Weeks,* 73; Killick, *The United States and European Reconstruction,* 130; Brice Mace to Harry Price, September 15, 1954, Box 2, Price Papers, GCML; U.S. Mutual Security Agency (MSA), *The Story of the American Marshall Plan in Greece* (Washington, D.C., 1950), 21.

5. Jones, *The Fifteen Weeks,* 68; Mee, *The Marshall Plan,* 16.

6. James C. Warren Oral History, NSA, GWU; John Nuveen to Paul Hoffman and Averell Harriman, March 22, 1949, Box 271, Harriman Papers, LC; L. S. Stavrianos, *Greece: American Dilemma and Opportunity* (Chicago, 1952), 4; Queen Frederica to George C. Marshall, July 20, 1950, a copy in Box 51, Folder 11, Van Fleet Papers, GCML. Greece voted in September 1946 to retain its king and queen.

7. MSA, *The Story of the American Marshall Plan,* 56; Paul R. Porter Oral History (November 1971), HSTL.

8. Mace to Price, September 15, 1954, Box 2, Price Papers, GCML; interviews with Brice Mace and Walter Packard, Price Papers, GCML; MSA, *The Story of the American Marshall Plan*; Bickham Sweet-Escott, *Greece: A Political and Economic Survey, 1939–1953* (London, 1954) 119 n. 2.

9. Brice to Price, September 15, 1954, Box 2, Price Papers, GCML; Constantinos Doxiadis (May 1964) and Spyros Markezinis (July 1970) Oral Histories, HSTL; James Warren Oral History, NSA, GWU; McNeill, *Greece: American Aid in Action,* 40; MSA, *The Story of the American Marshall Plan,* 8–9; Vetsopoulos, "The Economic Dimensions of the Marshall Plan in Greece, 1947–1952," 185.

10. MSA, *The Story of the American Marshall Plan,* 7; John O. Iatrides, "The Doomed Revolution: Communist Insurgency in Postwar Greece," in Roy Licklider, ed., *Stopping the Killing* (New York, 1993), 211–15, 219–20; Paul F. Braim, "General James A. Van Fleet and the U.S. Military Mission to Greece," in Rossides, ed., *The Truman Doctrine of Aid to Greece,* 117–27. In equating America's postwar policy in Greece with the Soviet Union's in East Europe, Lawrence Wittner's *American Intervention in Greece, 1943–1949* (New York, 1982) is too slanted to be a reliable source.

11. Stavrianos, *Greece: American Dilemma and Opportunity,* 198–204; McNeill, *Greece,* 42–44; Iatrides, "The Doomed Revolution," 215; Braim, "General James A. Van Fleet and the U.S. Military Mission to Greece," 126; Harriman to SecState, February 21, 1949, Box 271, Harriman Papers, LC; James C. Warren Oral History, NSA, GWU.

12. Alexander Papagos, "Guerrilla Warfare," *Foreign Affairs* 30 (January 1952): 226–27; James A. Van Fleet, "How We Won in Greece," *Balkan Studies* (Thessaloniki) 8 (1967): 391; Nuveen, "Answering the Greek Tragedians," 1238; ECA Mission to Greece, Information Division, "Morning Press Headlines," August 20, 1948, Box 52, Folder 25, Van Fleet Papers, GCML.

13. Interviews with Robert Hirschberg, Carroll Hinman, and Paul A. Jenkins, Price Papers, GCML; Menges, ed., *The Marshall Plan from Those Who Made It Succeed,* 133; MSA, *The Story of the American Marshall Plan,* 21–23.

14. Economic Cooperation Administration (ECA), *European Recovery Program: Greece, Country Study* (Washington, D.C., 1949), 30; interviews with Hirschberg, Hinman, and Jenkins, Price Papers, GCML; Paul R. Porter Oral History (November 1971) and Markezinis Oral History (July 1970), HSTL; McNeill, *Greece,* 73; MSA, *The Story of the American Marshall Plan,* 32; Vetsopoulos, "The Economic Dimensions of the Marshall Plan in Greece," 197–200, 264–65.

15. Mace to Price, September 15, 1954, Box 2, Price Papers, GCML; interview with Paul A. Jenkins, Price Papers, GCML; McNeill, *Greece,* 182; MSA, *The Story of the American Marshall Plan,* 68–69.

16. Dioxidis (May 1964) and Markezinis (July 1970) Oral Histories, HSTL; MSA, *The Story of the American Marshall Plan,* 66; James C. Warren, "Origins of the 'Greek Economic Miracle:' The Truman Doctrine and Marshall Plan Development and Stabilization Programs," 86–87, in Rossides, ed., *The Truman Doctrine of Aid to Greece.* In 1948 Greece's annual rice production was just seven thousand tons. See ECA Mission to Greece, Information Division, "Morning Press Headlines," September 11, 1948, Box 52, Folder 25, Van Fleet Papers, GCML; Vetsopoulos, "The Economic Dimensions of the Marshall Plan in Greece," 344, 376.

17. Brice Mace to Harry Price, September 15, 1954, Box 2; interviews with John O. Walker and Paul A. Jenkins, Price Papers, GCML; Harold F. Alderfer, *I Like Greece* (State College, Pa., 1956), 79–83, 99–107; William M. Rountree Oral History (September 1989), HSTL; McNeill, *Greece,* 74–75, 183; Munkman, *American Aid to Greece,* 253–54; MSA, *The Story of the American Marshall Plan,* 57–58.

18. Interview with Douglas A. Strachan, Price Papers, GCML; Paul R. Porter Oral History (November 1971), HSTL; James C. Warren Oral History, NSA, GWU.

19. Interview with Paul A. Jenkins, Price Papers, GCML; ECA, *European Recovery Program: Greece*, 33.

20. Leland Barrows Oral History (January 1971), HSTL; Menges, ed., *The Marshall Plan from Those Who Made It Succeed,* 169; Warren, "Origins of the 'Greek Economic Miracle,'" 100. For analysis of the successful 1952 Stabilization Program that involved curtailing the investment program inherited from ECA, closing the balance of payments gap, and balancing the government's budget, consult Vetsopoulos, "The Economic Dimensions of the Marshall Plan in Greece," 286–324, 350.

21. Interview with Constantin Tsatsos, Price Papers, GCML; Munkman, *American Aid to Greece,* 277.

22. Porter, "Greece's Vital Role in the Triumph of the Democracies," 229; interviews with Paul R. Porter (November 15, 1952) and John O. Coppock, Price Papers, GCML; "Greek Mission" and "Turkish Mission," Box 9, Folder 7, William C. Foster Papers, GCML; "Organization Directory," June 21, 1949, Box 52, Folder 37; "Speech by John Nuveen, Jr., at Meeting of ECA Mission Chiefs, February 16, 1949, a copy in Box 52, Folder 22, Van Fleet Papers, GCML; "Summary and Recommendations" of Paul A. Porter Report, n.d., Box 52, Folder 27, ibid.; "A Factual Summary Concerning the American Mission for Aid to Greece," June 15, 1948, Box 52, Folder 35, ibid. Marshall Plan aid to Greece in 1950 was an astonishing 50% of the country's GNP. See Judt, *Postwar,* 96.

23. Interviews with John O. Coppock and Constantin Tsatsos, Price Papers, GCML; Markezinis Oral History (July 1970), HSTL; Nuveen, "Answering the Greek Tragedians," 1236; Warren, "Origins of the 'Greek Economic Miracle'," 103.

24. Interview with Paul R. Porter, Price Papers, GCML; Howard K. Smith, *The State of Europe* (New York, 1949), 225; Nuveen, "Answering the Greek Tragedians," 1236; Vetsopoulos, "The Economic Dimensions of the Marshall Plan in Greece," 30, 131–32.

25. Interviews with Paul R. Porter and Constantin Tsatsos, Price Papers, GCML; McNeill, *Greece,* 62–63; Queen Frederica to George C. Marshall, July 20, 1950, a copy in Box 51, Folder 11, Van Fleet Papers, GCML. The whole Grady-Venizelos-Plastiras-Palace "mess" can be best understood by first consulting, U.S. Department of State, *Foreign Relations of the United States, 1950,* vol. 5, "Greece" (Washington, D.C., 1978), 356, 426–31 (hereafter cited as *FRUS: 1950*); and then Vetsopoulos, "The Economic Dimensions of the Marshall Plan in Greece," 169–75.

26 Clayton, "Is the Marshall Plan 'Operation Rathole'?" 27; interview with John O. Coppock, Price Papers, GCML; Markezinis Oral History (July 1970), HSTL; James C. Warren to author, February 18, 2006; McNeill, *Greece,* 182.

27. James C. Warren Oral History, NSA, GWU; Alderfer, *I Like Greece,* 12, 80, 84, 198; interviews with Constantin Tsatsos and Sefik Bilkur, Price Papers, GCML; Menges, ed., *The Marshall Plan from Those Who Made It Succeed,* 148, 153.

28. Theodore H. White, "The Marshall Plan: Springtime in a New World," in White, *In Search of History,* 293; Vera Zamagni, "Betting on the Future: The Reconstruction of Italian Industry, 1946–1952," in Becker and Knipping, eds., *Power in Europe?,* 288; Economic Cooperation Administration (ECA), *Italy: A Country Study* (Washington, D.C., 1949), 2; Federico Romero, "Migration as an Issue in European Interdependence and Integration: The Case of Italy," in Alan S. Milward et al., eds., *The Frontier of National Sovereignty: History and Theory, 1945–1992* (London, 1994), 36. Luciano Segreto, "The Importance of the Foreign Constraint: Debates About a New Social and Economic Order in Italy, 1945–1955," in Dominik Geppert, ed., *The Postwar Challenge* (London, 2005), 141–42. Segreto is my source for the 8% figure. Segreto to author, June 20, 2006.

29. Interview with Giovanni Malagodi (1952), Price Papers, GCML; Malagodi Oral History (July 1970), HSTL; Eichengreen and Uzan, "The Marshall Plan," 201; Marcello DeCecco and Francesco Giavazzi, "Inflation and Stabilization in Italy: 1946–1951," in Rudiger Dornbusch et al., eds., *Postwar Economic Reconstruction and Lessons for the East Today* (Cambridge, Mass., 1993), 60–61.

30. Harriman to Hoffman and Lovett, June 14, 1948, Box 270, Harriman Papers, LC.

31. ECA, *Italy: A Country Study*, 1–2, 4–5, 42–43; Memorandum of Conversation, December 19, 1949, Box 271, Harriman Papers, LC; Giovanni Malagodi Oral History (July 1970), HSTL.

32. Pisani, *The CIA and the Marshall Plan*, 114–15; Mario Rossi, "ECA's Blunders in Italy," *The Nation* 172 (April 7, 1951): 324; Romero, "Migration as an Issue in European Interdependence and Integration: The Case of Italy," 33–58.

33. Esposito, "Influencing Aid Recipients," 68–92; Pisani, *The CIA and the Marshall Plan*, 113–14; Carew, *Labour Under the Marshall Plan*, 95–96.

34. *Current Biography*, April 1960, 24–26; Memorandum of Conversation, February 8, 1950, Box 271, Harriman Papers, LC; Ellwood, "From 'Re-education' to the Selling of the Marshall Plan in Italy," in Pronay and Wilson, eds., *The Political Re-education of Germany and Her Allies After World War II*, 228–29; David Ellwood, "The 1948 Elections in Italy: A Cold War Propaganda Battle," *Historical Journal of Film, Radio and Television* 13 (1993): 26; Smith, *The State of Europe*, 204.

35. Ellwood, "From 'Re-education' to the Selling of the Marshall Plan in Italy," 230; Ellwood, "E.R.P. Propaganda in Italy: Its History and Impact in an Official Survey," 274–302, in Ekkehart Krippendorff, ed., *The Role of the United States in the Reconstruction of Italy and West Germany, 1943–1949* (Berlin, 1981); see also *Film Details* for *Talking to the Italians* (b&w, 1950, OSR, Paris) in Marshall Plan Filmography at www.marshallfilms.org.

36. Ellwood, "From 'Re-education to the Selling of the Marshall Plan in Italy," 235; Ellwood, "The Marshall Plan and the Politics of Growth," in Stirk and Willis, eds., *Shaping Postwar Europe*, 18–24; Ellwood, "You Too Can Be Like Us: Selling the Marshall Plan," 33–39; Schain, ed., *The Marshall Plan*, 286–87.

37. Killick, *The United States and European Reconstruction, 1945–1960*, 118; interview with Vincent Barnett, Price Papers, GCML; Rossi, "ECA's Blunders in Italy," 324.

38. Harriman to Forrestal, January 4, 1949, Box 271, Harriman Papers, LC; "Italian Mission," Box 9, Folder 7, William C. Foster Papers, GCML; Ronald L. Filippelli, *American Labor and Postwar Italy, 1943–1953* (Stanford, Calif., 1989), 110.

39. Carew, *Labour Under the Marshall Plan*, 102–3; interview with Thomas Lane, Price Papers, GCML. Comprehensive treatments of the ECA's rupture of the Italian labor movement, with AFL and CIO assistance, are Filippelli, *American Labor and Postwar Italy*, and Federico Romero, *The United States and the European Trade Union Movement, 1944–1951* (Chapel Hill, N.C., 1992).

40. Carew, *Labour Under the Marshall Plan*, 104; interview with James Toughill, Price Papers, GCML.

41. ECA, *Italy: A Country Study*, 31; Federico Romero, "When the Marshall Plan Fell Short: Industrial Relations in Italy," Paper Delivered at "The Marshall Plan and Its Consequences" Conference, University of Leeds, England, May 23–24, 1997; Pisani, *The CIA and the Marshall Plan*, 119; Carew, *Labour Under the Marshall Plan*, 212, 214; interview with Thomas Lane, Price Papers, GCML.

42. Harriman to Hoffman and Lovett, June 14, 1948, Box 270, Harriman Papers, LC; Killick, *The United States and European Reconstruction, 1945–1960*, 102; Esposito, *America's Feeble Weapon*, 125, 170.

43. Memorandum of Conversation, Harriman, Walters, Tasca, and Senator Restagno, February 8, 1950, Box 271, Harriman Papers, LC.

44. Banco di Roma, *Review of the Economic Conditions in Italy: Ten Years of Italian Economy, 1947–1956* (Rome, 1956), 91, 123, 126–27; Smith, *The State of Europe*, 213, 221–22; Judt, *Postwar,* 78; Charles S. Maier, "From Plan to Practice," 43; Pier Paulo D'Attorre, "The European Recovery Program in Italy: Research Problems," 88–89, in Krippendorff, ed., *The Role of the United States in the Reconstruction of Italy and West Germany.*

45. Banco di Roma, *Review of the Economic Conditions in Italy,* 6, 37–39, 47, 214–15; Luigi Barzini, *The Italians* (New York, 1964), 101; Judt, *Postwar,* 703, 755; Lincoln Gordon Oral History (July 22, 1975), 121–24, HSTL; interview with Bartlett Harvey, Price Papers, GCML.

46. Carew, *Labour Under the Marshall Plan,* 211; Segreto, "The Importance of the Foreign Constraint," in Geppert, ed., *The Postwar Challenge,* 144–46.

47. Pier Paulo D'Attorre, "Americanism and Anti-Americanism in Italy," in Stirk and Willis, eds., *Shaping Postwar Europe,* 43–52; Pier Paulo D'Attorre, "The European Recovery Program in Italy: Research Problems," in Krippendorff, ed., *The Role of the United States in the Reconstruction of Italy and West Germany,* 80; Roy Palmer Domenico, "'For the Cause of Christ Here in Italy': America's Protestant Challenge in Italy and the Cultural Ambiguity of the Cold War," *Diplomatic History* 29 (September 2005): 625–54; Patrick McCarthy, "The Church in Post-War Italy," in Patrick McCarthy, *Italy Since 1945* (New York, 2000), 136, 139, 142; Barzini, *The Italians,* 183; William L. Shirer, *Midcentury Journey* (New York, 1952), 106.

48. Economic Cooperation Administration (ECA), *Turkey, A Country Study* (Washington, D.C., 1949), 21–23; Max W. Thornburg et al., *Turkey: An Economic Appraisal* (New York, 1949), 27; George S. Harris, *Troubled Alliance: Turkish-American Problems in Historical Perspective, 1945–1971* (Washington, D.C., 1972), 24; Memorandum of Conversation, Harriman and Sadak, February 1, 1950, Box 271, Harriman Papers, LC; U.S.Department of State, *Foreign Relations of the United States: 1949,* vol. 6, "Turkey" (Washington, D.C., 1977), 1663 (hereafter cited as *FRUS: 1949*).

49. Harris, *Troubled Alliance,* 31; Sulzberger, *A Long Row of Candles,* 396.

50. Harris, *Troubled Alliance,* 33; *FRUS: 1950,* 5: 1318; Orren McJunkins to American Embassy, Paris, August 16, 1950, Economic Cooperation Administration, Office of Chief of Mission to Turkey, Subject Files–Central Files, Box 11, Record Group 469, National Archives and Records Administration, College Park, Maryland (hereafter, cited as ECA, RG, and NARA). Also consult "Statement of Mr. Russell H. Dorr . . . on 1949/50 Marshall Plan Program," n.d., and "Speech by Russell Dorr at Robert College, Istanbul," November 19, 1949, RG 469, NARA. Examples of government criticism are Zorlu Press Conference, May 25, 1950, and Menderes interview, December 24, 1951, Box 40, RG 469, NARA. A representative sample of unfavorable press treatment is *Hürriyet,* December 26, 1951. Other negative editorial coverage of the Marshall Plan is in Box 37, RG 469, NARA. Among Marshall Plan recipients, only Ireland's and Portugal's loan-to-grant ratios surpassed Turkey's. Ireland received $164,000,000 in aid, of which 89% were loans, according to Bernadette Whelan, "Marshall Plan Publicity and Propaganda in Italy and Ireland, 1947–1951," *Historical Journal of Film, Radio and Television* 23 (October 2003): 315. I have calculated the figure at 87%. See Appendix D. That wartime neutrals were disqualified from grants during the first year of the Marshall Plan is disclosed in Lincoln Gordon Oral History (July 22, 1975), 83, HSTL.

51. Russell Dorr to Foreign Minister Zorlu, December 19, 1951, ECA, Office of Chief of Mission to Turkey, Subject Files–Central Files, Box 37, RG 469, NARA. Dorr repeated his

charge of "belittlement" by prominent Turks in a letter to George McGhee, January 17, 1952, Box 9, RG 469; *Vatan* (Istanbul), June 16, 1951, clipping in Box 37, RG 469, NARA.

52. Interview with Russell Dorr, Price Papers, GCML; ECA, *Turkey, A Country Study*, 3; Harris, *Troubled Alliance*, 31–32; Menges, ed., *The Marshall Plan from Those Who Made It Succeed*, 335.

53. Interviews with Russell Dorr, Heyder Bey, Camal Bark, and Clifton Day, Price Papers, GCML; Harris, *Troubled Alliance*, 33–34; Wadsworth to Secretary of State, July 25, 1949, *FRUS: 1949*, 6: 1676; Harris, *Troubled Alliance*, 35.

54. Russell Dorr Press Conference, April 29, 1950, ECA, Office of Chief of Mission to Turkey, Box 40, RG 469, NARA.

55. Interviews with Gideon Hadary and Russell Dorr, Price Papers, GCML; Harriman to Hoffman and Lovett, January 6, 1949, Box 270, Harriman Papers, LC; Dorr, "Turkish Viability After 1954," May 2, 1952, RG 469, NARA; Turkey, Ministry of State, *Quarterly Report on Marshall Plan in Turkey: First Quarter, 1950* (Ankara, 1950), 12–13 (hereafter cited as *Quarterly Report: Jan./March 1950*).

56. ECA, *Turkey, A Country Study*, 24; Thornburg, *Turkey: An Economic Appraisal*, 80, 222; Memorandum of Conversation, Harriman and Sadak, December 28, 1948, Box 271, Harriman Papers, LC.

57. Interview with Dewain L. Delp, Price Papers, GCML; Harry S. Truman, "Radio and Television Address to the American People on the Mutual Security Program," March 6, 1952, *Public Papers of the Presidents: Harry S. Truman* at www.trumanlibrary.org/publicpapers; Elmer Starch, "The Future of the Great Plains Reappraised," *Journal of Farm Economics* 31 (November 1949): 917–27. Biograpical information on Starch can be found in the Elmer Starch Papers at the National Agricultural Library, Beltsville, Maryland. The collection sheds no light on his years in Turkey.

58. Interview with George McGhee, Price Papers, GCML.

59. Mace to Price, September 15, 1954, Box 2, Price Papers, GCML; Memorandum, Hugh Richwine to R. H. Allen, n.d; F. M. Coray to R. H. Allen, June 9, 1952, ECA, Office of Chief of Mission to Turkey, Box 2, RG 469, NARA; Thornburg, *Turkey*, 222; International Bank for Reconstruction and Development, *The Economy of Turkey: An Analysis and Recommendations for a Development Program* (Baltimore, Md., 1951), 18, 73 (hereafter cited as World Bank, *Report on Turkey* [1951]).

60. Interviews with Dewain Delp, Russell Dorr, and Ahmet Yalman, Price Papers, GCML; Thornburg, *Turkey*, 82; World Bank, *Report on Turkey* (1951), 125.

61. Turkey, *Quarterly Report: Jan./March 1950*, 9; ECA, *Turkey, A Country Study*, 29–30; Thornburg, *Turkey*, 96, 108, 111; World Bank, *Report on Turkey* (1951), 102; Dorr to Robert Huse, December 2, 1949, ECA, Office of Chief of Mission to Turkey, Box 27, RG 469, NARA; Memorandum of Conversation, Harriman and Sadak, December 29, 1948; Harriman, Hoffman, and Sadak, February 1, 1950, Box 271, Harriman Papers, LC.

62. Russell Dorr to C. W. Jeffers, August 7, 1950, Box 27; Russell Dorr, "Turkish Viability after 1954," May 2, 1952, Box 12, both in ECA, Office of Chief of Mission to Turkey, RG 469, NARA; Turkey, *Quarterly Report: Jan./March 1950*, 25; Winks, *The Marshall Plan and the American Economy*, 42–43; Donovan, *The Second Victory*, 97; Thornburg, *Turkey*, 136; World Bank, *Report on Turkey* (1951), 111, 143. For more technical details on Zonguldak Project, see Box 29, RG 469, NARA.

63. Harriman to McCloy, September 17, 1948, Box 267; Harriman to Hoffman and Lovett, January 6, 1949, Box 270, Harriman Papers, LC; *FRUS: 1949*, 5: 1639–40.

64. Memorandum of Conversation, February 4; June 7, 1950, *FRUS: 1950*, 5: 1229–30, 1264–69.

65. Memorandum of Conversation, Harriman, Hoffman, and Sadak, February 1, 1950, Box 271, Harriman Papers, LC; *FRUS: 1949,* 6: 1643–44; *FRUS: 1950,* 5: 1224–28; Department of State, *Foreign Relations of the United States, 1951* (Washington, D.C., 1982), 5: 1108–9 (hereafter cited as *FRUS: 1951*); "Progress Reports and Statistics," Office of the Secretary of Defense, May 29, 1950, Box 272, Harriman Papers, LC; interview with Russell Dorr, Price Papers, GCML; Russell Dorr to George McGhee, January 17, 1952, ECA, Office of Chief of Mission to Turkey, Box 9, RG 469, NARA.

66. Interview with Russell Dorr, Price Papers, GCML. Owner/editor of *Vatan* agreed with Dorr. The 1950 election was "probably the first instance," Ahmet Yalman wrote, "when absolute power yielded, without violence, to the will of the people freely expressed by secret ballots." Ahmet Yalman, *Turkey in My Time* (Norman, Okla., 1956), 239.

67. Interviews with Leon Dayton, Fuat Koprulu, Thomas Flanagan, and Lawrence Hall, Price Papers, GCML; *FRUS: 1950,* 5: 1262–63.

68. Interviews with Russell Dorr and Bulent Yazici, Price Papers, GCML; Russell Dorr, "Turkish Viability after 1954," May 2, 1952, Box 12, RG 469, NARA.

69. Interview with Irene Walker, Price Papers, GCML.

70. Interview with Sefik Bilkur, Price Papers, GCML; Sulzberger, *A Long Row of Candles,* 512.

71. Michael J. Hogan, "European Integration and German Reintegration: Marshall Planners and the Search for Recovery and Security in Western Europe," 119, in Maier and Bischof, eds., *The Marshall Plan and Germany.*

72. Maier and Bischof, eds., *The Marshall Plan and Germany,* 7; Herbert C. Mayer, *German Recovery and the Marshall Plan, 1948–1952* (New York, 1969), 9; Manfred Knapp, "US Economic Aid and the Reconstruction of West Germany," 41, in Krippendorff, ed., *The Role of the United States in the Reconstruction of Italy and West Germany.*

73. Herbert Giersch et al., "Openness, Wage Restraint, and Macroeconomic Stability: West Germany's Road to Prosperity, 1948–1959," 20, in Dornbusch et al., eds., *Postwar Economic Reconstruction and Lessons for the East Today.*

74. Milton Katz Oral History (July 1975); Lincoln Gordon Oral History (July 22, 1975), 164–65, HSTL.

75. Lucius Clay Oral History (July 1974), HSTL; Smith, *The State of Europe,* 127; Gerd Hardach, "The Marshall Plan in Germany, 1948–1952," *Journal of European Economic History* 16 (1987): 443.

76. Lucius Clay Oral History (July 1974), HSTL; Alexander Cairncross, "The Marshall Plan," paper delivered at "The Marshall Plan and Its Consequences" Conference, University of Leeds, England, May 23–24, 1997.

77. Lucius Clay Oral History (July 1974), HSTL; Kindleberger, *Marshall Plan Days,* 37.

78. Gustav Sonnenhol Oral History (May 1964), HSTL; interview with Hans W. Buttner, Price Papers, GCML; Boris Shishkin to Harriman, June 13, 1949, with attachment "Roundtable Discussion Between Military Government Officials and Wuerttemberg-Baden Trade Union Representatives, May 17, 1949," Box 271, Harriman Papers, LC. On currency reform, a classic is "Currency and Economic Reform, West Germany after World War II: A Symposium," edited by Rudolf Richter in *Zeitschrift für die Gesamte Staatswissenschaft* 135 (September 1979): 297–373.

79. Giersch, "Openness, Wage Restraint, and Macroeconomic Stability," 2–3; Alan Kramer, *The West German Economy, 1945–1955* (New York, 1991), 134–35; Herman Abs, "Germany and the Marshall Plan," in Clesse and Epps, eds., *Present at the Creation,* 93; Killick, *The United States and European Reconstruction, 1945–1960,* 117.

80. Hardach, "The Marshall Plan in Germany," 456; Holger C. Wolf, "Post-War Germany in the European Context: Domestic and External Determinants of Growth," 323–24, in Eichengreen, ed., *Europe's Postwar Recovery*.

81. Mayer, *German Recovery and the Marshall Plan*, 99; Holger C. Wolf, "The Lucky Miracle: Germany, 1945–1951," in Dornbusch et al., eds., *Postwar Economic Reconstruction and Lessons for the East Today*, 45, 47; Wolf, "Post-War Germany in the European Context," 330–36.

82. Lucius Clay Oral History (July 1974), HSTL; Shirer, *Midcentury Journey*, 22.

83. Helge Berger and Albrecht Ritschl, "Germany and the Political Economy of the Marshall Plan, 1947–52: A Re-revisionist View," in Eichengreen, ed., *Europe's Postwar Recovery*, 220–21; Ralph Willett, *The Americanization of Germany, 1945–1949* (London, 1989), 13–14; Kunz, "The Marshall Plan Reconsidered," 168–69; Wolf, "Post-War Germany in the European Context," 340–41; Wolf, "The Lucky Miracle," 47–48; Giersch et al., "Openness, Wage Restraint, and Macroeconomic Stability," 8–12.

84. Hans-Georg Sachs Oral History (May 1964), HSTL.

85. Milton Katz Oral History (July 1975), HSTL; interview with Martin Tank, Price Papers, GCML; Everett Bellows Oral History, FAOHP, Georgetown University; Mayer, *German Recovery and the Marshall Plan*, 24; Memorandum of Discussion, Royall and Foster, December 31, 1948, Box 271, Harriman Papers, LC; Thomas Schwartz, "European Integration and the 'Special Relationship': Implementing the Marshall Plan in the Federal Republic," in Maier and Bischof, eds., *The Marshall Plan and Germany*, 177.

86. Clay to Harriman, August 21, 1948, Box 271, Harriman Papers, LC; Lincoln Gordon Oral History (July 22, 1975), 164–65, HSTL; Jaques J. Reinstein, "Germany: Solving Problems," in Menges, ed., *The Marshall Plan from Those Who Made It Succeed*, 183; Schwartz, "European Integration and the 'Special Relationship,'" 175–76.

87. Harriman to Clay, January 11, 1949; Clay to Harriman, January 12, 1949, Box 271, Harriman Papers, LC; Schwartz, "European Integration and the 'Special Relationship,'" 174.

88. Interview with Martin Tank, Price Papers, GCML; Memorandum of Discussion, Royal and Foster, December 31, 1948; Harriman to SecState, December 22, 1948, Box 271, Harriman Papers, LC.

89. Harriman to Lovett, December 22, 1948, Box 271, Harriman Papers, LC; Schwartz, "European Integration and the 'Special Relationship,'" 183; Mayer, *German Recovery and the Marshall Plan*, 62; Hardach, "The Marshall Plan in Germany," 474; Giersch, "Openness, Wage Restraint, and Macroeconomic Stability," 7–9; Wolf, "The Lucky Miracle," 42.

90. Economic Cooperation Administration (ECA), *Western Germany, Country Study* (Washington, D.C., 1949), 1.

91. Memorandum of Conversation, Harriman and Erhard, November 11, 1949, Box 271, Harriman Papers, LC; Berger and Ritschl, "Germany and the Political Economy of the Marshall Plan," 214, 229, 232, 240; Hardach, "The Marshall Plan in Germany," 435.

92. ECA, *Western Germany, Country Study*, 45; interview with Karl Albrecht and others, December 3, 1952, Price Papers, GCML; interview with Carl Bode, Price Papers, GCML; Hardach, "The Marshall Plan in Germany," 447, 455; Mayer, *German Recovery and the Marshall Plan*, 34, 44, 98; Berger and Ritschl, "Germany and the Political Economy of the Marshall Plan," 206.

93. Memorandum for Harriman from Walters, January 31, 1950, Box 271, Harriman Papers, LC.

94. Mayer, *German Recovery and the Marshall Plan*, 77, 90–93; Killick, *The United States and European Reconstruction, 1945–1960*, 102; Price, *The Marshall Plan and Its*

Meaning, 264; interview with Karl Albrecht, December 3, 1952, Box 4, Price Papers, GCML; ECA, *Western Germany, Country Study,* 4, 12, 19, 60; Abs, "Germany and the Marshall Plan," in Clesse and Epps, eds., *Present at the Creation,* 97.

95. Berger and Ritschl, "Germany and the Political Economy of the Marshall Plan," 199; Wolf, "Post-War Germany in the European Context," 341–42.

96. Interview with Franz Blücher, Price Papers, GCML.

97. Gustav Sonnenhol (May 1964) and Konrad Adenauer (June 1964) Oral Histories, HSTL; interview with Karl Albrecht and others, December 3, 1952, Price Papers, GCML.

98. Kunz, "The Marshall Plan Reconsidered," 168–69; Berger and Ritschl, "Germany and the Political Economy of the Marshall Plan," 200; Wolf, "Post-War Germany in the European Context," 342.

Chapter V: An Unusable Marshall Plan?

1. Smith, *The State of Europe,* 354.

2. Whelan, "Marshall Plan Publicity and Propaganda in Italy and Ireland, 1947–1951," 313; Ellwood, "The 1948 Elections in Italy: A Cold War Propaganda Battle," 24–26; Patrick McCarthy, "The Church in Post-War Italy," in McCarthy, ed., *Italy Since 1945,* 133–41; Smith, *The State of Europe,* 204–5; Judt, *Postwar,* 228.

3. Anna J. Merritt and Richard L. Merritt, eds., *Public Opinion in Occupied Germany: The OMGUS Surveys, 1945–1949* (Urbana, Ill., 1970), 26–29, 248–49, 263–64, 270, 297; Anna J. Merritt and Richard L. Merritt, eds., *Public Opinion in Semisovereign Germany: The HICOG Surveys, 1949–1955* (Urbana, Ill., 1980), 66–68, 85; Judt, *Postwar,* 128; Hoffman, *Peace Can Be Won,* 27.

4. On the impact of the Korean War, see Holger C. Wolf's "The Lucky Miracle," 29–56, "Postwar Germany in the European Context," 339–41, 344; and Judt, *Postwar,* 151–53, 159. The conventional wisdom represented by Wolf has its detractors. In Peter Temin's view, aggregate trade data refutes the theory of "Koreaboom," which he calls "mythical." See Peter Temin, "The 'Koreaboom' in West Germany: Fact or Fiction?" *Economic History Review* 48 (1995): 737–53. On the Berlin Airlift, consult Berger and Ritschl, "Germany and the Political Economy of the Marshall Plan, 1947–1952," 220–21. Red Army misconduct and mistreatment of locals in Austria and the Soviet zone of occupation in Germany, including indiscriminate dismantling of industrial plant, also provoked great sympathy for the Marshall Planners and receptivity to their particular gospel of reconstruction.

5. Baron Jean-Charles Snoy Oral History (May 1964) and Erik Von Sydow Oral History (July 1970), HSTL. The head of ECA's Payments Section and Trade and Payments Division in Paris graded as "first rate" his European counterparts: "The Europeans we had to deal with were, generally speaking, I must say, of a very high quality. I was amazed at the expertise the Europeans had," particularly an "imaginative, competent, broad-minded" Robert Marjolin. See Hubert F. Havlik Oral History (June 1973), 161, 163–64, HSTL. Marjolin was also "highly regarded" by Norwegian officials. See Knut Getz Wold Oral History (May 1964), 39, HSTL.

6. Harriman to Lewis Douglas and Thomas Finletter, July 17, 1948, Box 272, Harriman Papers, LC. A short but revealing feature on Marjolin is in *Time* 53 (January 24, 1949): 21–22.

7. Ernst van der Beugel Oral History (June 1964), HSTL.

8. Robert Marjolin Oral Histories (May 1964 and July 1971), HSTL; Marjolin, *Architect of European Unity,* xi, 25–27, 35–43, 116–19, 143–58, 175–81; Hirschman, *Crossing Boundaries,* 34; Eric Roll, *Crowded Hours* (London, 1985), 73; Gordon, "Recollections of a

Marshall Planner," 241. In 1946 Monnet was put in charge of the "Commissariat du Plan, de Modernisation et d'Equipement."

9. *Foreign Affairs* 76 (May-June 1997): 210, 218; Menges, ed., *The Marshall Plan from Those Who Made It Succeed,* 185, 305; Bissell, *Reflections,* 30–31; Clesse and Epps, eds., *Present at the Creation,* x–xi; Hoffmann and Maier, eds., *The Marshall Plan: A Retrospective,* 89, 94; Hogan, *The Marshall Plan,* 443.

10. Bissell, *Reflections,* 30.

11. *Foreign Affairs* 76 (May-June 1997): 210; Bissell, *Reflections,* 71–72; C. Tyler Wood Oral History, Box 36, Folder 12, C. Tyler Wood Papers, GCML; George F. Kennan, *Memoirs (1925–1950)* (Boston, Mass., 1967), 370–71.

12. Schain, ed., *The Marshall Plan,* 131–41.

13. McGlade, "Confronting the Marshall Plan," 172; McGlade, "From Business Reform Programme to Production Drive," 18–34; McGlade, "A Single Path for European Recovery?," 192–95; McGlade, "Whose Plan Anyway? An Examination of Marshall Plan Leadership in the United States and Western Europe," paper delivered at "The Marshall Plan and Its Consequences" Conference, University of Leeds, England, May 23–24, 1997; Sanford, "The Marshall Plan," 12.

14. Sanford, "The Marshall Plan," 12–14; Thomas and Isaacson, *The Wise Men,* 444; Bonds, *Bipartisan Strategy,* 132, 142 n. 27.

15. Robert Marjolin Oral History (May 1964), HSTL; Knut Getz Wold Oral History (May 1964), 34–36, HSTL.

16. Walter J. Levy, *Oil Strategy and Politics, 1941–1981* (Boulder, Colo., 1982), 64.

17. David S. Painter, "Oil and the Marshall Plan," *Business History Review* 58 (Autumn 1984): 359–83; Gordon, "ERP in Operation," 139; Daniel Yergin, *The Prize: The Epic Quest for Oil, Money, and Power* (New York, 1991), 424, 459; Marjolin, *Architect of European Unity,* 394–96; Levy, "Petroleum Under the ECA Program," 63–69, and "One Year of ECA's Oil Operations," in *Oil Strategy and Politics,* 70–76. For more on Walter Levy, consult Charles Kindleberger Oral History (July 1973), 15–16, HSTL.

Chapter VI. A Usable Marshall Plan

1. Jules Moch Oral History (April 1970), 6–10, HSTL.

2. Hoffmann and Maier, eds., *The Marshall Plan: A Retrospective,* 54–55; Reuss, *When Government Was Good,* 30; Valentine, *Trial Balance,* 163–82.

3. Josef Joffe, *Überpower: The Imperial Temptation of America* (New York, 2006), 205.

4. Wilson, *The Marshall Plan,* 4; Agnew and Entrikin, eds., *The Marshall Plan Today,* 20; Reuss, *When Government Was Good,* 29.

5. Raucher, *Paul G. Hoffman,* 67.

6. Dirk Stikker Oral History (April 23, 1964), 4, HSTL; Menges, ed. *The Marshall Plan from Those Who Made It Succeed,* 169; Marjolin, *Architect of European Unity,* 180; Hoffman, *Peace Can Be Won,* 42; Valentine, *Trial Balance,* 164, 169, 171, 167.

7. Joffe, *Überpower,* 147–61, 226, 237, 240; Sulzberger, *A Long Row of Candles,* 487.

8. Donovan, *The Second Victory,* 6; Hoffmann and Maier, eds., *The Marshall Plan: A Retrospective,* 55; Judt, *Postwar,* 70, 97; Sulzberger, *A Long Row of Candles,* 373, 682.

9. Hoffman, *Peace Can Be Won,* 90–105.

10. Marjolin, *Architect of European Unity,* 175.

11. See Gordon S. Wood, *Revolutionary Characters: What Made the Founding Fathers Different* (New York, 2006); and Jon Meacham, "Original Intent," *New York Times Book Review,* June 25, 2006, 19.

12. Marshall to Ulio, January 18, 1941, in Larry I. Bland et al., eds., *The Papers of George Catlett Marshall* (Baltimore, Md., 1986), 2: 394–95.

13. Cray, *General of the Army,* 621.

Bibliography

I. Primary Sources

A. Manuscript Collections and Government Archives

Foreign Affairs Oral History Program (FAOHP), Georgetown University Washington, D.C. (copies also deposited at George C. Marshall Library)

Everett Bellows (February 1989)   David S. Brown (March 1989)
Vincent V. Checchi (July 1990)   Lincoln Gordon (January 1988)
John J. Grady (August 1989)   William Parks (November 1988)
Melbourne Spector (December 1988)   Joseph Toner (October 1989)

Library of Congress, Washington, D.C.

W. Averell Harriman Papers

George C. Marshall Library, Lexington, Virginia

Dowsley Clark Collection
European Recovery Plan Commemoratives Collection
William C. Foster Papers
George C. Marshall Papers
Marshall Plan Photograph Collection
Forrest Pogue Interviews (Paul Hoffman and John McCloy)
Harry B. Price Interviews (conducted 1952–54)

ECA and OEEC

Leland Barrows   Richard M. Bissell
Samuel Board   Harlan Cleveland
H. Van B. Cleveland   John O. Coppock
Glenn Craig   D. A. Fitzgerald
William C. Foster   Theodore Geiger
Lincoln Gordon   W. Averell Harriman
Carroll Hinman   Paul Hoffman
E. N. Holmgren   John Lindeman
Shaw Livermore   Robert Marjolin
Orbun V. Powell   MacDonald Salter
Melbourne Spector   Harold Stein
Donald C. Stone   Allan Swim
Samuel Van Hyning

Greece (Americans)

Michael H. B. Adler   Leland Barrows
Dowsley Clark   John O. Coppock
Helene Granby   Joseph F. Heath
Robert Hirschberg   Paul A. Jenkins
Brice M. Mace   Lawrence B. Myers
Walter E. Packard   Paul R. Porter

Greece (Americans—continued)
    Alan D. Strachan   Edward A. Tenenbaum
    John O. Walker
Greece (Greeks)
    Costa Hadjiagyras   Constantin D. Tsatsos
Italy (Americans)
    Vincent M. Barnett   William E. Corfitzen
    Henry J. Costanzo   Bartlett Harvey
    Thomas A. Lane   Dominic J. Marcello
    Walter C. McAdoo   Guido Nadzo
    Chauncey Parker   Donald Simmons
    James Toughill
Italy (Italians)
    Giovanni Malagodi   Donato Menichella
    Ernesto Rossi
Turkey (Americans)
    Clifton H. Day   Leon Dayton
    Dewain L. Delp   Russell H. Dorr
    Thomas Flanagan   Gideon Hadary
    Lawrence J. Hall   George McGhee
    Alonzo E. Taylor   Irene Walker
    Henry W. Wiens
Turkey (Turks)
    Cemal Bark   Heyder Bey
    Sefik Bilkur   Fuat Koprulu
    Ahmet Emin Yalman   Bulent Yazici
West Germany (Americans)
    F. M. Bianco   Carl Bode
    Lucius D. Clay   E. J. Epstine
    Michael Harris   Carl R. Mahder
    Martin Tank   Harry C. Thomas
West Germany (Germans)
    Karl Albrecht   Franz Blücher
    Hans W. Buttner   Gunther Harkort
    Paul Hertz   Friedrich Wesemann
Harry B. Price Papers
James A. Van Fleet Papers
C. Tyler Wood Papers

National Archives and Records Administration II, College Park, Maryland
    Record Group 469—Records of U.S. Foreign Assistance Agencies, 1948–61

National Agricultural Library, U.S. Department of Agriculture History Collection, Beltsville, Maryland
    Elmer Starch Papers

Bibliography

National Security Archive, George Washington University, Washington, D.C.
(also on web at www.gwu.edu/~nsarchiv/coldwar/interviews). Interviews
conducted February-April 1996.

Gianni Agnelli (Italy)   Marianne Debouzy (France)
Theodore Geiger   George McGhee
James Warren   Mark Wyatt

Harry S. Truman Library, Independence, Missouri,Oral History Collection
(also on web at www.trumanlibrary.org/oralhist).
Economic Cooperation Administration (ECA)
Richard M. Bissell (July 1971)
David K. E. Bruce (March 1972)
Thomas K. Finletter (January 1972)
Dennis A. Fitzgerald (June 1971)
Lincoln Gordon (July 17 and 22, 1975)
W. Averell Harriman (1971)
Hubert F. Havlik (June 1973)
Paul G. Hoffman (October 1964)
Milton Katz (July 1975)
W. John Kenney (November 1971)
Charles P. Kindleberger (July 1973)
Shaw Livermore (March 1974)
Organization for European Economic Cooperation (OEEC)
Gerard Bauer (Switzerland, July 1970)
Sir Alexander Cairncross (U.K., June 1970)
Sir Frank Figgures (U.K., August 1970)
Knut Getz Wold (Norway, May 1964)
Sir Edmund Hall-Patch (U.K., June 1964)
Robert Marjolin (France, May 1964 and July 1971)
Roger Ockrent (Belgium, July 1971)
Sir Eric Roll (U.K., August 1970)
Baron Jean-Charles Snoy (Belgium, May 1964 and June 1970)
Dirk U. Stikker (Netherlands, April 1964 and July 1970)
Erik von Sydow (Sweden, July 1970)
Ernst H. van der Beugel (Netherlands, June 1964)
Contemporary European Officials
Klas E. Book (Sweden, July 1970)
Herve De Gruben (Belgium, May 1964)
Per Haekkerup (Denmark, May 1964)
Etienne Hirsch (France, June 1970)
Thorkil Kristensen (Denmark, April 1964)
Halvard M. Lange (Norway, May 1964)
Jules Moch (France, April 1970)
Konrad Nordahl (Norway, May 1964)
Eelco van Kleffens (Netherlands, June 1964)
Povl Westphall (Denmark, May 1964)
Erling Wikborg (Norway, May 1964)

Country Study: Greece
   Anthony Bernaris (April 1964)
   Leland Barrows (January 1971)
   Theodore Christidis (July 1970)
   Constantinos Doxiadis (May 1964)
   Spyros Markezinis (July 1970)
   John Pesmazoğlu (April 1964)
   Paul R. Porter (November 1971)
   William M. Rountree (September 1989)
   Constantine Tsaldaris (May 1964)
Country Study: Italy
   Giovanni Malagodi (July 1970)
   Franco Mattei (May 1964)
   Giuseppe Pella (August 1964)
Country Study: Bizonia and West Germany
   Konrad Adenauer (June 1964)
   Lucius D. Clay (July 1974)
   Gunther Harkort (November 1970)
   Hans-Georg Sachs (May 1964)
   Gustav Adolf Sonnenhol (May 1964)
   Alexander Von Susskind-Schwendi (May 1964)

B. Memoirs, Autobiographies, and Eyewitness Accounts

Acheson, Dean G. *Present at the Creation: My Years in the State Department.* New York, 1969.

Bailey, Thomas A. *The Marshall Plan Summer.* Stanford, Calif., 1977.

Ball, George W. *The Past Has Another Pattern: Memoirs.* New York, 1982.

Bissell, Richard M. "European Recovery and the Problems Ahead," *Papers and Proceedings of the American Economic Association* 42 (May 1952): 306–26.

———. "Foreign Aid: What Sort? How Much? How Long?" *Foreign Affairs* 31 (October 1952): 15–38.

———. With Jonathan E. Lewis and Frances T. Pudlo. *Reflections of a Cold Warrior.* New Haven, Conn., 1996. Chapter 3—"The Marshall Plan," 30–73.

Bland, Larry I., ed. *George C. Marshall Interviews and Reminiscences for Forrest C. Pogue,* 3d. ed. Lexington, Va., 1996.

Bland, Larry I., et al., eds. *The Papers of George Catlett Marshall.* Baltimore, Md., 1986.

Cairncross, Alexander. "The Marshall Plan." Paper delivered at "The Marshall Plan and Its Consequences" Conference, University of Leeds, England, May 23–24, 1997.

Chenery, Hollis. "Remarks," Eastern Economic Association Meeting. Hartford, Conn., April 1977.

Clayton, Will. "Is the Marshall Plan 'Operation Rathole'?" *Saturday Evening Post* 222 (November 29, 1947): 26–27, 137–38.

Bibliography

Cleveland, Harold Van B. "If There Had Been No Marshall Plan . . ." in Stanley Hoffman and Charles Maier, eds., *The Marshall Plan: A Retrospective.* Boulder, Colo., 1984, 59–64.

Dulles, Allen W. *The Marshall Plan.* Providence, R.I., 1993.

Fox, Paula. *The Coldest Winter: A Stringer in Liberated Europe.* New York, 2005.

Geiger, Theodore "The Lessons of the Marshall Plan for Development Today," *Looking Ahead* 15 (1967): 1–4.

Gordon, Lincoln. "ERP in Operation," *Harvard Business Review* 27 (March 1949): 129–50.

———. "Lessons From the Marshall Plan: Successes and Limits," in Stanley Hoffman and Charles Maier, eds., *The Marshall Plan: A Retrospective* (Boulder, Colo., 1984), 53–58.

———. "The Marshall Plan Legacy," *NATO Review* 35 (June 1987): 14–19.

———. "Recollections of a Marshall Planner," *Journal of International Affairs* 41 (Summer 1988): 233–45.

Harriman, W. Averell. "The Marshall Plan: Self-Help and Mutual Aid," *Foreign Service Journal* 44 (June 1967): 21.

Hemsing, Albert. "The Marshall Plan's European Film Unit, 1948–1955: A Memoir and Filmography," *Historical Journal of Film, Radio and Television* 14 (August 1994): 269–97.

Hirschman, Albert O. *Crossing Boundaries.* Cambridge, Mass., 1998. Chapter 2— "Fifty Years After the Marshall Plan," 33–44.

Hoffman, Paul G. "The Marshall Plan: Peace Building—Its Price and Its Profits," *Foreign Service Journal* 44 (June 1967): 19–21.

———. *Peace Can Be Won.* Garden City, N.Y., 1951.

Kaplan, Jacob J., and Gunther Schleiminger. *The European Payments Union: Financial Diplomacy in the 1950s.* Oxford, U.K., 1989.

Katz, Milton. "The Marshall Plan: After Twenty Years," *Foreign Service Journal* 44 (June 1967): 22–26, 47.

Kennan, George F. *Memoirs (1925–1950).* Boston, 1967.

Kindleberger, Charles P. "In the Halls of the Capitol: A Memoir," *Foreign Affairs* 76 (May-June 1997): 185–90.

———. "The Marshall Plan and the Cold War," *International Journal* (Canada) 23 (Summer 1968): 369–81.

———. *Marshall Plan Days.* Boston, Mass., 1987.

———. "The Marshall Plan Seen from the United States, 1947 and 1987," *Okonomi Og Politik* (Denmark) 60 (1987): 224–30.

———. "The One and Only Marshall Plan," *National Interest* 11 (1988): 113–15.

Levy, Walter. *Oil Strategy and Politics, 1941–1981.* Boulder, Colo., 1982.

Marjolin, Robert. *Architect of European Unity: Memoirs, 1911–1986.* Trans. by William Hall. London, 1989.

Marjolin, Robert. *Europe and the United States in the World Economy.* Durham, N.C., 1953.

—. *Le Travail d'Une Vie.* Paris, 1986.

Menges, Constantine, ed. *The Marshall Plan From Those Who Made It Succeed.* Lanham, Md., 1999.

Monnet, Jean. *Memoirs.* Garden City, N.Y., 1978.

Nitze, Paul. *From Hiroshima to Glasnost: At the Center of Decision, A Memoir.* New York, 1989.

Porter, Paul R. "Greece's Vital Role in the Triumph of the Democracies," in Eugene T. Rossides, ed., *The Truman Doctrine of Aid to Greece: A Fifty-Year Retrospective.* New York and Washington, D.C., 1998, 170–73.

Reuss, Henry S. *When Government Was Good: Memoirs of a Life in Politics.* Madison, Wisc., 1999.

Roll, Eric. *Crowded Hours.* London, 1985.

Rostow, Walt W. "Lessons of the Plan: Looking Forward to the Next Century," *Foreign Affairs* 76 (May-June 1997): 205–12.

Schlesinger, Arthur, Jr. *A Life in the Twentieth Century: Innocent Beginnings, 1917–1950.* Boston, Mass., 2000, 464–76.

Schorr, Daniel. "Marshall Plan Memories," *The New Leader* 80 (June 30, 1997): 4–5.

Schulberg, Stuart. "Making Marshall Plan Movies," *Film News,* September 1951, 10, 19.

Shirer, William L. *Midcentury Journey.* New York, 1952.

Smith, Howard K. *The State of Europe.* New York, 1949.

Spaak, Paul-Henri. *The Continuing Battle: Memoirs of a European, 1936–1966.* London, 1971.

Stikker, Dirk U. *Men of Responsibility: A Memoir.* New York, 1966.

Stone, Donald C. "The Impact of US Assistance Programs on the Political and Economic Integration of Western Europe," *American Political Science Review* 46 (December 1952): 1100–1116.

Sulzberger, C. L. *A Long Row of Candles: Memoirs and Diaries, 1934–1954.* New York, 1969.

Valentine, Alan. *Trial Balance: The Education of an American.* New York, 1956.

Van der Beugel, Ernst H. *From Marshall Aid to Atlantic Partnership: European Integration as a Concern of American Foreign Policy.* New York, 1966.

Walters, Vernon, "The Marshall Plan and Harriman," in Vernon Walters, *Silent Missions.* Garden City, N.Y., 1978, 170–89.

Warren, James C., Jr. "Origins of the 'Greek Economic Miracle': The Truman Doctrine and Marshall Plan Development and Stabilization Programs," in Eugene T. Rossides, ed., *The Truman Doctrine of Aid to Greece: A Fifty-Year Retrospective.* New York and Washington, D.C., 1998, 76–105.

White, Theodore H. *Fire in the Ashes: Europe in Midcentury.* New York, 1953.

————. "The Marshall Plan: Springtime in a New World," in Theodore H. White, *In Search of History: A Personal Adventure.* New York, 1978, 263–306.

II. Secondary Sources

Agnew, John, and J. Nicholas Entrikin, eds., *The Marshall Plan Today: Model and Metaphor on International Relations.* London, U.K., 2004.

Arkes, Hadley. *Bureaucracy, the Marshall Plan, and the National Interest.* Princeton, N.J., 1972.

Barber, Joseph, ed.. *The Marshall Plan as American Policy: A Report on the Views of Community Leaders in Twenty-One Cities.* New York, 1948.

Barbezat, Daniel. "The Marshall Plan and the Origins of the OEEC," in Richard T. Griffiths, ed., *Explorations in OEEC History.* Paris, 1997, 33–44.

Barjot, Dominique, ed. *Catching Up With America: Productivity Missions.* Paris, 2002.

Bonds, John Bledsoe. *Bipartisan Strategy: Selling the Marshall Plan.* Westport, Conn., 2002.

Burk, Kathleen. "The Marshall Plan: Filling in Some of the Blanks," *Contemporary European History* 10 (2001): 267–94.

————. "The Marshall Plan from the European Perspective." The 1995 Sir Alec Cairncross Lecture, St. Peter's College, Oxford, England, September 22, 1995.

Burnham, James, ed. *What Europe Thinks of America.* New York, 1953.

Carew, Anthony B. *Labour Under the Marshall Plan: The Politics of Productivity and the Marketing of Managerial Science.* Detroit, Mich., 1987.

————. "The Politics of Productivity and the Politics of Anti-Communism: American and European Labour in the Cold War," *Intelligence and National Security* 18 (2003): 73–91.

Chace, James. "An Extraordinary Partnership: Marshall and Acheson," *Foreign Affairs* 76 (May-June 1997): 191–94.

Clesse, Armand, and Archie Epps, eds. *Present at the Creation: 40th Anniversary of the Marshall Plan.* New York, 1990.

Comite pour l'histoire economique et financiere, Ministere des Finances (CHEFF). *Le Plan Marshall.* Paris, 1993.

Cray, Ed. *General of the Army: George C. Marshall, Soldier and Statesman.* New York, 1990.

Culbert, David. "Albert E. Hemsing (1921–1997)," *Historical Journal of Film, Radio and Television* 17 (August 1997): 401–2.

DeLong, J. Bradford, and Barry Eichengreen, "The Marshall Plan: History's Most Successful Structural Adjustment Program," in Rudiger Dornbusch et al., eds.,

Postwar Economic Reconstruction and Lessons for the East Today. Cambridge, Mass., 1993, 189–230.

Diebold, William. "The Marshall Plan in Retrospect: A Review of Recent Scholarship," *Journal of International Affairs* 41 (Summer 1988): 421–35.

———. *Trade and Payments in Western Europe: A Study in European Economic Cooperation.* New York, 1952.

Doherty, Thomas. "A Symposium on the Marshall Plan Films in New York City," *Historical Journal of Film, Radio and Television* 25 (March 2005): 151–54.

Donovan, Robert J. *The Second Victory: The Marshall Plan and the Postwar Revival of Europe.* Lanham, Md., 1987.

Duignan, Peter, and L. H. Gann. *The Rebirth of the West: The Americanization of the Democratic World, 1945–1958.* Cambridge, Mass., 1992.

Eichengreen, Barry J., ed. *Europe's Postwar Recovery.* Cambridge, U.K., 1995.

———, ed. *The Reconstruction of the International Economy, 1945–1960.* Cheltenham, U.K., 1996.

———, and Marc Uzan. "The Marshall Plan: Economic Effects and Implications for Eastern Europe and the Soviet Union," *Economic Policy* 14 (April 1992): 13–75.

Ellwood, David W. "From the Revolt of the Masses to the Revolution of Rising Expectations." Paper delivered at the Annual SHAFR Conference, June 23–25, 2005.

———. "The Impact of the Marshall Plan," *History* 74 (October 1989): 427–36.

———. "The Limits of Americanisation and the Emergence of an Alternative Model: The Marshall Plan in Emilia-Romagna," in Matthias Kipping and Ove Bjarnar, eds., *The Americanisation of European Business: The Marshall Plan and the Transfer of U.S. Management Models.* London, 1998, 149–67.

———. "The Marshall Plan and the Politics of Growth," in Peter M. R. Stirk and David Willis, eds., *Shaping Postwar Europe: European Unity and Disunity, 1945–1957.* New York, 1991, 15–26, 163–66. Reissued in Richard T. Griffiths, ed., *Explorations in OEEC History.* Paris, 1997, 99–107.

———. *The Marshall Plan Forty Years After: Lessons for the International System Today.* Bologna, Italy, 1988.

———. *Rebuilding Europe: Western Europe, America and Postwar Reconstruction.* New York, 1992.

———. "You Too Can Be Like Us: Selling the Marshall Plan," *History Today* 48 (October 1998): 33–39.

Fay, Sidney B. "The Marshall Plan," *Current History* 88 (January 1989): 30–31, 51–52.

Fossedal, Gregory A. "A Modest Magician: Will Clayton and the Rebuilding of Europe," *Foreign Affairs* 76 (May-June 1997): 195–99.

———. *Our Finest Hour: Will Clayton, the Marshall Plan, and the Triumph of Democracy.* Palo Alto, Calif., 1993.

Freeland, Richard M. *The Truman Doctrine and the Origins of McCarthyism.* New York, 1970.

Garrett, Amy. "Marketing America: Public Culture and Public Diplomacy in the Marshall Plan Era, 1947–1954." Ph.D. dissertation, University of Pennsylvania, 2004.

Gay, James T. "Rebuilding Europe," *American History* 32 (May-June 1997): 44–50, 68.

Gourvish, Terence, and Nick Tiratsoo, eds. *Missionaries and Managers: American Influences on European Management Education, 1945–1960.* Manchester, U.K., 1998.

Griffiths, Richard T., ed. *Explorations in OEEC History.* Paris, 1997.

———. "Washington, the Hague, and the Politics of Productivity, 1945–1955." Paper delivered at Annual SHAFR Conference, June 23–25, 2005.

Grose, Peter. "The Marshall Plan—Then and Now," *Foreign Affairs* 76 (May-June 1997): 159.

Harris, Seymour E. *Economic Planning: The Plans of 14 Countries with Analysis of the Plans.* New York, 1949.

Hitchens, Harold L. "Influences on the Congressional Decision to Pass the Marshall Plan," *Western Political Quarterly* 21 (March 1968): 51–68.

Hoffmann, Stanley, and Charles Maier, eds. *The Marshall Plan: A Retrospective.* Boulder, Colo., 1984.

Hogan, Michael J. *The Marshall Plan: America, Britain, and the Transformation of Western Europe, 1947–1952.* Cambridge, U.K., 1987.

Isaacson, Walter, and Evan Thomas, *The Wise Men: Six Friends and the World They Made.* New York, 1986.

Joffe, Josef. *Überpower: The Imperial Temptation of America.* New York, 2006.

Jones, Joseph M. *The Fifteen Weeks.* New York, 1955.

Judt, Tony. *Postwar: A History of Europe Since 1945.* New York, 2005.

Killick, John. *The United States and European Reconstruction, 1945–1960.* Edinburgh, U.K., 1997.

Kipping, Matthias, and Ove Bjarner, eds. *The Americanisation of European Business: The Marshall Plan and the Transfer of U.S. Management Models.* London, 1998.

Kunz, Diane B. "The Marshall Plan Reconsidered," *Foreign Affairs* 76 (May-June 1997): 162–70.

Labohm, Hans H. J., ed. *The Fiftieth Anniversary of the Marshall Plan in Retrospect and in Prospect.* The Hague, 1997.

Leffler, Melvyn. "The United States and the Strategic Dimensions of the Marshall Plan," *Diplomatic History* 12 (Summer 1988): 277–306.

Maier, Charles S. "American Visions and British Interests: Hogan's Marshall Plan," *Reviews in American History* 18 (March 1990): 102–11.

————. "From Plan to Practice: The Context and Consequences of the Marshall Plan," *Harvard Magazine* 99 (May-June 1997): 40–43.

————. "The Marshall Plan and the Division of Europe," *Journal of Cold War Studies* 7, no.1 (2005): 168–74.

————. "The Politics of Productivity: Foundations of American International Economic Policy after World War II," *International Organization* 31 (1977): 607–33.

————. "Premises of the Recovery Program," in CHEFF, *Le Plan Marshall.* Paris, 1993, 15–30.

McGlade, Jacqueline. "The Big Push: The Export of American Business Education to Western Europe after World War II," in Vera Zamagni and L. Engwall, eds., *Management Education in an Historical Perspective.* Manchester, U.K., 1998.

————. "Confronting the Marshall Plan: US Business and European Recovery," in John Agnew and J. Nicholas Entrikin, eds., *The Marshall Plan Today: Model and Metaphor.* London, 2004, 171–90.

————. "From Business Reform Programme to Production Drive: The Transformation of United States Technical Assistance to Western Europe," in Matthias Kipping and Ove Bjarner, eds., *The Americanisation of European Business.* London, 1998, 18–34.

————. "A Single Path for European Recovery? American Business Debates and Conflicts Over the Marshall Plan," in Martin Schain, ed., *The Marshall Plan: Fifty Years After.* New York, 2001, 185–204.

————. "The United States Technical Assistance and Productivity Program and the Education of Western European Managers, 1948–1958," in Terence Gourvish and Nick Tiratsoo, eds., *Missionaries and Managers.* Manchester, U.K., 1998.

————. "Whose Plan Anyway? An Examination of Marshall Plan Leadership in the United States and Western Europe." Paper delivered at "The Marshall Plan and its Consequences" Conference, University of Leeds, England, May 23–24, 1997.

Mee, Charles L. *The Marshall Plan: The Launching of the Pax Americana.* New York, 1984.

Milward, Alan S. "The Marshall Plan and Europe's Foreign Trade," in CHEFF, *Le Plan Marshall.* Paris, 1993, 641–50.

————. *The Reconstruction of Western Europe, 1945–1951.* Berkeley, Calif., 1984.

————. "Was the Marshall Plan Necessary?" *Diplomatic History* 13 (1989): 231–53.

Painter, David S. "Oil and the Marshall Plan," *Business History Review* 58 (Autumn 1984): 359–83.

Pogue, Forrest C. *George C. Marshall: Statesman, 1945–1959.* New York, 1987.

Pells, Richard. *Not Like Us: How Europeans Have Loved, Hated, and Transformed American Culture Since World War II.* New York, 1997.

Pisani, Sallie. *The CIA and the Marshall Plan.* Lawrence, Kans., 1991.

Potter, David. "The Marshall Plan and American Foreign Policy," *Current Affairs* (London) 48 (February 21, 1948): 5–18.

Price, Harry B. *The Marshall Plan and Its Meaning.* Ithaca, N.Y., 1955.

Raucher, Alan. *Paul G. Hoffman: Architect of Foreign Aid.* Lexington, Ky., 1985.

Reichlin, Lucrezia. "The Marshall Plan Reconsidered," in Barry Eichengreen, ed., *Europe's Postwar Recovery.* Cambridge, U.K., 1995, 39–67.

Reynolds, David. "The European Response," *Foreign Affairs* 76 (May-June 1997): 171–84.

Sanford, William F. *The American Business Community and the European Recovery Program, 1947–1952.* New York, 1987.

———. "The Marshall Plan: Origins and Implementation," *Department of State Bulletin* 82 (June 1982): 17–33.

Schain, Martin, ed. *The Marshall Plan: Fifty Years After.* New York, 2001.

Schipper, Frank. "You Too Can Be Like Us: Americanizing European (Road) Transport after World War II." Paper delivered at the T2M Conference, York, England, 6–9 October, 2005.

Schmidt, Helmut. "Miles to Go: From American Plan to European Union," *Foreign Affairs* 76 (May-June 1997): 213–21.

Schulberg, Sandra, and Richard Pena. *Selling Democracy: Films of the Marshall Plan, 1948–1953.* New York, 2004.

Scott-Smith, Giles, and Hans Krabbendam, eds. *The Cultural Cold War in Western Europe, 1945–1960.* London, 2003.

Smith, Richard Norton. *The Colonel: The Life and Legend of Robert R. McCormick.* Boston, Mass., 1997.

Snyder, David J. "A Model of Licentiousness: Growth, Redistribution, and the Critique of the American Model in Postwar Dutch Economic Thought." Paper delivered at Annual SHAFR Conference, June 23–25, 2005.

Stirk, Peter M. R., and David Willis, eds. *Shaping Postwar Europe: European Unity and Disunity, 1945–1957.* New York, 1991.

Strunk, Mildred, ed. "The Quarter's Polls," *Public Opinion Quarterly* 12 (Summer 1948): 348–70.

Tarnoff, Curt. "The Marshall Plan: Design, Accomplishments, and Relevance to the Present," in Constantine Menges, ed., *The Marshall Plan from Those Who Made It Succeed.* Lanham, Md., 1999, 349–80.

Tomlinson, Jim. "Another Lost Opportunity? Marshall Aid and the British Economy in the 1940s." Paper delivered at "The Marshall Plan and its Consequences" Conference, University of Leeds, England, May 23–24, 1997.

Wala, Michael. "Selling the Marshall Plan at Home," *Diplomatic History* 10 (Summer 1986): 247–65.

———. *The Council on American Foreign Relations and American Foreign Policy in the Early Cold War.* Providence, R.I., 1994.

Wasser, Solidelle F., and Michael L. Dolfman. "BLS and the Marshall Plan: The Forgotten Story," *Monthly Labor Review* 128 (June 2005): 44–52.

Weiss, Charles. *The Marshall Plan: Lessons for US Assistance to Central and Eastern Europe and the Former Soviet Union.* Washington, D.C., 1996.

Wexler, Imanuel. *The Marshall Plan Revisited: The European Recovery Program in Economic Perspective.* Westport, Conn., 1983.

Wilson, Theodore A. *The Marshall Plan, 1947–1951.* New York, 1977.

Winks, Robin W. *The Marshall Plan and the American Economy.* New York, 1960.

Woods, Randall B. *The Marshall Plan: A Fifty Year Perspective.* Washington, D.C., 1987; reprint, 1997.

Zamagni, Vera. *The Marshall Plan: An Overview of its Impact on National Economies.* Bologna, Italy, 1992.

III. Country Studies

A. Greece

Alderfer, Harold F. *I Like Greece.* State College, Pa., 1956.

Bigart, Homer. "Are We Losing Out in Greece?" *Saturday Evening Post* 221 (January 1, 1949): 19, 49–51.

Braim, Paul F. "General James A. Van Fleet and the U.S. Military Mission to Greece," in Eugene T. Rossides, ed., *The Truman Doctrine of Aid to Greece: A Fifty-Year Retrospective.* New York and Washington, D.C., 1998, 117–27.

Candilis, Wray O. *The Economy of Greece, 1944–66: Efforts for Stability and Development.* New York, 1968.

Close, David H. "War, Medical Advance and the Improvement of Health in Greece, 1944–53," *South European Society and Politics* 9 (Winter 2004): 1–27.

Delivanis, D. J. "Marshall Plan in Greece," *Balkan Studies* [Thessaloniki] 8 (1967): 333–38.

Freris, A. F. *The Greek Economy in the Twentieth Century.* London, 1986.

Iatrides, John O. "The Doomed Revolution: Communist Insurgency in Postwar Greece," in Roy Licklider, ed., *Stopping the Killing.* New York, 1993, 205–34.

———, ed. *Greece in the 1940s: A Nation in Crisis.* Hanover, N.H., 1981.

———, ed. *Greece at the Crossroads: The Civil War and Its Legacy.* University Park, Pa., 1995.

———. "The United States and Greece in the Twentieth Century," in Theodore Couloumbis et al., eds., *Greece in the Twentieth Century.* Portland, Oreg., 2003, 69–110.

Maddison, Angus, et al. *Foreign Skills and Technical Assistance in Greek Development.* Paris, 1966.

Matthews, Kenneth. *Memories of a Mountain War: Greece, 1944–1949*. London, 1972.

McGhee, George C. "Implementation of the Aid Program," in Eugene T. Rossides, ed., *The Truman Doctrine of Aid to Greece: A Fifty-Year Retrospective*. New York and Washington, D.C., 1998, 60–66.

McNeill, William H. *Greece: American Aid in Action, 1946–1956*. New York, 1957.

———. *The Metamorphosis of Greece Since World War II*. Chicago, 1978.

Munkman, C. A. *American Aid to Greece: A Report on the First Ten Years*. New York, 1958.

Nuveen, John. "Answering the Greek Tragedians," *Christian Century* 85 (October 2, 1968): 1236–39.

Papagos, Alexander "Guerrilla Warfare," *Foreign Affairs* 30 (January 1952): 215–30.

Schmidt, Dana Adams. "Griswold—'Most Powerful Man in Greece,' Head of the American Mission to Greece," *New York Times Magazine*, October 12, 1947, 10.

Stathakis, George. "The Marshall Plan in Greece," in CHEFF, *Le Plan Marshall*. Paris, 1993, 577–89.

Stavrianos, L. S. *Greece: American Dilemma and Opportunity*. Chicago, 1952.

Sweet-Escott, Bickham. *Greece: A Political and Economic Survey, 1939–1953*. London, 1954.

Tsoukalas, Constantine. *The Greek Tragedy*. Baltimore, Md., 1969.

United States, Department of State. *Foreign Relations of the United States: 1948–1951*, "Greece." Washington, D.C., 1974–82.

———. Economic Cooperation Administration. *European Recovery Program: Greece, Country Study*. Washington, D.C., 1949.

———. Mutual Security Agency. *The Story of the American Marshall Plan in Greece*. Washington, D.C., 1952.

Van Fleet, James A. "How We Won in Greece," *Balkan Studies* [Thessaloniki] 8 (1967): 387–93.

Vetsopoulos, Apostolos. "The Economic Dimensions of the Marshall Plan in Greece, 1947–1952." Ph.D. dissertation, University College London, 2002.

Warren, James C., Jr. "Origins of the 'Greek Economic Miracle': The Truman Doctrine and Marshall Plan Development and Stabilization Programs," in Eugene T. Rossides, ed., *The Truman Doctrine of Aid to Greece: A Fifty-Year Retrospective*. New York and Washington, D.C., 1998, 76–105.

Wittner, Lawrence S. *American Intervention in Greece, 1943–1949*. New York, 1982.

B. Italy

Aga-Rossi, Elena, ed. *Il Piano Marshall e l'Europa*. Roma, 1983, part 3, 119–201.

Bibliography

Banco di Roma. *Review of the Economic Conditions in Italy: Ten Years of Italian Economy, 1947–1956*. Rome, 1956.

Barzini, Luigi. *Americans Are Alone in the World*. New York, 1953.

———. *The Italians*. New York, 1964.

Becker, Josef, and Franz Knipping, eds. *Power in Europe? Great Britain, France, Italy, and Germany in a Postwar World, 1945–1950*. Berlin, 1986.

Brogi, Alessandro. *A Question of Self-Esteem: The United States and Cold War Choices in France and Italy, 1944–1958*. Westport, Conn., 2002.

Cheles, Luciano, ed. *The Art of Persuasion: Political Communication in Italy from 1945 to the 1990s*. Manchester, U.K., 2001.

D'Attorre, Pier Paulo. "Americanism and Anti-Americanism in Italy," in Peter M. R. Stirk and David Willis, eds., *Shaping Postwar Europe: European Unity and Disunity, 1945–1957*. New York, 1991, 43–52.

———. *ERP Aid and the Politics of Productivity in Italy during the 1950s*. Florence, Italy, 1985.

———. "The European Recovery Program in Italy: Research Problems," in Ekkehart Krippendorff, ed., *The Role of the United States in the Reconstruction of Italy and West Germany, 1943–1949*. Berlin, 1981, 77–105.

———. *Italian Reconstruction and Depressed Areas: The Marshall Plan in the Mezzogiorno*. Cambridge, Mass., 1987.

De Cecco, Marcello. "Italian Economic Policy in the Reconstruction Period," in Stuart J. Wolfe, ed., *The Rebirth of Italy, 1943–1950*. New York, 1972, 156–80.

———, and Francesco Giavazzi. "Inflation and Stabilization in Italy, 1946–1951," in Rudiger Dornbusch et al., eds., *Postwar Economic Reconstruction and Lessons for the East Today*. Cambridge, Mass., 1993, 57–81.

Domenico, Roy Palmer. "For the Cause of Christ Here in Italy: America's Protestant Challenge in Italy and the Cultural Ambiguity of the Cold War," *Diplomatic History* 29 (September 2005): 625–54.

Ellwood, David W. "ERP Propaganda in Italy: Its History and Impact in an Official Survey," in Ekkehart Krippendorff, ed., *The Role of the United States in the Reconstruction of Italy and West Germany, 1943–1949*. Berlin, 1981, 274–302.

———. "From 'Re-education' to the Selling of the Marshall Plan in Italy," in Nicholas Pronay and Keith Wilson, eds., *The Political Re-education of Germany and Her Allies After World War II*. Totowa, N.J., 1985, 219–39.

———. "The Impact of the Marshall Plan on Italy; The Impact of Italy on the Marshall Plan," *European Contributions to American Studies* [Netherlands] 25 (1993): 100–24. Also in R. Kroes et al., eds., *Cultural Transmissions and Receptions: American Mass Culture in Europe*. Amsterdam, 1993.

———. "Italian Modernization and the Propaganda of the Marshall Plan," in Luciano Cheles, ed., *The Art of Persuasion: Political Communication in Italy from 1945 to the 1990s*. Manchester, U.K., 2001,

————. "The 1948 Elections in Italy: A Cold War Propaganda Battle," *Historical Journal of Film, Radio and Television* 13 (1993): 19–34.

————. "The Propaganda of the Marshall Plan in Italy in a Cold War Context," *Intelligence and National Security* 18 (Summer 2003): 225–36.

Esposito, Chiarella. *America's Feeble Weapon: Funding the Marshall Plan in France and Italy, 1948–1950.* Westport, Conn., 1994.

————. "Influencing Aid Recipients: Marshall Plan Lessons for Contemporary Aid Donors," in Barry Eichengreen, ed., *Europe's Postwar Recovery.* Cambridge, U.K., 1995, 68–92.

Filippelli, Ronald L. *American Labor and Postwar Italy, 1943–1953: A Study of Cold War Politics.* Stanford, Calif., 1989.

Grindrod, Muriel. *The Rebuilding of Italy: Politics and Economics, 1945–1955.* New York, 1955.

Harper, John L. *America and the Reconstruction of Italy, 1945–1948.* Cambridge, Mass., 1986.

————. "Italy and the World Since 1945," in Patrick McCarthy, ed., *Italy Since 1945.* New York, 2000, 95–117.

Hildebrand, George H. *Growth and Structure in the Economy of Modern Italy.* Cambridge, Mass., 1965.

Kogan, Norman. *A Political History of Postwar Italy.* New York, 1981.

Krippendorff, Ekkehart, ed. *The Role of the United States in the Reconstruction of Italy and West Germany, 1943–1949.* Berlin, 1981.

McCarthy, Patrick. "The Church in Post-War Italy," in Patrick McCarthy, ed., *Italy Since 1945.* New York, 2000, 133–52.

Miller, James Edward. "Taking Off the Gloves: The United States and the Italian Elections of 1948," *Diplomatic History* 7 (Winter 1983): 35–55.

————. *The United States and Italy, 1940–1950.* Chapel Hill, N.C., 1986.

Oliva, Juan Carlos Martinez. *Italy and the Political Economy of Cooperation: The Marshall Plan and the European Payments Union.* Rome, 2003.

Romero, Federico. "Migration as an Issue in European Interdependence and Integration: The Case of Italy," and "Interdependence and Integration in American Eyes: From the Marshall Plan to Currency Convertibility," in Alan S. Milward et al., eds., *The Frontier of National Sovereignty: History and Theory, 1945–1992.* London, 1994, 33–58 and 155–81.

————. *The United States and the European Trade Union Movement, 1944–1951.* Chapel Hill, N.C., 1992.

————. "Where the Marshall Plan Fell Short: Industrial Relations in Italy." Paper delivered at "The Marshall Plan and its Consequences" Conference, University of Leeds, England, May 23–24, 1997.

Rossi, Mario. "ECA's Blunders in Italy," *The Nation* 172 (April 7, 1951): 324–26.

Segreto, Luciano. "Changing a Low Consumption Society: The Impact of US Advertising Methods and Techniques in Italy," in Matthias Kipping and Nick

Tiratsoo, eds., *Americanisation in Twentieth Century Europe: Business, Culture, Politics*. Lille, France, 2001, 2: 75–87.

————. "The Importance of the Foreign Constraint: Debates About a New Social and Economic Order in Italy, 1945–1955," in Dominik Geppert, ed., *The Postwar Challenge: Cultural, Social and Political Change in Western Europe, 1945–58*. London, 2005, 129–50.

United States, Economic Cooperation Administration. *Italy: A Country Study*. Washington, D.C., 1949.

————. *Trieste: A Country Study*. Washington, D.C., 1949.

United States, Mutual Security Agency. *The Structure and Growth of the Italian Economy*. Rome, 1953.

Whelan, Bernadette. "Marshall Plan Publicity and Propaganda in Italy and Ireland, 1947–1951," *Historical Journal of Film, Radio and Television* 23 (October 2003): 311–28.

Willis, F. Roy. *Italy Chooses Europe*. New York, 1971.

Wolf, Stuart J., ed. *The Rebirth of Italy, 1943–1950*. New York, 1972.

Zamagni, Vera Negri. "Betting on the Future: The Reconstruction of Italian Industry, 1946–1952," in Josef Becker and Franz Knipping, eds., *Power in Europe? Great Britain, France, Italy, and Germany in a Postwar World, 1945–1950*. Berlin, 1986, 283–300.

————. *The Economic History of Italy, 1860–1990*. Oxford, U.K., 1993.

C. Turkey

Chenery, Hollis B., et al. *Turkish Investment and Economic Development*. Ankara, 1953.

Frey, Frederick. "Surveying Peasant Attitudes in Turkey," *Public Opinion Quarterly* 27 (Fall 1963): 335–55.

Harris, George S. *Troubled Alliance: Turkish-American Problems in Historical Perspective, 1945–1971*. Washington, D.C., 1972.

Hartmann, Robert T. *Uncle Sam in Turkey*. New York, 1952.

International Bank for Reconstruction and Development. *The Economy of Turkey: An Analysis and Recommendations for a Development Program*. Baltimore, Md., 1951.

Robinson, Richard D. "Impact of American Military and Economic Assistance Programs in Turkey," *Report to the American Universities Field Staff*, 1956.

Starch, Elmer. "The Future of the Great Plains Reappraised," *Journal of Farm Economics* 31 (November 1949): 917–27.

Thobie, Jacques. "La Turquie et le Plan Marshall," in CHEFF, *Le Plan Marshall*. Paris, 1993, 565–75.

Thornburg, Max W., et al. *Turkey: An Economic Appraisal*. New York, 1949.

Turkey, Ministry of State. *Quarterly Report on Marshall Plan in Turkey: First Quarter, 1950*. Ankara, 1950.

United States, Department of State. *Foreign Relations of the United States: 1948–1951*, "Turkey." Washington, D.C., 1974–82.

United States, Economic Cooperation Administration. *Turkey: A Country Study*. Washington, D.C., 1949.

Yalman, Ahmet Emin. *Turkey in My Time*. Norman, Okla., 1956.

D. Germany

Abelshauser, Werner. "The Re-entry of West Germany into the International Economy and Early European Integration," in Clemens Wurm, ed., *Western Europe and Germany: The Beginnings of European Integration, 1945–1960*. Washington, D.C., 1995, 27–53.

Abs, Herman. "Germany and the Marshall Plan," in Armand Clesse and Archie C. Epps, eds., *Present at the Creation: 40th Anniversary of the Marshall Plan*. New York, 1990, 91–98.

Adenauer, Konrad. *Memoirs, 1945–1953*. Chicago, 1966.

Backer, John H. *Winds of History: The German Years of Lucius DuBignon Clay*. New York, 1983.

Becker, Josef, and Franz Knipping, eds. *Power in Europe? Great Britain, France, Italy, and Germany in a Postwar World, 1945–1950*. Berlin, 1986.

Berger, Helge, and Albrecht Ritschl, "Germany and the Political Economy of the Marshall Plan, 1947–52: A Re-visionist View," in Barry J. Eichengreen, ed., *Europe's Postwar Recovery*. Cambridge, U.K., 1995, 199–245.

Berghahn, Volker R. *The Americanisation of West German Industry, 1945–1973*. Cambridge, U.K., 1986.

Buhrer, Werner. "German Industry and European Integration in the 1950s," in Clemens Wurm, ed., *Western Europe and Germany: The Beginnings of European Integration, 1945–1960*. Washington, D.C., 1995, 87–113.

Castillo, Greg. "Domesticating the Cold War: Household Consumption as Propaganda in Marshall Plan Germany," *Journal of Contemporary History* 40 (April 2005): 261–88.

Clay, Lucius D. *Decision in Germany*. Garden City, N.Y., 1950.

"Currency and Economic Reform, West Germany After World War II: A Symposium," ed. Rudolf Richter, in *Zeitschrift für die Gesamte Staatswissenschaft* 135 (September 1979): 297–373.

Diefendorf, Jeffrey M., et al., eds. *American Policy and the Reconstruction of West Germany, 1945–1955*. Cambridge, U.K., 1993.

Dobbins, James, et al. *America's Role in Nation-Building: From Germany to Iraq*. Santa Monica, Calif., 2003. Chapter 2, "Germany," and Chapter 9, "Lessons Learned."

Dornbusch, Rudiger, et al., eds. *Postwar Economic Reconstruction and Lessons for the East Today.* Cambridge, Mass., 1993.

Eisenberg, Carolyn. "Working Class Politics and the Cold War: American Intervention in the German Labor Movement, 1945–1949," *Diplomatic History* 7 (Fall 1983): 283–306.

Giersch, Hubert, et al. "Openness, Wage Restraint, and Macroeconomic Stability: West Germany's Road to Prosperity, 1948–1959," in Rudiger Dornbusch et al., eds., *Postwar Economic Reconstruction and Lessons for the East Today.* Cambridge, Mass., 1993, 1–28.

Hardach, Gerd. "The Marshall Plan in Germany, 1948–1952," *Journal of European Economic History* 16 (1987): 433–85.

Knapp, Manfred. "US Economic Aid and the Reconstruction of West Germany," in Ekkehart Krippendorff, ed., *The Role of the United States in the Reconstruction of Italy and West Germany, 1943–1949.* Berlin, 1981, 40–55.

Kramer, Alan. *The West German Economy, 1945–1955.* New York, 1991.

Lademacher, Horst. "The AFL in Germany," in Ekkehart Krippendorff, ed., *The Role of the United States in the Reconstruction of Italy and West Germany, 1943–1949.* Berlin, 1981, 120–26.

Maier, Charles S., and Günter Bischof, eds. *The Marshall Plan and Germany.* New York, 1991.

Major, Patrick. "From Punishment to Partnership: New Studies on the Americans and the Reconstruction of Postwar Germany, 1945–1955," *German History* 14 (1996): 67–83.

Mayer, Herbert C. *German Recovery and the Marshall Plan, 1948–1952.* New York, 1969.

Merritt, Anna J., and Richard L. Merritt, eds. *Public Opinion in Occupied Germany: The OMGUS Surveys, 1945–1949.* Urbana, Ill., 1970.

———. *Public Opinion in Semisovereign Germany: The HICOG Surveys, 1949–1955.* Urbana, Ill., 1980.

Morgan, Roger P. *The United States and West Germany, 1945–1973.* New York, 1974.

Pommerin, Reiner, ed. *The American Impact on Postwar Germany.* Providence, R.I., 1995.

Schafer, Axel. "The Study of Americanisation after German Reunification: Institutional Transfer, Popular Culture and the East," *Contemporary European History* 12 (February 2003): 129–44.

Schröder, Hans-Jürgen. "The Economic Reconstruction of West Germany in the Context of International Relations, 1945–1949," in Josef Becker and Franz Knipping, eds., *Power in Europe? Great Britain, France, Italy, and Germany in a Postwar World, 1945–1950.* Berlin, 1986, 303–21.

———. "Marshall Plan Propaganda in Austria and Western Germany," *Contemporary Austrian Studies* 8 (2000): 212–46.

Schwartz, Thomas A. *America's Germany: John J. McCloy and the Federal Republic of Germany.* Cambridge, Mass., 1991.

————. "European Integration and the 'Special Relationship': Implementing the Marshall Plan in the Federal Republic," in Charles S. Maier and Gunter Bischof, eds., *The Marshall Plan and Germany.* New York, 1991, 171–215.

Temin, Peter. "The 'Koreaboom' in West Germany: Fact or Fiction?" *Economic Historical Review* 48 (1995): 737–53.

United States, Economic Cooperation Administration. *Western Germany, Country Study.* Washington, D.C., 1949.

Willett, Ralph. *The Americanization of Germany, 1945–1949.* London, 1989.

Wolf, Holger C. "The Lucky Miracle: Germany, 1945–1951," in Rudiger Dornbusch et al., eds., *Postwar Economic Reconstruction and Lessons for the East Today.* Cambridge, Mass., 1993, 29–56.

————. "Post-War Germany in the European Context: Domestic and External Determinants of Growth," in Barry Eichengreen, ed., *Europe's Postwar Recovery.* Cambridge, U.K., 1995, 323–52.

Wurm, Clemens, ed. *Western Europe and Germany: The Beginnings of European Integration, 1945–1960.* Washington, D.C., 1995.

Index